MW01232695

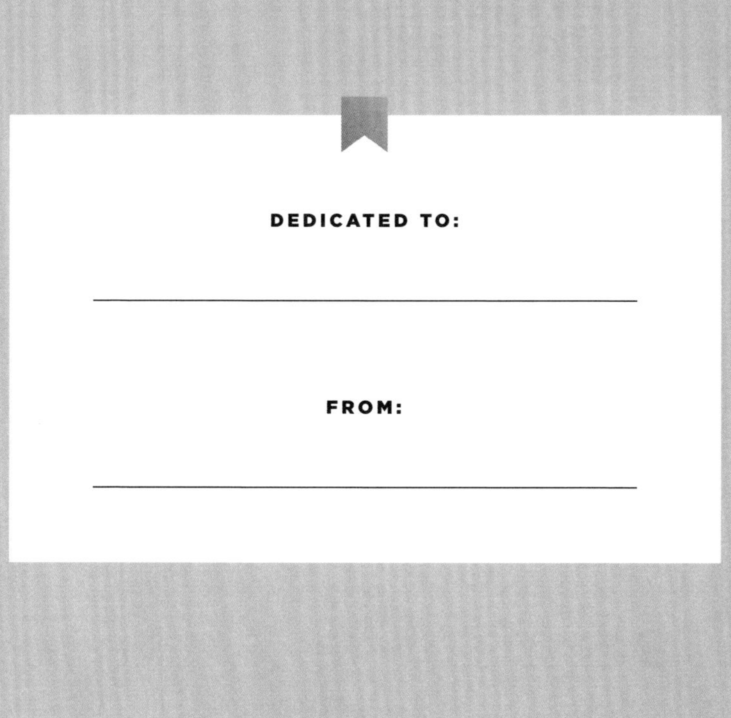
DEDICATED TO:
FROM:

3 Minute Mornings

START YOUR DAY IN FAITH

JOEL OSTEEN

3-Minute Mornings: Start Your Day in Faith

ISBN: 978-1-963492-19-4

Created and assembled for Joel Osteen Ministries by
Breakfast for Seven
breakfastforseven.com

Printed in China.

For additional resources by Joel Osteen, visit JoelOsteen.com.

INTRODUCTION

Every day is a gift, and we get to choose how to live it.

The Bible promises in Hebrews 11:6 that *"He is a rewarder of those who diligently seek Him"* (NKJV). God rewards people that get up every morning and thank Him for His goodness, people that go through the day meditating on His promises, people that acknowledge Him in all of their ways.

When you diligently seek God, there's a reward. He will take you where you could not go on your own. What's amazing about God is He says you don't even have to find Him; if you'll just seek Him, He'll give you a reward. If you'll just get up early and take time to thank Him, if you'll just acknowledge Him throughout the day, He'll reward you for making an effort.

Proverbs 3:6 says, *"In all your ways acknowledge Him, and He will make your paths straight"* (NASB). Not in some of your ways, not just the big things . . . but if you'll acknowledge God in all of your ways, He will crown your efforts with success.

It doesn't have to be some long, drawn-out thing. Just say throughout the day, "Lord, thank you for a good day today." Driving to work, "God help me to have a safe trip." That's acknowledging God. Going to a restaurant, "God help us to have a good dinner; bless this time together." When You show this dependency on God, relying on Him in your everyday life, that's what allows Him to make things easier.

Your Heavenly Father cares about all the moments of your day. With *3-Minute Mornings: Start Your Day in Faith*, you can start each day with a power boost and a fresh anointing from the Holy Spirit. The Scripture, devotions, prayers, and declarations will set a course for your day that you can carry with you in all the moments, challenges, conflicts, and even the simple daily tasks you face.

It's my prayer that this devotional will be a blessing to you in each and every day. As you acknowledge God, He'll go before you and make your crooked places straight. He can cause the right people to show up. He can open doors that you can't open on your own. He can crown your efforts with success. Yes, He will be your rewarder in your relationships, your work, and most of all, in giving you overflowing peace and joy throughout every day.

Let today and every day begin
and be filled with abounding faith.

January

JANUARY 1

Make God a Part of Everyday Life

In all your ways acknowledge Him,
and He will make your paths straight.

PROVERBS 3:6, NASB

As we start this new year, remember that you can celebrate God every day of the coming year. God can help you in the big things and the small things. He is near and available — as you cook dinner, drive in traffic, study at school, or work at the office. A lot of people keep God in a Sunday morning box. That's when they come to church, pray, and think about God. Then they go out during the week and never really include God in their life. They love God and revere Him, but they think there's nothing spiritual about cleaning the house, going to the grocery store, or meeting with a client. As you acknowledge God in all of your ways, He will crown your efforts with success.

PRAY & DECLARE

Father, thank You that I am acknowledging You in all the moments of my life. I know as I do this, I will be empowered in life by the life You placed within me through Your Son, Jesus. Thank You for making all the twisted parts of my life straight. In Jesus' Name, Amen.

JANUARY 2

Bold Prayers

On the day the Lord *gave the Amorites over to Israel, Joshua said to the* Lord *in the presence of Israel: "Sun, stand still over Gibeon."*

JOSHUA 10:12, NIV

When Joshua and the Israelite army were fighting a battle late in the day, he wasn't going to be able to finish the enemy off unless he had more daylight. He could have thought, *Too bad.* No, he knew that he had God's favor and authority and prayed a bold prayer: *"Sun, stand still."* The sun didn't go down until Joshua completely defeated the enemy.

Would you do as Joshua did and ask God to do something out of the ordinary to bring those dreams to pass that seem too far out? It may not look logical for an average person, but God is for you. Ask in spite of what the enemy keeps whispering in your ears.

PRAY & DECLARE

Father, thank You that when the odds are against me, You are for me. Thank You that nothing and no one is more powerful than You, and I can dare to pray bold prayers energized by Your authority. In Jesus' Name, Amen.

JANUARY 3

The Reward of Integrity

A good name is more desirable than great riches;
to be esteemed is better than silver or gold.
PROVERBS 22:1, NIV

Your reputation is one of the most valuable things you have. You can have great riches and yet be despised and looked down on. But when you're a person of integrity, other people say, "I can trust them. They'll always do the right thing. They're honest, fair, and consistent. They don't talk one way and live another." Your name is too important to let it become tarnished. A life of integrity will take you much further than being dishonest and manipulating. There's a lot we can get away with, hide, manipulate, and exaggerate. People may not see it, but God does. Be honest. Be trustworthy. Be a person of your word.

PRAY & DECLARE

Father, thank You that You are not limited to seeing me as other people see me. Thank You that You see my heart, and You know I am faithful. Thank You for inspiring me to live a life of integrity. My integrity is a reflection of You. I give You all the praise. In Jesus' Name, Amen.

JANUARY 4

Listening in Your Spirit

For the things which are seen are temporary,
but the things which are not seen are eternal.
2 CORINTHIANS 4:18, NKJV

Just as we have physical ears, we have spiritual ears. God speaks to us in our spirit. Many times He will speak things that contradict what we see with our eyes. You're struggling in your finances, but His voice says, "You're blessed." It doesn't look like you'll ever get well, but God says, "You're healthy. You're whole." God calls you what you are before it happens. Abraham didn't have any children when God called him *"a father of many nations"* (Genesis 17:5, NIV). Gideon was afraid, yet God called him *"mighty hero"* (Judges 6:12, NLT). Don't be discouraged by what you see, which is temporary, and start being encouraged by what you hear. What God speaks to us is permanent.

PRAY & DECLARE

Father, thank You for how You speak to my spirit directly as well as through Your Word. Yes, I love listening to Your voice in my spirit. I believe what I hear and not what I see with my eyes. Your voice stirs my deepest longing and reveals Your eternal truth. In Jesus' Name, Amen.

JANUARY 5

To the Next Level

God is our refuge and strength,
a very present help in trouble.
PSALM 46:1, NKJV

When troubles come our way, it's easy to get frustrated. But God wouldn't allow it if it weren't going to work to your advantage. That's why you don't need to be discouraged when life deals you a tough hand. The reason you have big challenges is that you have a big destiny. Average people have average challenges. But you're not ordinary; you're extraordinary. You're a child of the Most High God. The Creator of the universe breathed His life into you. He crowned you with His favor. Don't be surprised if you face extraordinary challenges.

God knows what He's doing. You may not like the trouble; it may not be fair, and you're uncomfortable, but that trouble is actually taking you to the next level of your destiny. You wouldn't be who you are today without all the things you've been through.

PRAY & DECLARE

Father, thank You that You are the Most High God who breathed life into me. Thank You that the trouble that comes my way is transporting me to the next level of my destiny. I believe that You are preparing me for an extraordinary destiny. In Jesus' Name, Amen.

Ask in spite of what the enemy keeps whispering in your ears.

JANUARY 6

Who Do You Believe You Are?

But now, O Jacob, listen to the Lord *who created you. O Israel, the one who formed you says, "Do not be afraid, for I have ransomed you. I have called you by name; you are mine."*

ISAIAH 43:1, NLT

It's easy to go through life letting people and circumstances put names on us, such as average, unqualified, or poor. Sometimes our own thoughts have named us as unattractive, not talented, not good enough. As long as you're wearing these names and believing the lies that people and circumstances have told you, it will keep you from your potential. Yes, God has a different name for you. When He breathed life into you, He named you blessed, prosperous, talented, victorious, one of a kind, and a masterpiece. People may call you ordinary. If you accept that name, you'll become exactly that.

Call yourself what God calls you. As you do this, strongholds that have held you back will be broken. You will step into who you were created to be.

PRAY & DECLARE

Father, thank You that You have called me by name, and I am Yours. Thank You that You call me blessed, redeemed, forgiven, victorious, overcomer, and a masterpiece. I refuse to let life name me anything less than what You have named me. In Jesus' Name, Amen.

JANUARY 7

Stand Still in Faith

"Now then, stand still and see this great thing the Lord is about to do before your eyes!"
1 SAMUEL 12:16, NIV

Maybe you come from a family line of depression, addictions, divorce, or poverty. It could continue with you, but there's a blessing on your life that's going to thrust you to a new level. Forces that have stopped your family are being broken right now. You're going to take new ground in your finances, in your health, and in your relationships. Areas that looked as though they would never change are shifting. Favor is coming in new ways — opportunities, breakthroughs, the right people.

God is going to do something that surpasses anything you've ever seen. You're not going to have to make this happen through your own efforts, your strength, your talent, and your determination. It's going to be the hand of God. Stand still and watch Him show out in your life.

PRAY & DECLARE

Father, thank You for the great things You are about to do before my eyes. I choose to be still, to be quiet before You, and to watch You work. Give me the grace to accept Your timing and rest in the fact that You want me to stand in faith. In Jesus' Name, Amen.

JANUARY 8

Shift the Winds

The LORD answered Moses, "Is the LORD's arm too short? Now you will see whether or not what I say will come true for you."

NUMBERS 11:23, NIV

When the Israelites were in the desert, they complained that there was no meat to eat. God told Moses that He was going to give them meat, not just for a day but for a whole month. When Moses expressed his disbelief, God responded by saying, "Do you think the unfavorable conditions somehow limit Me? Nothing is too difficult for Me." God shifted the winds and caused a huge flock of quail to show up in their camp.

You may not see how your situation can work out, and none of the conditions are favorable, but stay encouraged. God knows how to shift the winds. He knows how to bring the quail, the right people, good breaks, and restoration. He's not limited because you're in a desert place.

PRAY & DECLARE

Father, thank You that You control the winds and bring Your blessings to me. When it looks too big for me, I know that with You, all things are possible. I believe that You are not limited by any unfavorable conditions that I face. In Jesus' Name, Amen.

JANUARY 9

Turn the Page

Weeping may endure for a night,
but joy comes in the morning.
PSALM 30:5, NKJV

The Scripture talks about how God has written every day of our life in His book. When we go through things we don't understand, things that aren't fair, things that are painful, it's easy to get stuck on that page and think it's never going to change. Can I encourage you that it's just one chapter, not your whole book? God will help you turn the page. As you keep moving forward, being your best in spite of what didn't work out, in spite of who did you wrong, you'll come into another place where the light comes bursting in. Joy will replace the darkness. God will do exceedingly, abundantly more than you can imagine.

PRAY & DECLARE

Father, thank You that in times of trouble, in times of weeping, when I don't see the way out, I can know that it's only for a night, for a chapter of my life. You will come bursting in with light and transform my situation. I believe that I have Your favor, and as You inspire me to turn the page, joy will come. In Jesus' Name, Amen.

JANUARY 10

Kept from Defeat

"Simon, Simon! Indeed, Satan has asked for you, that he may sift you as wheat. But I have prayed for you, that your faith should not fail . . ."

LUKE 22:31–32, NKJV

Jesus warned Peter that the enemy was focused on him and was going to attack him and do his best to take him down. But Jesus went on to say, *"But I have prayed for you, that your faith should not fail"* (v. 32). Jesus was saying in effect, "The enemy is coming against you, to distract you, to discourage you, to get you off course, but don't worry. I'm praying for you, and I'm going to strengthen you. I'm going to keep you from being defeated. I'm the God who overrules." When life gets tough and things come against you, you have an advantage. Jesus is at the right hand of the Father right now, praying for you so your faith will not fail.

PRAY & DECLARE

Father, thank You for being the God who has the authority and power to overrule the attacks of the enemy on my life. Thank You that Jesus is praying for me that my faith will not fail. I know that You are strengthening me to stand in the battle. In Jesus' Name, Amen.

God calls you what you are before it happens.

JANUARY 11

Stay Faithful

But Elisha said, "As surely as the LORD lives and as you live, I will not leave you."

2 KINGS 2:2, NIV

When the prophet Elijah was about to be taken up to Heaven in a whirlwind, three times he told his assistant Elisha that he did not need to go with him to Bethel. But Elisha, who had walked with Elijah faithfully, wouldn't hear of it. His attitude was, "I'm committed to you. I was with you in the good times of miracles, and I'm going to be with you to the end." Elisha had plenty of reasons to walk away, but he was committed. Because he stayed committed to serving Elijah, Elisha received a double portion of Elijah's anointing and ended up performing twice as many miracles as Elijah did. When you stay committed to your marriage, to your church, or to your job even though it's hard, a double portion is coming — double favor, double honor, double resources.

PRAY & DECLARE

Father, thank You for the double portion that You have reserved for those who stay committed when it would be easy to walk away. Help me to do the right thing when the wrong thing is happening. I believe that my breakthrough is coming. In Jesus' Name, Amen.

JANUARY 12

Change Your Name

The baby's father, however, called him Benjamin (which means "son of my right hand").

GENESIS 35:18, NLT

Just before Rachel died while giving birth, she was in so much pain and distress that she named the baby Ben-Oni, which means *"son of my sorrow."* Back in those days, a child's name set the direction for their life. She had pronounced that he would live a sorrowful, painful, depressing life. But Jacob intervened and changed his name to Benjamin, which means *"son of my right hand,"* or son of my strength. Jacob would not allow his son to see himself as a son of sorrow, as limited and defeated. Perhaps the people who could have been speaking faith over you — affirming you, naming you victorious and strong — did just the opposite. If they named you a failure or not talented, the good news is that what God names you overrides what people name you.

PRAY & DECLARE

Father, thank You that You alone have the right to name me. Thank You that what You name me supersedes all the other names I've been called and all the mistakes of my past. I will call myself what You call me, for I am who You say I am. In Jesus' Name, Amen.

JANUARY 13

He Walks Through Doors

When the disciples were together, with the doors locked for fear of the Jewish leaders, Jesus came and stood among them and said, "Peace be with you!"

JOHN 20:19, NIV

After Jesus was crucified, the disciples were huddled together in a room behind locked doors for fear of being arrested. They did everything they could to keep people out, but Jesus suddenly walked through the door. He didn't unlock it, open it, or try to beat it down. He just came through it. Even closed doors can't keep us from what He has for us.

A loved one may have shut the door in your relationship. Forces of darkness may be trying to keep you from your destiny. The good news is that God comes through any locked door. He's not limited by what's limiting us. Closed doors can't stop Him. God is going to walk right through it and declare peace in your most fearful and defeated moments.

PRAY & DECLARE

Father, thank You that You see every detail of my life, and You know when I'm fearful and hiding behind closed doors. Thank You that any of the closed rooms in my life are still wide open to You. In Jesus' Name, Amen.

JANUARY 14

It's Not Too Late

"So I will restore to you the years
that the swarming locust has eaten . . ."
JOEL 2:25, NKJV

The Israelites had labored over their crops, but for years at harvest time, swarms of locusts came in and ate up all the crops. We've all been through seasons in life where it feels like we've lost time. Perhaps it's the years lost in a relationship that didn't work out or the years of struggle with an illness or an addiction. Or it's the years we let fear and opposition hold us back from pursuing our dreams. But God says He will restore those years to you. We serve a supernatural God who knows how to make up for lost time. He's not going to just restore the years you lost. He promises you abundance of joy, an overflow of peace, and more than enough resources to restore all that seems lost.

PRAY & DECLARE

Father, thank You that nothing is too hard for You to work out in my life, not even the time I've lost in the past for many different reasons. Thank You that You work in ways so far beyond anything I can think or imagine. In Jesus' Name, Amen.

JANUARY 15

Receive It

"May the Lord repay you for what you have done.
May you be richly rewarded by the Lord, the God of Israel,
under whose wings you have come to take refuge."

RUTH 2:12, NIV

A young Moabite widow named Ruth moved to Bethlehem to take care of her elderly mother-in-law, Naomi. To survive, she went into the harvest fields every day to pick up whatever wheat the workers missed. God brought her to the attention of Boaz, the owner of the fields, who began to help her and then fell in love with her. God's blessing was on Ruth, and she and Naomi went from poverty and disappointment to abundance and joy.

Like Ruth, you may have been through disappointments, but things are about to turn in your favor. It's going to happen by the Spirit of the living God. He's breathing on your life right now. There are breakthroughs already en route — healing, promotions, contracts — the right people are already headed your way.

PRAY & DECLARE

Father, thank You that You know every hardship and difficult situation I have faced and will face. Thank You that I can take refuge under Your wings. You have more blessings and favor for me than I can dream. In Jesus' Name, Amen.

The reason you have big challenges is that you have a big destiny.

JANUARY 16

It's in the Obedience

"The master of the banquet tasted the water that had been turned into wine. He did not realize where it had come from, though the servants who had drawn the water knew."

JOHN 2:9, NIV

When Jesus turned water into wine, He told the staff at the wedding to fill up the large stone pots with water, which didn't make sense. They could have said, "Jesus, we need wine, not water. What good is this going to do?" Without them filling the water pots, without their obedience, there wouldn't have been a miracle.

Is God asking you to step out in faith into a brand-new venture, or to forgive someone who did you wrong, or to pray for others who need healing when you're not feeling well? Is He asking you to fill pots with water when you need wine? As you step out even when it's hard, even when it doesn't make sense, you're going to see God do awesome things in your life.

PRAY & DECLARE

Father, thank You that You are a miracle-working God. Thank You for calling me to be faithful and obedient when things aren't changing. I believe that the wine is coming, that I am going to see You do something life-changing. In Jesus' Name, Amen.

JANUARY 17

It Really Doesn't Matter

The devil said to Jesus, "If you are God's Son,
tell this stone to turn into bread."

LUKE 4:3, CEV

After Jesus was baptized, God the Father said, *"This is My beloved Son, in whom I am well pleased"* (Matthew 3:17, NKJV). Then Jesus was led into the desert to be tempted. After forty days, the enemy said, *"If you are the Son of God, tell these stones to become bread"* (Matthew 4:3, NIV). Jesus refused. He said, *"Man shall not live on bread alone"* (v. 4, NIV).

He was saying, "I don't have anything to prove. My Father announced who I am. I was His Son in the waters of the Jordan River, and I'm His Son in the wilderness of the Judean Desert. I won't waste My time trying to convince you of who I am. I have a destiny to fulfill." As with Jesus, it really doesn't matter what the enemy or other people think of you. You have nothing to prove. When God looks at you, He says, "That's My child, in whom I am well pleased."

PRAY & DECLARE

Father, thank You that I can be free from trying to prove who I am to others. I'm overjoyed to be Your child and to keep moving in my destiny you have already ordained for me. In Jesus' Name, Amen.

JANUARY 18

Pour the Oil

They brought the jars to her and she kept pouring. When all the jars were full, she said to her son, "Bring me another one." But he replied, "There is not a jar left." Then the oil stopped flowing.

2 KINGS 4:5–6, NIV

Things were so bad for this poor widow that creditors were coming to take her two sons as payment for her bills. When the prophet Elisha told her to get as many jars as possible and pour her little remaining oil in them, it didn't make sense. But when she obeyed, the miracle happened, and the oil kept flowing till every jar was full. She sold the oil, paid the creditors, and had plenty left over to live on. Has God put a promise in your heart, but it hasn't made sense? Don't talk yourself out of what you know God is telling you to do. Yes, pour the oil. From your little bit, God will create more than enough.

PRAY & DECLARE

Father, thank You that You are the true and living God. Thank You that you provide oil when there seems to be none. You turn emptiness into fullness and overflowing. In Jesus' Name, Amen.

JANUARY 19

Don't Forget

They soon forgot what he had done
and did not wait for his plan to unfold.
PSALM 106:13, NIV

The Israelites did not enter the Promised Land because they got impatient, afraid, and complained against God, thinking He had forgotten about them in the wilderness. If something we're hoping for hasn't happened yet, it might be that it just hasn't been the right time. When God is ready, all the forces of darkness cannot stop Him.

When we go through difficulties that we don't understand, it's easy to sit around discouraged and anxious, wondering if it's ever going to change. Remember: People who oppose you don't determine your destiny. Bad breaks, disappointments, or even mistakes you've made don't cancel what God has ordained for you. As you wait for God's plan to unfold, know that it is going to exceed your greatest expectations.

PRAY & DECLARE

Father, thank You that when You created me, You also ordained a plan for my life. Thank You that You are working behind the scenes and unfolding Your plan at just the right time. Help me to be patient and know that You are always on schedule. In Jesus' Name, Amen.

JANUARY 20

On the Verge of a Miracle

"As soon as the priests who carry the ark of the LORD — the Lord of all the earth — set foot in the Jordan, its waters flowing downstream will be cut off and stand up in a heap."

JOSHUA 3:13, NIV

When Joshua and the Israelites came to cross the Jordan River, it was in flood stage, with violent currents rushing down from the melting snow on Mount Hermon. It looked impassable. When the people wanted to turn around, Joshua told them, "Keep on walking." As soon as the priests got their feet wet, the miracle happened, and they were given entrance into the Promised Land.

You may be at the Jordan River right now. The problem in your health, finances, or relationships is bigger than it's ever been, and you don't see how it can work out. But take that first step. Get your feet wet. That Jordan River is setting you up for your promised land.

PRAY & DECLARE

Father, thank You for the promise that You will part my Jordan Rivers as I step into the water. When things look impossible, I know that You want me to be bold and keep taking steps forward, to keep praying and expecting. In Jesus' Name, Amen.

God is not limited because you're in a desert place.

JANUARY 21

Surely We Will Prevail

And Caleb silenced the people before Moses and said, "Surely, let us go up and let us take possession of it because surely we will be able to prevail over it."

NUMBERS 13:30, LEB

When Moses sent twelve men to spy out the Promised Land, ten spies came back saying though it was more than they ever dreamed, the inhabitants were too big and strong and the cities too fortified. They were fully persuaded that they couldn't defeat the opposition. The two other spies, Joshua and Caleb, came back fully persuaded that they could surely overcome and take the land. They were the only two Israelites of that generation who made it into the Promised Land. There may be giants on your land — a sickness, a debt, an addiction. Do as Caleb did and put a "surely" on the front of what you're believing for. "Surely I will defeat this giant. Surely God is on my side."

PRAY & DECLARE

Father, thank You that You are so much greater than any giants in the land, and the facts are never a reason to keep me from Your purposes for my life. Thank You that because You are with me, I can be fully persuaded that victory is coming. In Jesus' Name, Amen.

JANUARY 22

Always

Therefore, my beloved brethren, be steadfast, immovable, always abounding in the work of the Lord, knowing that your labor is not in vain in the Lord.

1 CORINTHIANS 15:58, NKJV

What can you say about yourself that's "always"? Are you always worried? Always late? Always hot-tempered? Always undisciplined? Or are you always joyful, always encouraging, always helping others? God has empowered you, through Christ, to be consistent, abounding in His work. As you bring forth His consistency that's already within you, you won't be ruled by your feelings. Feelings go up and down. Feelings would tell people off, eat the whole gallon of ice cream, and sit around in self-pity. Don't let those feelings control you. You have to put your foot down and say, "Feelings — through Christ — I'm in control. I will do the right thing when it's hard. I will treat people with respect even when they don't deserve it."

PRAY & DECLARE

Father, thank You that You have always been steadfast and immovable in Your love for me. Thank You for calling and equipping me to be the same. Thank You that my labor in the Lord is not in vain. I am empowered to make Your "always" abound in "all ways" in my life. In Jesus' Name, Amen.

JANUARY 23

Invisible

As the Aramean army advanced toward him, Elisha prayed, "O Lord, please make them blind." So the Lord struck them with blindness as Elisha had asked.

2 KINGS 6:18, NLT

The prophet Elisha was so hated by the king of Syria that he sent a great army with chariots and horses to surround Elisha's house and capture him. Elisha had no chance against them in the natural, but he understood that plans that were sent to stop him cannot stand against our God. Elisha didn't pray, "Lord, stop this army." He said, "Lord, please make them blind." He was saying, "Lord, make me invisible to the enemy." What a powerful prayer.

We can pray that every day. "Lord, make my family invisible to the enemy. Make my health, my finances, and my dreams invisible to the enemy." When you ask God to make you invisible, He can do the impossible.

PRAY & DECLARE

Father, thank You that no matter what trouble I face, I can stay in peace knowing that You will make me invisible to it. I ask You to blind the enemy now and prevent his purposes. I declare that You are greater than any force that comes against me. In Jesus' Name, Amen.

JANUARY 24

By This I Know

By this I know that You are well pleased with me,
because my enemy does not triumph over me.
PSALM 41:11, NKJV

Are you facing difficulties that seem too big? Perhaps you never dreamed you would be battling a sickness, that your marriage would be in trouble, or the company wouldn't need you. God is saying, "It's not a surprise to Me." I've learned to recognize that God is pleased with me not by the battles that He's stopped, but by the battles that didn't stop me. You can't judge God's favor by the battles He kept you out of, but by the battles He brought you through. The Scripture says you will go through the fire and not be burned, and you will go through the waters and not drown. God won't allow you to get in a difficulty that He can't bring you out of.

PRAY & DECLARE

Father, thank You for every time You have not allowed the enemy to triumph over me. It pleases me to know that You are pleased with me. I can declare, "By this I know . . . Your favor, protection, and love are forever mine." In Jesus' Name, Amen.

JANUARY 25

Change How You See Yourself

"No longer will you be called Abram; your name will be Abraham, for I have made you a father of many nations."
GENESIS 17:5, NIV

After Abram and Sarai had waited for the promise of a baby boy for over twenty years, God changed Abram's name to Abraham, which means "the father of many nations," and Sarai's name to Sarah, which means "princess." He didn't feel like a father, and she didn't feel like a princess. But God called them what they were before it happened. As they spoke their names and heard others speak their names, the words pointed to the promise that seemed impossible. God was changing how they saw themselves through the names He gave them. They kept declaring those words over and over, and Sarah finally conceived and gave birth to Isaac. What are you saying about your dreams? "I'm too old. I've made too many mistakes. I don't have the talent." Let these negative words go and declare what God says about you.

PRAY & DECLARE

Father, thank You that You call me blessed, redeemed, forgiven, healthy, and an overcomer. I will declare what You call me for You have already purposed a glorious destiny for me. In Jesus' Name, Amen.

What God names you overrides what people name you.

JANUARY 26

Not a Watered-Down Version

So Sarai said to Abram, "The Lord has prevented me from having children. Go and sleep with my servant. Perhaps I can have children through her." And Abram agreed with Sarai's proposal.

GENESIS 16:2, NLT

God told Abraham that He was going to give him and Sarah a son. The problem was that they were already too old to have children in the natural. Finally Sarah told Abraham to sleep with her maid. She watered down the promise, and Abraham went along with it. Instead of believing for the extraordinary, they settled for what they thought was good enough. But the baby Ishmael was not the promised child, and trying to help God out caused many problems.

Sometimes we take what God put in our heart, and instead of believing for the impossible, we bring it down to what makes sense to us. Be assured: What God promises will come to pass — not a watered-down version. Get ready for the fullness of what God said.

PRAY & DECLARE

Father, thank You that You are not limited by what limits me. Yes, I declare that You can do the impossible when I'm tempted to water down Your promises. In Jesus' Name, Amen.

JANUARY 27

It's Your Love

"By this all will know that you are My disciples, if you have love for one another."
JOHN 13:35, NKJV

It's easy to write off someone because they don't believe as we do. Too often we try to make them believe, but their heart may not be open yet. Know that at the right time God will soften their heart. Will you keep sowing seeds of love in that friend or family member who shows no sign of changing? Will you keep praying for that coworker who ridicules believers? It's not by your doctrine, not by how many scriptures you can quote, not by how right you are, but by how much you love them. You don't judge them. You don't look down because they don't believe as you do. You just keep loving and being good to them. They're in your life because God is pouring out His light on them through you.

PRAY & DECLARE

Father, thank You for Your unconditional love for me. Thank You for the people You've brought into my life that I might love and encourage in their journey to faith. Thank You that I am a reflection of Your love and, through Christ, I will be there for them. In Jesus' Name, Amen.

JANUARY 28

Share It With Others

Blessed be the God and Father of our Lord Jesus Christ, the Father of mercies and God of all comfort, who comforts us in all our tribulation, that we may be able to comfort those who are in any trouble, with the comfort with which we ourselves are comforted by God.

2 CORINTHIANS 1:3–4, NKJV

There are times when God will allow us to go through a painful season so He can birth something new inside. If you go through something you don't understand, God allowed this to happen because He trusts you. He knows His Spirit within you will empower you to take the same comfort, the same healing, and the same encouragement that helped you overcome this trouble and share it with others. Don't get caught up in a painful situation wondering, "Where does this piece of my puzzle go? It's ugly, and it doesn't make sense." Keep moving forward. There's a blessing in that pain. When you've been through something, you're uniquely qualified to help and comfort somebody else in that situation.

PRAY & DECLARE

Father, thank You that You are using the painful situations I experience to help others. Thank You that I have something to give, some encouragement to share, and Your love to impart. In Jesus' Name, Amen.

JANUARY 29

New Beginnings

He told them, "My soul is crushed with grief to the point of death. Stay here and keep watch with me."
MATTHEW 26:38, NLT

On the night before Jesus went to the cross, He was so deeply troubled in the garden of Gethsemane that He asked His disciples to stay there and pray for Him. But they couldn't stay awake. It was disappointing, but He accepted that He wasn't going to have their encouragement and moved forward toward His crucifixion and resurrection.

In life we all have disappointments, some that deeply trouble us. But God gives you grace for every Gethsemane, for every person who falls asleep. It's very freeing when you can look at the frustration, look at the business that slowed down, look at the people who left you, and know that amazing things are ahead. Yes, there are crosses to bear, betrayals, and setbacks, but keep moving forward. You may be in Gethsemane, but know that resurrection is coming.

PRAY & DECLARE

Father, thank You that Jesus did not allow His disappointment over the disciples' lack of support to keep Him from His purpose. Thank You for the grace to go through times of betrayal and crosses, knowing that new beginnings are coming. In Jesus' Name, Amen.

JANUARY 30

Mind Your Own Business

This should be your ambition: to live a quiet life, minding your own business and doing your own work, just as we told you before.

1 THESSALONIANS 4:11, TLB

Moses' sister, Miriam, and his brother, Aaron, began to criticize him and question his leadership. Perhaps Miriam felt Moses was getting some of the recognition she deserved. She focused her criticism on the fact that many years before, Moses had married a Cushite woman, a foreigner. It was none of her business who he had married, and because of it, her skin suddenly became leprous. That may seem extreme, but that is how much God dislikes it when we sow discord and stir up trouble. Fortunately for Miriam, Moses prayed for her, and God restored her skin to health. The apostle Paul says to mind your own business. It's hard enough to run our own life. Don't try to run somebody else's.

PRAY & DECLARE

Father, thank You for all the people You have placed in my life. Thank You that You want me to love them like You do. Help me to mind my own business, as well as be about minding Your business throughout the world. In Jesus' Name, Amen.

JANUARY 31

Before You Even Ask

"I will answer them before they even call to me.
While they are still talking about their needs,
I will go ahead and answer their prayers!"
ISAIAH 65:24, NLT

Joseph's brothers hated him so much that they threw him into a deep pit and were going to leave him there to die. But just then they saw a caravan of Ishmaelite merchants coming their way, and they decided to sell Joseph to them. What's interesting is that the trade caravan had been traveling for months on their way to sell their goods in Egypt. Long before Joseph had the problem, God had the answer already set up. God knows what you're going to need, when you're going to need it, and how to get it to you. The problem you're worried about, God has the answer already en route. It may not have happened yet, but what God has ordained is on the way.

PRAY & DECLARE

Father, thank You that before I even ask You for my needs and desires, You've already lined up solutions and have them headed my way. Thank You for the people, the favor, and the promotion You've ordained to come across my path. I believe that even now, answers to my prayers are on the way. In Jesus' Name, Amen.

February

FEBRUARY 1

No Pretenders

"Blessed are the pure in heart, for they will see God."

MATTHEW 5:8, NIV

The Pharisees went to the temple all the time and did the right religious things outwardly, but they had wrong motives. They went to be seen and to impress people. They prayed long prayers out loud, but only because they wanted everybody to hear them. They gave their money so they would look good. And in the process, they failed to see God right in front of them in Jesus.

Our inner life is more important than our outer life. And through Christ, God places a pure heart within us. Unlike the Pharisees, we are compelled to help a person out of love, not to impress them and get something from them. We volunteer as a service to God, not to get other people's applause. We have pure motives and actions because Christ through us is empowering us.

PRAY & DECLARE

Father, thank You for blessing me through Christ with a pure heart. Thank You that I can see You, even as I reach out to the world around me. I don't have to pretend or be puffed up because You are moving out through me. In Jesus' Name, Amen.

FEBRUARY 2

What's New?

"Behold, the former things have come to pass, and new things I now declare; before they spring forth I tell you of them."

ISAIAH 42:9, ESV

Are you just going through the motions, stuck on a job where you're not fulfilled and still doing things the same way you did years ago? It's time to refocus and make adjustments. God has new dreams, new mindsets, new friendships, and new ways of doing things. Ask yourself, "What am I excited about?" Sometimes we're not passionate because we're stuck in the past. New things are springing forth, ready to take you out of your comfort zone to a new level. It may mean starting that business or doing things differently in your personal life. Look for open doors and be willing to walk away from what's stagnant. His favor is on the new.

PRAY & DECLARE

Father, thank You for the great things that You've done in my past, but I don't want to get stuck there. Thank You that You are the God who is always doing something new. I declare that this is a new day and my dreams and vision are being renewed. In Jesus' Name, Amen.

FEBRUARY 3

What's in Your Plan?

"For I know the plans I have for you,"
declares the LORD, *"plans to prosper you and not*
to harm you, plans to give you hope and a future."
JEREMIAH 29:11, NIV

God has a plan for your life, but He doesn't show you all the details. If He showed you what He has in store, where He's taking you, it would excite and amaze you. But if you saw what it's going to take to get you there — the giants and Pharaohs you'll face, the lonely nights, the betrayals, the closed doors — you would think, *I'll just stay where I am*. God doesn't show us the details because He knows we would talk ourselves out of it. Be comfortable not knowing the details but embracing and knowing the God who has wonderful plans for you. Start each day declaring: "God, I don't see a way or have the answer for how this situation can work out, but I trust You."

PRAY & DECLARE

Father, thank You for Your plan for my life, a plan that is full of hope and an abundant future. Thank You that You are calling me to trust You and to be comfortable not knowing how everything will work out. In Jesus' Name, Amen.

FEBRUARY 4

Chained but Not Bound

And because I preach this Good News, I am suffering and have been chained like a criminal. But the word of God cannot be chained.

2 TIMOTHY 2:9, NLT

Because the apostle Paul was sharing the Good News, he was put in prison. It looked as though God had forgotten him. But Paul didn't feel sorry for himself. Since he couldn't go out and speak publicly, he thought, *No problem. I'll start writing*. He wrote nearly half of the books in the New Testament, much of them from a prison cell. Even though he was in chains, his enemies couldn't stop what God wanted him to do. His voice actually became amplified. Some two thousand years later, we are still transformed by what Paul wrote from a dungeon. What his enemies meant for harm, God used for good. Remember: In the midst of your difficulties, you can shine and be a bright light. You may be chained, but you're never bound.

PRAY & DECLARE

Father, thank You that You are the Most High God and that Your work in my life is greater than any chains that might try to hold me back. I believe that, no matter what circumstances I face, Your Word cannot be bound in my life. In Jesus' Name, Amen.

FEBRUARY 5

Be the Bigger Person

"Brother Saul, the Lord Jesus, who appeared to you on the road, has sent me so that you might regain your sight and be filled with the Holy Spirit."

ACTS 9:17, NLT

Saul was the biggest enemy of the early church. He went around having believers arrested and put in jail. Yet when Saul was at the point of his deepest need, God sent a Christian named Ananias to pray for Saul and speak to his need. In praying for Saul, Ananias did good to someone who had done great harm to his fellow believers. Saul went on to become the apostle Paul.

You may have people like Saul in your life. They may not be that menacing or vocal, but they're condescending toward you and treat you as though you're less than. Be the bigger person and bless those who have cursed you. In their time of need, don't withhold your help.

PRAY & DECLARE

Father, thank You that no matter how badly I am treated at times, You are always my vindicator. Thank You that You love the Sauls in my life, and You are working in their lives as well as mine. I will be the bigger person and bless them. In Jesus' Name, Amen.

From your
little bit, God
can create more
than enough.

FEBRUARY 6

Blessed by Enemies

So David triumphed over the Philistine with a sling and a stone; without a sword in his hand he struck down the Philistine and killed him.

1 SAMUEL 17:50, NIV

Goliath was strategically placed in David's path — not to defeat him but to promote him. Without Goliath, David would never have taken the throne. What may look like a setback is really a setup to get you to your throne. We all know that God can bless us. But what we don't always realize is that God can use our enemies to bless us. There are Goliaths ordained to come across your path. If you don't understand this principle, you'll get discouraged and think, *God, why is this happening to me?* You may not like a disappointment someone caused — that person who left you, that coworker who's trying to make you look bad, or that friend who betrayed you — but you couldn't reach your destiny without it.

PRAY & DECLARE

Father, thank You that You are always greater than any adversity I will ever face. Thank You for the Goliaths that You have ordained to come across my path. I believe they were created to promote me and push me to my purpose. In Jesus' Name, Amen.

FEBRUARY 7

Release Your Faith

When he heard that it was Jesus of Nazareth, he began to shout, "Jesus, Son of David, have mercy on me!"

MARK 10:47, NIV

When a blind beggar named Bartimaeus heard that Jesus was passing by, he started to shout, *"Jesus, Son of David, have mercy on me!"* Technically, Jesus was the son of Joseph and Mary. Bartimaeus called him the *"Son of David,"* which was the Old Testament messianic title, because he recognized Jesus as the Messiah. Bartimaeus was declaring, "You are my Messiah, my deliverer, my healer, the Most High God." Jesus stopped in His tracks. I can imagine Him thinking, *Here's someone who knows who I am, someone who believes I have all power, someone who's expecting My goodness.* Bartimaeus was asking not just a man — but the Son of God. And Jesus responded by saying, *"Your faith has made you well"* (Mark 10:52, NKJV).

PRAY & DECLARE

Father, thank You that just as You restored the sight of Bartimaeus, You can do the impossible in my life. Thank You that I can bring You the desires of my heart. Help me be bold to ask You — the Son of David, the Messiah — for the big things only You can make happen. In Jesus' Name, Amen.

FEBRUARY 8

Go to Sleep

Suddenly there was an angel at his side and light flooding the room. The angel shook Peter and got him up: "Hurry!" The handcuffs fell off his wrists.

ACTS 12:7, MSG

The apostle Peter was chained between two soldiers in prison. The next day it looked as though Peter would be put to death. Yet when an angel appeared in the prison during the night, Peter was sleeping so soundly he had to be shaken awake. If you were Peter, would you be sleeping soundly? Peter must have thought, *God, I've done my best, believed and prayed, and now I'm going to rest in You.*

Worrying doesn't make anything better. Constantly reminding God about what's wrong only makes us depressed. Try a different approach and do what Peter did — go to sleep. Enter into the Lord's rest. Say, "God, I know You're bigger than anything I'm facing. You said You never sleep, so I'm going to sleep, knowing that You are fighting my battles."

PRAY & DECLARE

Father, thank You for Your strength and comfort in difficult times. I refuse to be overwhelmed by problems because You will bring me through to victory. I declare that I am resting in the Almighty God who is greater than anything I face. In Jesus' Name, Amen.

FEBRUARY 9

Turn Up Your Praise

He lifted me out of the slimy pit, out of the mud and mire; he set my feet on a rock and gave me a firm place to stand. He put a new song in my mouth, a hymn of praise to our God. Many will see and fear the Lord *and put their trust in him.*

PSALM 40:2–3, NIV

God gave Joseph a dream that one day his family would bow down before him, but his brothers' hatred toward him became so great that they threw him into a pit, intending to let him die there. But his brother Judah said, "Let's sell him to the Ishmaelites as a slave," which saved Joseph's life. The name Judah means "praise." Praise rose up and changed the opposition's mind; praise pushed back the forces of darkness. The dreams that God put in you are not going to come to pass without opposition. When you're in the pit, don't complain — turn up your Judah — your praise — and start thanking God that He's turning things around.

PRAY & DECLARE

Father, thank You that the pits I find myself in can never stop the dream You put in my heart. Thank You that I can turn up my praise and bless You that You're turning things around. In Jesus' Name, Amen.

FEBRUARY 10

Grasshopper Disease

"There we saw the giants (the descendants of Anak came from the giants); and we were like grasshoppers in our own sight, and so we were in their sight."

NUMBERS 13:33, NKJV

When Moses sent twelve men to spy out the Promised Land, ten came back with a negative report. Notice how they didn't say, "The giants called us grasshoppers." They said, "We were in our own sight as grasshoppers." They went in with a grasshopper mentality.

Opposition doesn't determine who you are; it simply reveals who you are. If you have a grasshopper mentality, all your challenges and problems will look too big. The problem is not the giants; the problem is your thinking. Joshua and Caleb saw the same giants, yet they said, "We are well able. Let us go in at once and take the land."

PRAY & DECLARE

Father, thank You that You are always greater than any difficulty or adversity I will ever face. Thank You that I am not a grasshopper, but I am well able to go in, overtake any giant, and take the land. I declare that I will move not based on what my eyes see before me but by the vision you have placed in my heart. In Jesus' Name, Amen.

You will go through the fire and not be burned.

FEBRUARY 11

The God of the Breakthrough

"The Lord *did it!" David exclaimed. "He burst through my enemies like a raging flood!" So he named that place Baal-perazim (which means "the Lord who bursts through").*

2 SAMUEL 5:20, NLT

When David was about to step into the fullness of his destiny as the king over all Judah and Israel, he found himself at the Valley of Rephaim, which means "giants." Many years earlier, he had killed Goliath in that valley. But now he not only faced one Goliath, he faced a valley of Goliaths.

The principle is that the closer you are to your destiny, the greater the opposition. When you overcome one challenge, don't be surprised if you face a bigger challenge. When David and his men defeated the Philistines, he renamed the valley of giants Baal-perazim, which means the Lord breaks through. When you face the valley of debt, struggle, and lack, rename it the valley of abundance, promotion, and increase.

PRAY & DECLARE

Father, thank You that a valley of giants and challenges is no match for You. Thank You that You are the God of the breakthrough, who bursts through like a raging flood and brings me to my destiny. In Jesus' Name, Amen.

FEBRUARY 12

Tame the Tongue

As long as an heir is underage, he is no different from a slave, although he owns the whole estate.

GALATIANS 4:1, NIV

It's easy to make excuses in relationships. "I was rude to her because she was rude to me. I shouldn't have said it, but I was so tired." No, you have God's grace to always treat others with love and not say hurtful things. Even though you're an heir of God with an incredible inheritance that belongs to you — joy, peace, favor, promotion, and abundance — if you remain a child, it won't be released. Sometimes we let small things keep us from the big things God has in store. In the big picture, it's a small thing to tame your tongue. God is simply asking you to use your words and actions to bless and not curse, to build up and not tear down.

PRAY & DECLARE

Father, thank You that You have given me Your grace and power to speak loving words. I declare that I will not be childish; I'll tame my tongue and walk in the incredible inheritance You have for me. In Jesus' Name, Amen.

FEBRUARY 13

Break the Bonds

Then the Spirit of the L*ORD* *came mightily upon him; and the ropes that were on his arms became like flax that is burned with fire, and his bonds broke loose from his hands.*

JUDGES 15:14, NKJV

For fear of the Philistines, the Israelites went to Samson, their friend and deliverer, and tied him up, with the intent of handing him over to the Philistines to stop more attacks. When the Philistines saw him bound, the Spirit of the Lord came on Samson. He snapped those ropes like threads before defeating a thousand Philistines. What's interesting is that he broke the restraints of his friends, not of his enemies.

Sometimes the people who are the closest to us, our family and friends, are the ones who limit us. Be emboldened to declare, "The power in me is greater than any power that's trying to stop me, including those close to me."

PRAY & DECLARE

Father, thank You for the power of the Holy Spirit in my life that is greater than any chains that are trying to hold me back — even those coming from family and friends. I break all unhealthy bonds, knowing that You have equipped and empowered me. In Jesus' Name, Amen.

FEBRUARY 14

He Is Love

And so we know and rely on the love God has for us. God is love. Whoever lives in love lives in God, and God in them.

1 JOHN 4:16, NIV

Sometimes religion tells us, "Clean yourself up, then God will love you. If you fail to do what's right, God won't have anything to do with you. If you're good enough, if you measure up, then God will help you." That's not real love; that's conditional love. Real love is not about your performance, what you do or don't do. It's about who God is and what He's already done. Nothing you can do will make Him love you more. When you know that God is love, you'll go to Him with confidence. You'll pray bold prayers, you'll ask Him for your dreams, you'll expect new doors to open — not because of who you are, but because of who your Father is.

PRAY & DECLARE

Father, thank You that You love me because You are love, that it's not just what You do but it is who You are. Thank You that I don't have to clean myself up to earn Your love or get You to love me more. I live knowing I can completely rely on and rest in Your abiding love. In Jesus' Name, Amen.

FEBRUARY 15

Conditional Trust

Trust in him at all times, you people; pour out your hearts to him, for God is our refuge.

PSALM 62:8, NIV

It's easy to trust God when things are going our way. But when our prayers aren't being answered the way we want, too often we get upset and ask, "God, why didn't You answer my prayers?" Conditional trust says, "God, if You answer my prayers in the way I want, I'll be happy; I'll be my best." The problem with conditional trust is that there will always be something that's not happening fast enough, something that doesn't work out the way we want. There will always be unanswered "why" questions. God is sovereign. He knows what He's doing. You may not understand everything that happens, but God has your best interest at heart. It's not random. It's a part of His plan. Therefore, you can rest and trust at all times.

PRAY & DECLARE

Father, thank You that You are sovereign and worthy of my unconditional trust. There are things in my life that I don't understand, but even if things don't happen the way I hope, I'm still going to trust You. I declare: You are my refuge, even in uncertainty. In Jesus' Name, Amen.

Use your words and actions to bless and not curse, to build up and not tear down.

FEBRUARY 16

Power in Connectivity

When the day of Pentecost came, they were all together in one place. Suddenly a sound like the blowing of a violent wind came from heaven and filled the whole house where they were sitting.

ACTS 2:1–2, NIV

Jesus had told His followers to wait for the promise of the Holy Spirit. Scholars say there were around 500 people there. But when the Holy Spirit came, only 120 were in the upper room. Maybe the others were busy or just tired. Whatever the reason, they missed the initial outpouring of what God promised. The Scripture says the people in the upper room were together in one place, in unity, and suddenly the Holy Spirit came like a rushing mighty wind.

When you're in unity, connected with other believers, there will be some "suddenlies." Suddenly, your health will improve. Suddenly, your business will take off. Suddenly, you'll meet the right person. You'll experience sudden turnarounds — things you couldn't make happen.

PRAY & DECLARE

Father, thank You that You ordained me to be in a community of faith so that my faith can be joined to others' faith. I know that, together, we will see Your power released and the "suddenlies" that transform each of us and the world. In Jesus' Name, Amen.

FEBRUARY 17

Positioned for Increase

Then the manna ceased on the day after they had eaten the produce of the land; and the children of Israel no longer had manna, but they ate the food of the land of Canaan that year.

JOSHUA 5:12, NKJV

For forty years in the wilderness, the Israelites depended upon God's supernatural provision of manna for their survival every day. But manna was only a temporary provision. God was taking them into a land flowing with milk and honey, with all kinds of fruits, vegetables, and resources. So when they ate their first produce from the Promised Land, the manna ceased. I can hear them crying out, "God, what's happening?" But God was saying, "From now on, I'm bringing you into abundance." When something ceases in your life — a friend walks away or a job ends — it's not the time to get discouraged. God never removes something unless He has something better coming.

PRAY & DECLARE

Father, thank You for all the ways You provide for me. Thank You that when one of those provisions ceases, You are getting me in a position to increase me. I believe You are stretching me to bring me into greater favor. In Jesus' Name, Amen.

FEBRUARY 18

Connect the Dots

We can make our plans, but the
Lord determines our steps.
PROVERBS 16:9, NLT

God doesn't always take us in a straight line. We make our plans going from A to B to C. But sometimes He'll take you from A to B, then to R, then back to D, then to S. Sometimes it's going to look like you're going backward. You have to trust Him when you don't understand. You have to know that God makes the final determination about your steps. Through the power of the Holy Spirit, you can stay in faith, believing that God is still in control, that He's working behind the scenes, and that what He started He will finish. Over time you're going to see how God connects the dots and how it was all part of His plan, strategically orchestrated.

PRAY & DECLARE

Father, thank You that when things don't go according to my plans, I can know that You are working behind the scenes and in charge of my steps. Thank You that You love me and have plans for me. I declare: You are determining my steps. You are strategically orchestrating and connecting the dots of my life. In Jesus' Name, Amen.

FEBRUARY 19

Keep on Walking

When Jesus saw the men, he said, "Go and show yourselves to the priests." As the ten men were going, they were healed.

LUKE 17:14, NCV

Jesus was met by ten lepers who began to shout, "Jesus, have mercy on us!" Jesus could have spoken a word and healed them, but instead He said, "Go show yourselves to the priests." They could have thought, *Once we're healed, we'll go to the priests.* But faith says you have to believe it and act on it before you see it. They kept walking even though there was no sign of healing. Finally, one of them looked at his skin and said, "It's getting better!" Another said, "My fingers are working!" The Scripture says, *"As the ten men were going, they were healed."* If they had waited for things to change, they wouldn't have seen the healing. Many times, the miracle is in the process of obedience to Jesus' word.

PRAY & DECLARE

Father, thank You for the promises You have put in my heart that haven't happened yet. Thank You that I'm going to keep praising, keep thanking, and I know that what I'm believing for is on the way. In Jesus' Name, Amen.

FEBRUARY 20

Times of Adversity

That You may give him power to keep himself calm in the days of adversity . . .

PSALM 94:13, AMPC

When trouble comes, you don't have to get upset. When your plans don't work out, you don't have to fall apart. When someone is rude, you don't have to get offended. You have the power to remain calm. You have the authority to rule over your kingdom — over your mind, your attitude, your responses. You can't rule over someone else. You can't rule over all your circumstances. That's not up to you. That's in God's hands. You control what you can control, and you have to trust God to take care of what you can't control. Make the decision at the first of the day that you're not going to let things upset you. You're going to be calm. You're going to stay in peace.

PRAY & DECLARE

Father, thank You that You have given me the power to keep calm in times of adversity. I declare and want to start this day and every day knowing the authority You have given me to rule over the kingdom of my thoughts, attitudes, and responses. In Jesus' Name, Amen.

God doesn’t always take us in a straight line.

FEBRUARY 21

Destiny Moments

So Joshua spared Rahab the prostitute and her relatives who were with her in the house, because she had hidden the spies Joshua sent to Jericho. And she lives among the Israelites to this day.

JOSHUA 6:25, NLT

When Joshua sent spies into the city of Jericho, it was Rahab the prostitute, who had the boldness to risk her life in hiding the spies from the king. She decided that this was a destiny moment, her opportunity to leave what was comfortable, to leave her dysfunction, to do the right thing and step into God's purpose for her life. In doing so, her whole world changed. Not only was Rahab and her family spared, but Rahab married a Jewish man and their descendants are in the family line of Jesus Christ.

Perhaps this is a destiny moment for you. Is God calling you to leave the things that have held you back and step into your calling to honor Him? You are one decision away from setting your family and your life on a new course to freedom, honor, blessing, and victory.

PRAY & DECLARE

Father, thank You that You break in with these destiny moments that can change everything. Thank You that You're orchestrating opportunities for me to step out of my comfort and into my calling. In Jesus' Name, Amen.

FEBRUARY 22

Find an Isaiah

"If two of you agree on earth concerning anything that they ask, it will be done for them by My Father in heaven. For where two or three are gathered together in My name, I am there in the midst of them."

MATTHEW 18:19–20, NKJV

When the king of Assyria invaded Judah with a huge army and threatened to destroy Jerusalem, King Hezekiah got together with the prophet Isaiah, and they started praying faith-filled prayers and speaking victory (2 Chronicles 32:20). Rather than panic, they declared God's favor, and He sent an angel to destroy the Assyrian army. When you feel bombarded by doubt, fear, and opposition, find someone full of faith who will stand in agreement with you. In difficult times, find an Isaiah. Find someone who declares, "I agree you're going to get well, overcome the setback, and do great things."

PRAY & DECLARE

Father, thank You that I can gather with the true believers You've brought into my life and we can agree together that Your will be done. I believe that as we come together, You are in our midst to bring victory. In Jesus' Name, Amen.

FEBRUARY 23

Do It Afraid

For God has not given us a spirit of fear and timidity, but of power, love, and self-discipline.

2 TIMOTHY 1:7, NLT

Does fear hold you back? Through Christ, we have the power to say, "I am not going to let fear, insecurity, what I don't have, or what I don't think I can do keep me in my limited environment. I'm going to stretch and make changes to follow the call." Your destiny is too great to let fear of what people will think stop you. The fear may still be there, but you have to act on your purpose, not on your fear. Fear will keep you from your destiny. Fear will keep you stuck. Sometimes, in your first steps forward, you may feel afraid. But as you step out, courage will come. Confidence will show up. The favor, the blessing, the healing — are waiting for you.

PRAY & DECLARE

Father, thank You that You have given me a spirit of power and courage to stretch and become all You created me to be. I declare that I will not let fear keep me in my comfort zone. In Jesus' Name, Amen.

FEBRUARY 24

Out of the Empty Places

"I went out full, and the Lord has brought me home again empty."

RUTH 1:21, NKJV

Naomi and her family had moved to the country of Moab because of a famine. Naomi's husband unexpectedly died. Then about ten years later, both of her sons died. Heartbroken, she decided to move back home. She returned bitter, but God turned her situation around and brought her great joy.

There are times when life deals us such a blow that we feel empty. We started out pursuing dreams, but a loss left us empty. The beauty is that our God is not going to leave you empty and feeling like you can't go on. He comes into our empty places with strength for the weary, fresh vision, fresh anointing. Even now, God is breathing on your life. You're about to come out of that empty place. He has something coming that's going to far outweigh the loss, the heartache, the disappointment.

PRAY & DECLARE

Father, thank You that You are able to take the empty places in my life and fill them with joy. Thank You for the new doors that You open. I start this day declaring that You are breathing fresh vision and strength into me. In Jesus' Name, Amen.

FEBRUARY 25

Freezing Time

There has never been a day like this one before or since, when the LORD answered such a prayer.

JOSHUA 10:14, NLT

Joshua and the Israelite army were winning a battle, but they were running out of time before it got dark and the enemy army would escape. Instead of conceding the situation, Joshua was bold and prayed, "Sun, stand still until the enemy is defeated." People who heard him must have thought he was crazy, but God answered his prayer and gave them the time they needed for a complete victory.

It may feel as though it's too late for you to accomplish a dream or to overcome an obstacle. God can even freeze time so you can finish what you started. Time is on your side, because God is on your side. He's not limited by a clock, by a calendar, by age, or by year. He's giving you a window of time to accomplish what He put in your heart.

PRAY & DECLARE

Father, thank You that when I feel that I am running out of time, time is actually on my side because You are on my side. Thank You that I can dare to pray bold prayers to accomplish my dreams. In Jesus' Name, Amen.

Praise is one
of God's great
gifts to us.

FEBRUARY 26

Be Faithful

When they had crossed, Elijah said to Elisha, "Tell me, what can I do for you before I am taken from you?" "Let me inherit a double portion of your spirit," Elisha replied.

2 KINGS 2:9, NIV

Elisha had left his family business to travel and serve the prophet Elijah. Year after year, he'd been faithful doing what could have been seen as insignificant, as less than what he was capable of doing. He kept serving with excellence in the background of Elijah's ministry. On the day when Elijah was taken to Heaven, Elisha asked for a double portion of Elijah's spirit, and God gave it to him. Elisha had twice the anointing and did twice as many miracles as Elijah.

Wherever God has you, be your best. Don't slack off because it's not where you want to be and it's less than what's in you. Keep being faithful. Your time is coming. God is going to take you from the background to the foreground. It's going to happen suddenly.

PRAY & DECLARE

Father, thank You for the double portion that You have for those who are faithful when it would be easy to walk away. Thank You for where I am today and for the increase that You will bring in the future. In Jesus' Name, Amen.

FEBRUARY 27

Travel Steadily

Don't be impatient for the Lord to act! Keep traveling steadily along his pathway and in due season he will honor you with every blessing . . .

PSALM 37:34, TLB

We all have things we're waiting on — for the promotion to come, our health to improve, to meet the right person. When it's taken longer than we thought, it's easy to get discouraged. But just because it hasn't happened yet doesn't mean it's not going to happen. What God promised you is still en route. He has empowered you to not get discouraged, to keep traveling steadily, to keep praying, to keep thanking God, to keep being your best at work, and to keep being good to coworkers.

You're not moved by what's not changing. You consistently have a good attitude. You may be dealing with many challenges, but you're not complaining. You're consistently praising God, consistently declaring His promises, consistently expecting His favor. That's what it means to travel steadily.

PRAY & DECLARE

Father, thank You that there is a purpose for times of waiting, whether I understand it or not. Help me to be patient, to keep traveling steadily along Your pathway, to be consistent, knowing that it's all part of Your process. In Jesus' Name, Amen.

FEBRUARY 28

What Are You Saying?

*She had heard the reports concerning Jesus,
and she came up behind Him in the throng and
touched His garment, for she kept saying, If I only
touch His garments, I shall be restored to health.*

MARK 5:27–28, AMPC

A lady had been sick for twelve years and spent all her money going to doctors, but nothing helped. When she heard that Jesus was passing through town, she kept saying, "If I only touch His garments, I'll be restored to health." She kept saying over and over, "This is my time. Healing is coming. Restoration is coming." Notice the principle that whatever you're constantly saying, you're moving toward. She finally reached out and touched Jesus' robe and instantly she was healed.

Pay attention to what you're saying, because your life is going in that direction. If you're always saying, "I'll never get out of debt," you're moving toward struggle and lack. But when you say, "I'm going to break this addiction," you are moving toward freedom, breakthrough, and victory.

PRAY & DECLARE

Father, thank You that I can reach out and touch You by faith. I believe that You are making a way, that things are changing in my favor, and that victory will be mine. In Jesus' Name, Amen.

March

MARCH 1

Green Pastures

He makes me to lie down in green pastures.
He leads me beside the still waters.
PSALM 23:2, NKJV

You can be in a desert, a difficult place, and God will have a green pasture for you. You know God is still on the throne. You know He holds victory in store for the upright. You know that what was meant for harm He's turning to your advantage. It may be barren all around you, but you're in a green pasture. While others are complaining and talking about how it's not going to work out, you have a song of praise; you're expecting God's favor; you're declaring His promises.

What you're up against may be difficult, but don't worry. God has a green pasture prepared for wherever He takes you. Going through a divorce, taking the medical treatment, or getting laid off from your job is hard, but you're going to discover a green pasture. God has grace for every season.

PRAY & DECLARE

Father, thank You that You are my Good Shepherd, and I can rest and lie down in green pastures wherever I go. Thank You that I never need to worry because You have grace for whatever I face. In Jesus' Name, Amen.

MARCH 2

First Place

In everything you do, put God first, and he will direct you and crown your efforts with success.
PROVERBS 3:6, TLB

The prophet Elijah asked a starving widow to do something that seemed selfish. He said, "Before you make your final meal from the last of your grain and oil, make me a loaf of bread." But with it came God's promise of overflowing provision if she would keep Him first place and do as Elijah asked.

God is saying, "Keep Me first place in your life; let Me direct your steps and decisions, and I'll crown your efforts with success." Start each morning meeting with God. Take time to thank Him for the day. Thank Him for who He is. Thank Him that He's the giver of all good things. All through the day, under your breath, you can talk to God and say, "Lord, direct me in everything I do and say."

PRAY & DECLARE

Father, thank You that You invited me into a relationship with You. I want, in everything I do, to put You first and have You direct my life. Thank You for speaking to me through Your Word. I believe that You will crown my efforts with success. In Jesus' Name, Amen.

MARCH 3

Step Into the Fight

"Don't be ridiculous!" Saul replied. "There's no way you can fight this Philistine and possibly win! You're only a boy, and he's been a man of war since his youth."

1 SAMUEL 17:33, NLT

God put the dream in David to defeat Goliath. When David told King Saul, you would think Saul would have been excited to finally have somebody take on the giant. But he did just the opposite. However, David refused to believe the limitations and declared his victory before bringing Goliath down.

The reason some people don't support you when you feel God has spoken something to you is because God didn't put the dream in them. They can't see what you see or feel what you feel. They may think they're protecting you and doing you a favor by telling you what you can't do. But you have an empowerment to step into the fight that will cause it to come to pass.

PRAY & DECLARE

Father, thank You that I am not limited by what the people around me say or think about me. Thank You that You have qualified me to do what You have destined me to do. I will not allow others to put a limitation on what You have put in my heart. In Jesus' Name, Amen.

MARCH 4

Faith Is Now

Now faith is the substance of things hoped for, the evidence of things not seen.

HEBREWS 11:1, NKJV

Think of all the people in the Scripture who didn't wait for Jesus to come to them but sought Him out passionately for their needs. God has a perfect time for each of us, but today's Scripture says, "*Faith is* . . ." Faith is always in the now. It may not bring the change overnight, for we all have waiting periods. But our faith should stay active, as we declare, "Lord, thank You that the secret petition of my heart is on the way. I'm looking for Your goodness and favor today, not next week, not next month, not next year." Stay in the now. Your faith is going to turn things around, open the right doors, and bring unexpected favor. Live with the anticipation that it could happen today.

PRAY & DECLARE

Father, thank You that in this present moment I walk by faith and not by sight. Thank You that Your power can turn impossible situations around, open the right door, and bring an abundance of unexpected favor. In Jesus' Name, Amen.

MARCH 5

Why Are You Favored?

"If you keep quiet at a time like this, deliverance and relief for the Jews will arise from some other place, but you and your relatives will die. Who knows if perhaps you were made queen for just such a time as this?"

ESTHER 4:14, NLT

Esther was a Jewish orphan girl who was living in exile in Persia. It didn't look as though she would ever do anything great. But God raised her up to become the queen over many other women who came from wealth, influence, and beauty. God's favor caused her to stand out, and it shows that favor is more powerful than your résumé. Later, Esther used her position to save the Jewish people from a plot to destroy them.

Favor is not about having a bigger house, a better car, or more stuff. Favor is given to fulfill your purpose and advance His Kingdom. When your dreams are tied to helping others, to making the world a better place, to lifting the fallen, you will come into some of those "such a time as this" moments.

PRAY & DECLARE

Father, thank You that You are Almighty God and the power of Your favor is working in my life. Thank You for the opportunities You will bring my way to step into "such a time as this" moments and fulfill my purpose and advance Your Kingdom. In Jesus' Name, Amen.

When you're in the pit, remember your dreams. The palace is coming.

MARCH 6

When You Fall Down

As they were going out, they met a man from Cyrene, named Simon, and they forced him to carry the cross.

MATTHEW 27:32, NIV

When Jesus was being led out of Jerusalem to be crucified, He had to carry his own cross. Jesus was so exhausted from the sleepless night and the suffering and pain of the trial that He fell down under the weight of the cross. God provided a man named Simon to carry the cross for Jesus.

God knows that sometimes the weight of what we're carrying gets too heavy. It's okay to say, "God, I don't think I can do this." When you're down, God will always have someone to help lift you back up, someone to encourage you, someone to help you carry the load that you can't carry. God will send a Simon to help lift you back up.

PRAY & DECLARE

Father, thank You that You don't fault me for the times when I don't have the strength on my own to do what I need to do. Thank You that You find a way to get me the help I need in times of trouble. I believe that You know just the right people to encourage and lift me up. In Jesus' Name, Amen.

MARCH 7

Mind Clutter

The Lord *is my shepherd, I lack nothing. He makes me lie down in green pastures, he leads me beside quiet waters.*

PSALM 23:1–2, NIV

You might think that King David had an easy life and that everything went his way. It was just the opposite. His life was full of challenges: people trying to push him down, armies trying to defeat him, and his own family against him at times. Yet, in his mind, he was made to lie down in green pastures and be led by still waters. Despite all that came against him, he lived out of a place of peace.

Our circumstances can create noise in our thoughts — worries, offenses, doubts, fears, jealousy. But you don't have to carry all the mind clutter. Come into the green pastures by the still waters and let the Lord clear it out. As you welcome His stillness, you'll know that He is God. Despite what's coming at you, you'll experience a peace that passes understanding.

PRAY & DECLARE

Father, thank You that You are my Good Shepherd, and You lead me to green pastures beside restful waters. Thank You that I can come to You and clear out all the mind clutter and live out of a place of peace. In Jesus' Name, Amen.

MARCH 8

A Life of Praise

I will bless the Lord *at all times;*
His praise shall continually be in my mouth.
PSALM 34:1, NKJV

Praise is one of God's great gifts to us. We can overcome life's difficulties through praise. He has empowered us to be grateful, have a smile, and be passionate about our dreams. We are elevated as we bless the Lord at all times. You can be in a pit, but nobody around you knows it.

Praise is the antidote for the poison of life. And it's readily available to anyone at all times. It's a gift that doesn't cost us anything. When we face a difficulty, it's so easy to become consumed by it. But the power — the life — of praise will lift us to a new dimension. It's our privilege to bless the Lord at all times, not focusing on what we've lost but thanking God for what we have left; by not complaining about what's behind us but by being grateful for what's in front of us.

PRAY & DECLARE

Father, thank You that You have given me the gift of praise. I love blessing You. Thank You that whether I'm on the mountaintop or in the valley, my whole life can be a praise to You. In Jesus' Name, Amen.

MARCH 9

The Palace Is Coming

Although Joseph recognized his brothers, they did not recognize him. Then he remembered his dreams about them . . .

GENESIS 42:8–9, NIV

Many years after being sold into slavery by his brothers, Joseph was put in charge over all the affairs of Egypt. When his brothers showed up at the palace looking to purchase food during the famine, you would think Joseph would be bitter and vindictive. But he remembered the dreams of promise God had shown him — not the betrayal, the hurts, the injustices. God had used all the difficulties to get him to where he was supposed to be.

When God gives you a dream, it doesn't mean it's going to come to pass without opposition, delays, and adversities. There will be things you don't understand. You'll have plenty of opportunities to get discouraged. However, in the tough times, remember your dreams. The palace is coming.

PRAY & DECLARE

Father, thank You that my hope and trust are in You. Even when I don't understand my circumstances, I know that You are working things out for my good and to fulfill my dreams. I lift my eyes to You and declare that You are directing my steps on the way to the palace. In Jesus' Name, Amen.

MARCH 10

What Is Prayer?

The Spirit you received does not make you slaves, so that you live in fear again; rather, the Spirit you received brought about your adoption to sonship. And by him we cry, "Abba, Father." The Spirit himself testifies with our spirit that we are God's children.

ROMANS 8:15–16, NIV

When we pray, something supernatural occurs. Prayer is the most powerful posture we can take in this earthly realm. When we pray, we connect the strongest part of ourselves with the strongest force in the universe — the Spirit of God. When we open ourselves to Him, God's Spirit testifies with our spirit that we are His children. Prayer, then, is simply talking to our Abba, Father. It is beautiful, unfettered intimacy with the Creator of the universe.

Remember, prayer is a most vibrant relationship. We don't need to be intimidated by a holy, all-powerful God because Jesus has graciously opened a wonderful pathway to the Father's heart. Our spirit poured out to His.

PRAY & DECLARE

Father, thank You that I can come into Your presence right now because Jesus has made a way for me. Thank You for being able to freely ask You for the things You have put on my heart. Speak to my spirit and show me the path for my life. In Jesus' Name, Amen.

Prayer is the most powerful posture we can take in this earthly realm.

MARCH 11

Turn It Around

"But as for me, I know that my Redeemer lives, and he will stand upon the earth at last."

JOB 19:25, NLT

Although Job had done nothing wrong, he lost his children, his business, and his health in a short period of time. At first, he got discouraged and started to get bitter, but Job turned it around. When it seemed as though he had lost all hope, he looked up to the Heavens and said, *"I know that my Redeemer lives."* He was saying, "I know God is still on the throne and will vindicate me." Job eventually came out with twice what he had before.

In difficult times, it's tempting to get sour. Yet, we can draw a line in the sand and say, "I am not going to let hurts and disappointments poison me with a bad attitude and keep me from becoming who I was created to be." Because my Redeemer lives, I can experience life in the midst of tough times.

PRAY & DECLARE

Father, thank You that no matter what I go through, You are my Redeemer and my vindicator. Thank You that You can bring me out of difficulties better off than I was before they showed up. In Jesus' Name, Amen.

MARCH 12

His Way Is Higher

"As the heavens are higher than the earth, so are my ways higher than your ways and my thoughts than your thoughts."

ISAIAH 55:9, NIV

Over the years, many things haven't turned out the way I had planned. I had it all figured out. I told God what to do, when to do it, what I needed, and how to get me there. The funny thing is that God didn't take my advice. He had His own plan, and it's always been better than my plan. His ways have always been more rewarding, more fulfilling, and bigger than my ways. If God had done what I asked, it would have limited my destiny.

Don't be discouraged when something doesn't work out the way you want. Know that God is in control. What He will do will be better than what you ever imagined.

PRAY & DECLARE

Father, thank You that You know best when it comes to the things I want and ask You for. Thank You that Your plans are always so much more fulfilling and bigger than my plan. I declare that You are in control, and You will get me to where You want me. In Jesus' Name, Amen.

MARCH 13

Prosper in All Things

Beloved, I pray that you may prosper in all things and be in health, just as your soul prospers.

3 JOHN 1:2, NKJV

Prosperity is so much more than having finances. It's having your health. It's having peace in your mind. It's being able to sleep at night. It's having good relationships. There are so many things that money cannot buy. But I also can't find a single verse in the Scripture that suggests we are supposed to drag around in the land of *Not Enough*.

God is called El Shaddai, the God of *More Than Enough*. He takes pleasure in prospering His people. He says we were created to be the head and not the tail. He says He will lavish us with good things. Jesus came that we might live an abundant life. God's dream for your life is that you would be blessed in such a way that you can be a blessing to others.

PRAY & DECLARE

Father, thank You that You are El Shaddai, the Almighty God, the God of abundance, not the God of barely enough. Thank You that You delight in prospering me and that I can use my finances as a tool for good. Help me to be generous in blessing others. In Jesus' Name, Amen.

MARCH 14

Only God Knows

And lest I should be exalted above measure by the abundance of the revelations, a thorn in the flesh was given to me, a messenger of Satan to buffet me, lest I be exalted above measure. Concerning this thing I pleaded with the Lord three times that it might depart from me. And He said to me, "My grace is sufficient for you, for My strength is made perfect in weakness."

2 CORINTHIANS 12:7–9, NKJV

Scholars have speculated about what the apostle Paul's *"thorn in the flesh"* was, but what we know is that it was a secret frustration that bothered him so much that he prayed three times for God to remove it. Paul says that he thought the thorn in his flesh was to keep him from getting puffed up because of the great revelations he had been given. Only God knows the reason He allows thorns to remain in our lives, but nothing happens by accident. Despite these "thorns," Jesus empowers you to keep giving even when you're not receiving, keep trying when every door is closing, and keep doing the right thing even when you're not seeing the right results.

PRAY & DECLARE

Father, thank You that You are the sovereign God who alone knows what is best for me. I declare that Your grace is sufficient for me. Whether it ever changes or not, I declare that I'm still going to be my best and stay in faith. In Jesus' Name, Amen.

MARCH 15

Taste and See

Taste and see that the Lord is good;
blessed is the one who takes refuge in him.
PSALM 34:8, NIV

When Moses led the Israelites toward the Promised Land, they never went in because they complained and had wrong mindsets. That generation wandered in the wilderness for forty years, only hearing about the land flowing with milk and honey. But they died without ever seeing it come to pass. Joshua led the next generation that had a different mindset into the Promised Land.

They didn't just hear about the land of abundance; they conquered and lived in it. Sometimes thoughts will tell you, *What you're dreaming about will always only be a dream, just a wish and a hope.* But you can be part of the Joshua generation. You're not going to just dream the dream; you're going to live your dream. You're going to taste the grapes, the abundance, the healing, and the freedom.

PRAY & DECLARE

Father, thank You for the invitation to taste and see just how good You are. Thank You that the dream You've put in my heart will come to pass and not remain just a dream. I believe You're taking me into my Promised Land. In Jesus' Name, Amen.

Prosperity is so much more than having finances.

MARCH 16

Stop the Leak

The start of a quarrel is like a leak
in a dam, so stop it before it bursts.
PROVERBS 17:14, MSG

One of the biggest challenges we all face is getting along with other people. We have different personalities and come from different backgrounds. When somebody doesn't agree with us, or they're doing what we don't like, it's easy to quarrel with them to prove our point. Before long we're at odds, mad at each other, and offended.

When we let our guard down and say things that are disrespectful, hurtful, and demeaning, we damage our relationship and open the door to strife. That's why the Scripture says, "*Give no opportunity to the adversary*" (1 Timothy 5:14, NKJV). Strife can't just come in whenever it wants; you have to open the door. To never have an argument or say a wrong word is not reality, but when we allow strife to become common, we're headed down the wrong path. Stop strife before it bursts and tears relationships apart.

PRAY & DECLARE

Father, thank You for the promise of blessedness when I take the high road and am a peacemaker in relationships. Give me wisdom to know when to keep my mouth closed and overlook something that bothers me. In Jesus' Name, Amen.

MARCH 17

Promotion

"For the Lord does not see as man sees;
for man looks at the outward appearance,
but the Lord looks at the heart."
1 SAMUEL 16:7, NKJV

People look on the outside. God looks on the heart. God knew that if He could trust David to take care of sheep and to be faithful when things weren't going his way, He could trust him to take care of His people. David went from being a shepherd to being the next king. Nobody voted for him. This wasn't a democracy. If it had been, he wouldn't have received one vote. His father didn't even believe in him.

When God is ready to promote you, He doesn't check to see who likes you or how popular you are. It's not a vote. It's an appointment. Promotion doesn't come from people. It comes from the Lord. When it's your time to be promoted, no person, no disappointment, and no enemy can stop you. God has the one and only vote.

PRAY & DECLARE

Father, thank You that You are not limited to seeing me as other people see me. Thank You that You see my heart. I believe that promotion comes from You, and You have the final say. In Jesus' Name, Amen.

MARCH 18

Clothed in Humility

... All of you, clothe yourselves with humility toward one another, because, "God opposes the proud but shows favor to the humble."

1 PETER 5:5, NIV

There are times when God asks us to do what seems hard — to be quiet when someone offends us, to not get even, to not prove we're right. Clothed in the Lord's humility, we can say to those we care about, "I will stop the argument. My happiness is not dependent on them doing it my way. I will say I'm sorry and ask for forgiveness."

The healing for many relationships is in humbling yourself and doing your part to get along. You can tap into the Lord's power by making the first move. You can't make them change, but if you treat them with respect and do what you can to honor them, be kind, and serve them, those seeds you're sowing will come back to you.

PRAY & DECLARE

Father, thank You that there is healing and restoration in my relationships when I clothe myself and walk in the humility that You have so graciously provided to me. Yes, I will be the one to sow seeds that build and restore relationships. In Jesus' Name, Amen.

MARCH 19

A Crown of Beauty

. . . and provide for those who grieve in Zion — to bestow on them a crown of beauty instead of ashes, the oil of joy instead of mourning, and a garment of praise instead of a spirit of despair. They will be called oaks of righteousness, a planting of the LORD for the display of his splendor.

ISAIAH 61:3, NIV

When someone you love leaves you or a friend walks away for some reason, it's easy to feel that you're somehow not smart enough, good enough, or talented enough. You may tell yourself, "If I'd only done this or that better." It can feel like it's all your fault. But when somebody leaves you, it doesn't necessarily mean there's something wrong with you. It could be the other person has the problem. Nevertheless, the accuser will work overtime trying to convince you that you don't measure up.

If this has happened to you, don't sit around feeling sorry for yourself. No more saying, "This person walked away. I'll never be happy again." Say, "No one is taking my crown. God is giving me beauty for these ashes. What God started in my life, He will finish!"

PRAY & DECLARE

Father, thank You that the past is over and done, and I can quit dwelling on it. I believe that You will always give me a crown of beauty instead of ashes and the oil of joy instead of mourning. In Jesus' Name, Amen.

MARCH 20

Darkness Cannot Stop the Light

Yes, happy is the man who delights in doing his commands. His children shall be honored everywhere, for good men's sons have a special heritage. He himself shall be wealthy, and his good deeds will never be forgotten. When darkness overtakes him, light will come bursting in.

PSALM 112:1–4, TLB

It may be dark in your life right now. You don't see how you will ever get well, get out of debt, or see the legal situation resolve. Here's the key: You are the righteous; you are a child of the Most High God. You have this promise from your Creator that when it's dark and you feel like giving up, light is about to burst in. It doesn't say it will barely get there. No, suddenly, unexpectedly, it will come bursting in. That means you won't see it coming, but God will turn it all around. Healing, favor, and restoration are going to burst in.

The God who spoke worlds into existence controls the darkness and the light. When it's your time for promotion, for abundance, all the forces of darkness cannot stop our God.

PRAY & DECLARE

Father, thank You that in times of darkness when I don't see the way out, I have Your promise that You will come bursting in with Your glorious light. I believe that all the forces of darkness cannot stop it. In Jesus' Name, Amen.

God is giving me beauty for these ashes.

MARCH 21

God's Character through Us

Then he broke down and wept. He wept so loudly the Egyptians could hear him, and word of it quickly carried to Pharaoh's palace.

GENESIS 45:2, NLT

Having God's favor doesn't mean you won't feel pain. Being blessed doesn't mean you won't have hurts. Joseph's brothers sold him into slavery, and for thirteen years he had his life taken away from him. He longed for freedom and to see his family; his nights were lonely, and his days felt forgotten in prison, yet he kept doing the right thing and never got bitter. Now when Joseph's brothers came before him, he wept so loudly that people all through the palace could hear it. But even though he was in a position of power to get even with his brothers, he used his power instead to be good to them.

Let God fight your battles; let Him be your vindicator. Be kind to the people who did you wrong, and God will take you further than you can imagine.

PRAY & DECLARE

Father, thank You that You use the really hard things in my life to bring out Your character in me. Thank You that with every unfair thing that comes my way, You empower and invigorate me with Your mercy and kindness. In Jesus' Name, Amen.

MARCH 22

Into the Unknown

"Go, gather together all the Jews who are in Susa, and fast for me. Do not eat or drink for three days, night or day. I and my attendants will fast as you do. When this is done, I will go to the king, even though it is against the law. And if I perish, I perish."

ESTHER 4:16, NIV

Esther was a Jewish orphan girl who was living in a foreign country. But God raised her up to become the queen. When a powerful official passed a law that all the Jewish people be killed, Esther's cousin Mordecai told her that she had to go in and plead with the king for their people. In those days, if you approached the king without his holding up his golden rod first, you could be killed. That included Esther. God was asking her to step into the unknown. We love that Esther put her life on the line and saved her people.

When God gives you opportunities to step into the unknown, don't let fear talk you out of it, and don't let the what-ifs silence you. Be bold, be courageous, and step into the unknown.

PRAY & DECLARE

Father, thank You for the opportunities You will bring my way to step into the unknown, and I expect to see Your hand of favor work powerfully on my behalf. I declare that the what-ifs will not stop me. In Jesus' Name, Amen.

MARCH 23

Love Lavished on Us

See what great love the Father has lavished on us, that we should be called children of God! And that is what we are! The reason the world does not know us is that it did not know him.

1 JOHN 3:1, NIV

The Scripture speaks of the *"great love the Father has lavished on us."* It wasn't a little love, an "I think" love, or a conditional love. It was and is a "great love." Before you were formed in your mother's womb, God knew and loved you. He took time to plan out all your days. He knows your thoughts before you think them. He knows your words before you speak them. Jesus said, *"Even the very hairs of your head are all numbered"* (Matthew 10:30, NIV).

Do you really think there's anything you can do to cause Him to stop loving you? We don't need to ever wonder, *I think He loves me. I think I'm good enough. I think I haven't done too much wrong.* Get rid of the "I think" mentality and start having an "I know" mentality. Live securely, knowing that your Heavenly Father loves you.

PRAY & DECLARE

Father, thank You for the great love that You have lavished on me that I should be called Your child. Thank You that nothing I've done can cancel out Your love. In Jesus' Name, Amen.

MARCH 24

A Father to All

Sing to God, sing in praise of his name, extol him who rides on the clouds; rejoice before him — his name is the LORD. A father to the fatherless, a defender of widows, is God in his holy dwelling.

PSALM 68:4–5, NIV

All of us have been wounded in some way. Life happens. People do us wrong. Perhaps the parent who should have been speaking life to you, empowering you, did just the opposite, or perhaps they just were never there. You may have faced rejection, abandonment, and dysfunction in your home. But it doesn't have to stop you.

People may have rejected you, but God has accepted you. They may have left you out, but God has brought you in. Don't have a victim mentality. Keep moving forward. People may not have given you what you needed, but the God who breathed life into you, the God who knew you before you were born, is your Father. He's going to make up for what people can't give.

PRAY & DECLARE

Father, thank You that You are watching over me, and You know what I didn't get and who wasn't there for me. Thank You that You can heal the wounds of the past and make me into Your masterpiece. I believe that because You are my Father, through Christ, I can do great things. In Jesus' Name, Amen.

MARCH 25

In the Potter's Hands

"What sorrow awaits those who argue with their Creator. Does a clay pot argue with its maker? Does the clay dispute with the one who shapes it, saying, 'Stop, you're doing it wrong!'"

ISAIAH 45:9, NLT

The Scripture says that God is the potter and we are the clay. The potter takes a lump of clay and spins it on his wheel. The clay could say, "I'm tired of going in circles. Let me off this wheel." The clay doesn't realize that while it's spinning, the potter is molding it. It's rising up from a lump of clay into a beautiful vase.

You may feel like you're spinning today. You're doing the same thing over and over and don't see much progress. But when it feels like you're going in circles, something is happening that you can't see. You're coming up higher. God is molding your character. It may seem routine, but the Potter is causing you to rise higher.

PRAY & DECLARE

Father, thank You that my life is in Your hands and You are shaping my life like a potter — not just my dreams and goals, but my character. Thank You that You are working in the routine to mold my life into Your image. In Jesus' Name, Amen.

God is going to bless you where you are. Just let down your net.

MARCH 26

Be Amazed

As the enemy came down toward him, Elisha prayed to the Lord, *"Strike this army with blindness." So he struck them with blindness, as Elisha had asked.*

2 KINGS 6:18, NIV

The king of Aram was so angry with the prophet Elisha that he sent an army to capture him. Elisha was only one man against an army, but he knew how to pray bold prayers. He had seen God open blind eyes, and now he prayed for the reverse. The soldiers were struck blind and were captured.

When you know that God is with you, you'll see God do amazing things. He can protect you, guide you, and make things happen that you could never make happen. Don't go around feeling weak, intimidated, and afraid of what you're up against. Just as with Elisha, you are so powerful, full of favor, that even when the enemy does his best to defeat you, his best will never be enough.

PRAY & DECLARE

Father, thank You that no matter what trouble I face, I can stay in peace knowing that You are with me, and You can turn every situation around and put an end to it. I declare that You are greater than any force that comes against me. In Jesus' Name, Amen.

MARCH 27

Take That Step of Faith

Jesus told him, "Stand up, pick up your mat, and walk!"

JOHN 5:8, NLT

When Jesus asked a disabled man, "*Would you like to get well?*" (v. 6, NLT) he made excuses and tried to justify his condition. After thirty-eight discouraging years of having this disability, the man had gotten comfortable in his dysfunction and lost his passion to be well. But when he heard Jesus' call to do the impossible and rise up and walk, something ignited within him to try; strength came into his legs and he was instantly healed.

As with this man, God is going to ask you to do things that you don't think you can do. In your own ability, you can't, but when you take that step of faith, God will step in and give you supernatural ability. That's because there's favor in your calling. In your calling, you'll break addictions, beat the cancer, and rise up and walk in ways you never thought were possible.

PRAY & DECLARE

Father, thank You that with Your calling upon my life comes the power to release any old thinking, old habits, discouragement, and dysfunction that would keep me stuck. I'm taking steps of faith for a new beginning today. In Jesus' Name, Amen.

MARCH 28

Let Down Your Net

Simon then gets his fellow fishermen to help him let down their nets, and to their surprise, the water is bubbling with thrashing fish — a huge school. The strands of their nets start snapping under the weight of the catch.

LUKE 5:6, THE VOICE

The disciples were professional fishermen, but they had fished all night and caught nothing. When we're not seeing things happen as we expect, it's easy to feel frustrated and discouraged. But God still has all the fish that belong to you. You tried all night, so to speak. It's been months, or even years, and you haven't seen good breaks, promotions, or things turning around.

Don't worry, your fish are being stored up. Jesus told His disciples to let their nets into the deep one more time, which means the fish were close. You don't have to do something drastically different. God is going to bless you where you are. As with those disciples, boatloads of prepared blessings are coming your way. Just let down your net.

PRAY & DECLARE

Father, thank You that You are the God who spoke worlds into existence, and You know how to bring net-breaking blessings to my net. I'm going to keep believing Your Word and letting down my net. In Jesus' Name, Amen.

MARCH 29

Mighty Hero

The angel of the LORD *appeared to him and said, "Mighty hero, the* LORD *is with you!"*

JUDGES 6:12, NLT

When God called Gideon a mighty hero, he was afraid, intimidated, insecure, hiding from the Israelites' enemy, and he hadn't done anything significant. It seemed as though he was just an ordinary farmer. But God calls us what we are before it happens. He knows what's in us. He's the One who put the potential, the gifts, and the talents in us. Gideon finally did what I'm asking you to do. Instead of seeing himself as ordinary, not able to, something rose up inside. He said, in effect, "If God says I'm a mighty hero, then I believe I'm a mighty hero."

God has already called you a "mighty hero." Agree with Him. God calls you what you are, even though you might not have felt that way about yourself. Step out and walk in the name He has given you.

PRAY & DECLARE

Father, thank You that You have equipped and are empowering me to be strong where I feel weak and afraid. I declare what You have already declared over me: that I am a mighty hero. In Jesus' Name, Amen.

MARCH 30

Give Him Some Time

For since the world began, no ear has heard and no eye has seen a God like you, who works for those who wait for him!

ISAIAH 64:4, NLT

God will work all things together for our good, including the closed doors, the breakups, and the failures. That's how awesome our God is. Don't live sour because of what didn't work out or bitter over the person who walked away. Let it go. God has beauty for the ashes and joy for the mourning. He just needs some time.

Don't judge the rest of your life by one difficult season. Thoughts will tell you, *It's never going to change.* Don't believe those lies. At the right time, you're going to be so blessed and fulfilled that you won't think about the negative things of your past. Keep waiting on God — He can do something beyond your imagining.

PRAY & DECLARE

Father, thank You for the promises You have put in my heart and for the dreams I want to accomplish. Thank You that there is no other God like You, the Most High God, and I can joyfully wait on You. In Jesus' Name, Amen.

MARCH 31

Who Do You Say You Are?

Oh, give thanks to the Lord, *for He is good! For His mercy endures forever. Let the redeemed of the* Lord *say so, whom He has redeemed from the hand of the enemy.*

PSALM 107:1–2, NKJV

There are a lot of voices in life trying to define us and tell us who we are. Some voices are uplifting, telling us that we're talented and can do great things. Others are negative, telling us that there's nothing special about us. Our own thoughts will try to label us with: *You made too many mistakes and missed your chance.* It's easy to wonder, *Who am I? Am I strong and confident or weak and insecure? Do I have a bright future, or have I blown it?*

Here's the key: The only voice that matters is the voice of God, proclaiming who we really are. Instead of letting people or circumstances define you, agree and affirm what God says about you. He declares unequivocally that you can do all things through Christ. You're equipped and empowered to fulfill your purpose.

PRAY & DECLARE

Father, thank You that nothing anyone says about me can change what You have said about me. Thank You that I am who You say I am, and I can say so. I believe that I am redeemed, a masterpiece, fearfully and wonderfully created in Your image. In Jesus' Name, Amen.

April

APRIL 1

Boldness

The wicked flee though no one pursues,
but the righteous are as bold as a lion.
PROVERBS 28:1, NIV

When Nehemiah heard that the walls of Jerusalem were still torn down, he was working as the cupbearer for the king of Persia. He was living a thousand miles from Jerusalem. He had no resources and wasn't a builder. He was normally reserved and never made any waves, but he suddenly had this boldness to do something that he had never done. He had the courage to ask the king to authorize him to go and rebuild the walls as well as supply the timbers to do it, and the king did. God gave Nehemiah the strength, ability, and favor to complete those walls in just fifty-two days.

Don't discount your future based on where you're at today. God has given you a dream and will catapult you ahead. Suddenly you'll have courage and boldness, favor, and doors will open. People will go out of their way to help you, and you will accomplish what you never imagined was possible.

PRAY & DECLARE

Father, thank You that I can come boldly before You, knowing that as Your child, as one of the righteous, this is my rightful place. I declare bold prayers and ask You to make a way to the boldest dreams. In Jesus' Name, Amen.

APRIL 2

Committed to Excellence

Whatever you do, work at it with all your heart, as working for the Lord, not for human masters, since you know that you will receive an inheritance from the Lord as a reward. It is the Lord Christ you are serving.

COLOSSIANS 3:23–24, NIV

We live in a society in which mediocrity is the norm. Many people do as little as they can to get by. Don't sink to that level. God doesn't bless mediocrity. God blesses excellence. When you have a spirit of excellence, you do your best whether anyone is watching or not. You go the extra mile. You do more than you have to. You're always taking steps to improve. You set the highest standard. You live your best because you are honoring God, and you're representing Almighty God to your loved ones, friends, coworkers, and neighbors. In everything you do, make the more excellent choices that give God praise.

PRAY & DECLARE

Father, thank You for calling me to be a person of excellence in everything I do, to go the second mile, and to always be my best. I declare and focus on Your excellence that flows out of my heart. In Jesus' Name, Amen.

APRIL 3

Not a Victim

"For the Lord of hosts has purposed, and who will annul it? His hand is stretched out, and who will turn it back?"

ISAIAH 14:27, NKJV

You may have come from generations of abuse, mistreatment, addictions, and things that were not fair. There's a victim mentality that can be passed from generation to generation that says, "We've always been poor, defeated, shortchanged, addicted. We can't do anything about it." This forever-the-victim mentality will continue to be passed down until someone rises up and puts an end to it.

Today is a new day! Your past doesn't have the power to keep you enslaved in what was. The reason you're reading this is because you're the one to break the cycle; you're the one to say, "I am not a victim. Through Christ, I am a victor. I'm going to live whole, free, and expecting favor."

PRAY & DECLARE

Father, thank You for the promise that You have a purpose for my life that nothing can annul or turn back. Thank You for Your call to leave the past behind and refuse to settle for less than Your best for me. I declare that I will have a victor's mindset and live out all You created me to be. In Jesus' Name, Amen.

APRIL 4

Be a Stander

Be on your guard; stand firm in the faith;
be courageous; be strong. Do everything in love.
1 CORINTHIANS 16:13–14, NIV

God is not necessarily looking for people who have great faith, but for people who simply stand with an attitude of faith. People who stand when the problem is not turning around, stand when their heart is breaking, stand when the bottom falls out — not bitter, not discouraged. God never said we wouldn't have times of trouble. But He did promise that if you just stand, He'll bring you out. He'll defeat your enemies. He'll give you beauty for ashes. He has joy coming in the morning.

The enemy cannot defeat a stander. He can't defeat you when you stand in praise, even when things are not working out. You stand unmoved by what you're up against; stand with your eyes on God, knowing that He has the final say, that He's working behind the scenes, and that what He promised you will come to pass.

PRAY & DECLARE

Father, thank You for Your promise that You will work out Your plans for my life. I know and declare that You have empowered me to stand firm in my faith even in the times when nothing seems to make sense. In Jesus' Name, Amen.

APRIL 5

Rule Your Response

But as for me, I will sing about your power. Each morning I will sing with joy about your unfailing love. For you have been my refuge, a place of safety when I am in distress. O my Strength, to you I sing praises, for you, O God, are my refuge, the God who shows me unfailing love.

PSALM 59:16–17, NLT

David was on the run in the desert, hiding from King Saul and his army. He had been good to Saul, but Saul was so jealous of David that he was trying to kill him. David said, "I've done them no wrong, but they come at me at night, snarling like vicious dogs." But then David declared today's scripture. He understood that he couldn't control Saul. He couldn't change the minds of his enemies, but he could rule his response. He didn't let in the worry, the fear, or the panic. He sang about God's great power and love, filled with the joy of the Lord.

You can't rule other people's attitudes or actions; you can't make them do what's right, but you can rule your response.

PRAY & DECLARE

Father, thank You that I am not at the mercy of anyone else or any situation I may be struggling with. I'm going to praise You in spite of what comes against me and stay in peace. In Jesus' Name, Amen.

Father, thank You that You are my healer.

APRIL 6

Release It

Let him have all your worries and cares,
for he is always thinking about you and
watching everything that concerns you.

1 PETER 5:7, TLB

God puts promises and dreams in our hearts. We know that we're going to get well or that our business is going to turnaround. But God doesn't tell us how or when it's going to happen. Too often, if it's not happening the way we think or on our timetable, we get anxious. Here's the key: Once you pray, once you believe, leave how and when God does it up to Him. God's ways are not our ways. Sometimes it's taking longer because He has something better in store. It may not happen the way you think or when you had planned. If you're trying to control the outcome and time frame, you're going to live worried. It's a blessed thing to release to Him all your worries and cares.

PRAY & DECLARE

Father, thank You that You are in control of all the situations in my life and that You are fighting my battles. I choose to let go of the anxious thoughts that trap me in worry and discouragement. In Jesus' Name, Amen.

APRIL 7

Keep the Negative Out

The Lord will fight for you, and you shall hold your peace and remain at rest.

EXODUS 14:14, AMPC

You may be in a situation that's unfair, somebody did you wrong, you're dealing with an illness, or you've gone through a loss. You couldn't control what happened, and you can't make that go away. You could be worried, bitter, and upset. But praise be to God! The Lord is fighting for you. You don't have to be controlled by what you don't have control over. Don't give away this power that God has already given you by letting the negative in.

Declare: "I'm keeping my walls up. I'm not letting that negative into my spirit. I'm going to keep singing praises and thanking God. I will remain at rest, and I know God will fight my battles." He'll pay you back for the unfair things. He'll bring beauty out of those ashes. He will take care of what is trying to stop you.

PRAY & DECLARE

Father, thank You that You have power over what I cannot control. When I face problems that seem overwhelming, thank you that I can remain in peace and at rest, knowing that You are fighting my battles. In Jesus' Name, Amen.

APRIL 8

A Power Far Greater

"Which of their gods was able to rescue its people from the destructive power of my predecessors? What makes you think your God can rescue you from me?"

2 CHRONICLES 32:14, NLT

The king of Syria had invaded Judah with a huge army, and Jerusalem was next to be attacked. He sent a letter to the Israelites, defying their trust in God. But King Hezekiah declared, "Don't be afraid of this mighty army, for there is a power far greater on our side. We have the Lord our God to fight our battle." And God sent an angel to destroy the whole Syrian army (v. 21).

The enemy will always try to defeat you in your thoughts first. If you are facing a big enemy, remind yourself that our God is bigger than the cancer, the opposition, the addiction, and the financial problem. Don't talk about how big the enemy is; talk about how big your God is.

PRAY & DECLARE

Father, thank You for the strength that rises within me whenever I remember how great You are and what You have done in my life. Thank You for the countless times You have delivered my mind from the clutter of fears and doubts. In Jesus' Name, Amen.

APRIL 9

Come Out of Your Shell

A man's gift makes room for him,
and brings him before great men.
PROVERBS 18:16, NKJV

God has entrusted us with gifts and talents, but too often we let fear hold us back. We're hiding our gifts, our talents, our personality. We're afraid to come out of our shell, afraid we may not be accepted. It's time to quit hiding. If God has given you the gift to sing, start singing. If you can write, start writing. If you can lead, start leading. If you can build, start building. If you can teach, start teaching.

Your gift may seem small, but that gift will open big doors. You don't have to have a great gift for God to use you in a great way. Whatever you have, as you exercise it, it will open doors of opportunity, promotion, and influence.

PRAY & DECLARE

Father, thank You for the gifts and talents You have given to me as well as my personality. Thank You that You created me to release my gift and make a difference in the world. I declare that through Your power I have and will come out of my shell. In Jesus' Name, Amen.

APRIL 10

Mind-Boggling

That is what is meant by Scriptures which say that no mere man has ever seen, heard, or even imagined what the wonderful things God has ready for those who love the Lord.

1 CORINTHIANS 2:9, TLB

God's dream for your life is so much bigger than your own. What He has in your future is going to boggle your mind. You can't imagine the places He's going to take you, the people you will meet, the levels you're going to reach. If you think you've reached your limits, you better think again. God is about to take you into overflow, into abundance, into more than enough. Whatever level you're at, get ready; another level is coming. What you haven't seen or imagined is on the way.

Circumstances may be against you, but the Most High God is for you. He's working behind the scenes. Things are happening that you can't see. Your time is coming. God will do wonderful things you haven't experienced and can't even imagine.

PRAY & DECLARE

Father, thank You that You are the Most High God and that Your dream for my life is much bigger than my own. I sit in amazement anticipating the wonderful things You have and will do in my life. In Jesus' Name, Amen.

Thank You that blessings will be released no matter if I have started late.

APRIL 11

The Power of His Resurrection

When they entered the tomb, they saw a young man clothed in a white robe sitting on the right side. The women were shocked, but the angel said, "Don't be alarmed. You are looking for Jesus of Nazareth, who was crucified. He isn't here! He is risen from the dead! Look, this is where they laid his body."

MARK 16:5–6, NLT

On Easter morning, we celebrate the resurrection day of our Lord and Savior, Jesus Christ. As three women approached the tomb that morning, where His crucified body had been laid, they were shocked to see that the stone had been rolled away. And even far better, they witnessed an empty tomb, an angel, and the amazing news that Jesus had risen from the dead just as He promised!

Nothing is more amazing or significant than the power of God displayed at the resurrection of our Savior. Jesus paid the ultimate price for our sins on the cross. He lived a perfect and sinless life and gave it as a sacrifice for the forgiveness of our sins. And when all hope seemed to be gone, Jesus miraculously overcame sin and death and came to life again to give us life!

PRAY & DECLARE

Father, thank You for Jesus' resurrection and triumph over the grave and all the forces of sin and darkness. Thank You that He made the ultimate sacrifice for the forgiveness of my sins to give me eternal life. In Jesus' Name, Amen.

APRIL 12

Surely He Was

When the centurion and those with him who were guarding Jesus saw the earthquake and all that had happened, they were terrified, and exclaimed, "Surely he was the Son of God!"

MATTHEW 27:54, NIV

When the Roman soldiers crucified Jesus, it looked as though His enemies had finally gotten rid of Him. Hanging on the cross, beaten, bleeding, wearing a crown of thorns, spit upon, mocked — Jesus seemed to have lost. When He bowed His head and took His last breath, all of Heaven went silent. Then the earth began to tremble. From noon until three in the afternoon, darkness covered the earth (v. 45). The soldiers were so overwhelmed that they exclaimed, *"Surely He was the Son of God!"*

Satan and the forces of darkness did not realize the power of Jesus' blood dripping down into the earth. He took all your mistakes, all your failures, all your weaknesses, all the times you blew it, every wrong thing you've said and ever will say, and He forgave them all.

PRAY & DECLARE

Father, thank You for the power of Jesus' shed blood that has secured an everlasting release from my sins. Thank You for the incredible price that He paid to set me free. I declare that Jesus is surely the Son of God. In Jesus' Name, Amen.

APRIL 13

As Strong as Ever

Moses was 120 years old when he died, yet his eyesight was clear, and he was as strong as ever.
DEUTERONOMY 34:7, NLT

When Moses was 120 years old, it was his time to die. God told him to climb to the top of Mount Nebo, and that's where he would pass. You would think at his age, Moses would be frail and weak, his knees would hurt, and his eyesight would be poor. You would think he would say, "God, I can't climb a mountain." But Moses was still strong as a young man, still healthy when God took him.

One of the names of God in Scripture is Jehovah Rophe, which means "the Lord the healer" (Exodus 15:26). Get rid of the notion that as you age, you're going to get frail, be overcome by sickness, and be unable to move. Trust God to keep you strong and healthy, still climbing mountains, taking new ground, making the world a better place.

PRAY & DECLARE

Father, thank You that You are my healer. Thank You that You are Jehovah Rophe, and that, even as I grow older, through Your power, I will be as strong as ever. I will trust You to keep me healthy, always taking new ground. In Jesus' Name, Amen.

APRIL 14

Encourage Them All

When he arrived and saw what the grace of God had done, he was glad and encouraged them all to remain true to the Lord with all their hearts. He was a good man, full of the Holy Spirit and faith, and a great number of people were brought to the Lord.

ACTS 11:23–24, NIV

Even though some people look like they're doing fine and don't need encouragement, the truth is that everybody needs somebody cheering them on, somebody who believes in them and supports them. You can be that person for the people in your life. Many times, you can see things in other people that they can't see in themselves. Your words of encouragement and words of blessing can help them step up to who they were created to be. You can be the one they can count on, because you're not going to find fault with them but reinforce the purpose and destiny God has for them.

Everybody is going through something difficult. Be on the lookout for those around you. There are people whom God has in your life right now who need your love, your encouragement, and your kindness.

PRAY & DECLARE

Father, thank You for the people in my life and the special role You have given me in their lives. Thank you that Your encouragement motivates me to bless someone else today. In Jesus' Name, Amen.

APRIL 15

A Full Day's Wage

"When those hired at five o'clock were paid, each received a full day's wage."

MATTHEW 20:9, NLT

Jesus told a parable about a landowner who hired laborers to work in his vineyard. He hired the first group at nine in the morning, and they agreed to work for a full day's wage. He hired other groups around noon, three in the afternoon, and five o'clock. That evening, the owner, who represents God, paid every worker a full day's wage, even those who only worked one hour. Some workers complained that it wasn't fair. The owner said, "I paid you what we agreed. It's my money. Don't fault me for my kindness."

You may feel that you've started late, that you missed some opportunities and made some mistakes, but God is not cutting your pay. If you just show up and work as the Lord leads, He will release all those past wages He has stored up — the blessings, the favor, the mercy, the healing, the freedom.

PRAY & DECLARE

Father, thank You for Your goodness and the many blessings You have stored up for me. Thank You that blessings will be released no matter if I have started late. In Jesus' Name, Amen.

When you come
to Me, ask for
big things,
knowing that
I'm a big God.

APRIL 16

Be Compassionate

Finally, all of you be of one mind, having compassion for one another; love as brothers, be tenderhearted, be courteous; not returning evil for evil or reviling for reviling, but on the contrary blessing, knowing that you were called to this, that you may inherit a blessing.

1 PETER 3:8–9, NKJV

Everywhere you go these days, people are hurting and discouraged, and many have broken dreams. They've made mistakes; their lives are in a mess. They need to feel God's compassion and unconditional love. They don't need somebody to judge them. They need somebody to bring hope, to bring healing, to show God's mercy, to encourage them, to take the time to listen and genuinely care.

Our world is crying out for people with compassion, people who love unconditionally. The apostle Paul says that God's love has been poured into our hearts through the Holy Spirit (Romans 5:5). You can make a difference in other people's lives. When God puts love and compassion in your heart toward someone, follow that love. Act on it. Somebody needs the great compassion of our Lord.

PRAY & DECLARE

Father, You have poured Your love into my heart through the Holy Spirit. You have opened my spirit to be compassionate and kind and merciful to others like You are. In Jesus' Name, Amen.

APRIL 17

Out of the Box

Yet the Lord longs to be gracious to you; therefore he will rise up to show you compassion. For the Lord is a God of justice. Blessed are all who wait for him!

ISAIAH 30:18, NIV

Sometimes we think it's selfish to ask God for big things — to pay your house off, to own your own company, to be healed of a sickness. The enemy would love to convince us to only pray small prayers and only believe for little things. Don't believe those lies. God doesn't say, "Who do you think you are?" It's just the opposite. Our God is an all-powerful God. He loves and welcomes our bold prayers. Yes, it's good to ask for your needs, but also ask for your dreams. Pray audacious, out-of-the-box prayers.

Remember that God created the universe, parted the Red Sea, and opened blind eyes. When you come to God, ask for big things, believing that He is a big God.

PRAY & DECLARE

Father, thank You that You are the all-powerful God who longs to be gracious to me and show me compassion. Thank You that it is Your pleasure to give me the Kingdom and to answer big prayers. I am coming to You with bold, out-of-the-box prayers. In Jesus' Name, Amen.

APRIL 18

The Night Shift

Indeed, he who watches over Israel
will neither slumber nor sleep.

PSALM 121:4, NIV

You've heard the phrase "the night shift." It refers to people who work during the night. Today's scripture says that God never sleeps. He doesn't just work the night shift; He shifts things in the night. You may be in a night season, and you may not see how the difficulties you face can work out. Don't worry. God specializes in shifting things in the dark. The God who works the night shift is going to shift things in your favor. There's going to be a shift in your health, your finances, and that addiction.

Right now, God is working the night shift for you. When you wake up and see what He's been up to, the first thing you're going to say is, "Wow, God, I never dreamed You'd take me here!"

PRAY & DECLARE

Father, thank You that You are the God who rules over my night seasons. Thank You that no matter what comes my way, You are working the night shift for me. I believe that You are shifting things in my favor right now. In Jesus' Name, Amen.

APRIL 19

Kingdom Greatness

Jesus called them together and said, "You know that the rulers of the Gentiles lord it over them, and their high officials exercise authority over them. Not so with you. Instead, whoever wants to become great among you must be your servant, and whoever wants to be first must be your slave — just as the Son of Man did not come to be served, but to serve, and to give his life as a ransom for many."

MATTHEW 20:25–28, NIV

Jesus said that the simple key to being great in the Kingdom is to serve other people as He did. He was talking about a lifestyle in which you're always looking for ways to serve. It becomes a part of who you are. You develop an attitude of giving to everyone you meet.

God has put people in your life on purpose so you can be a blessing to them. Don't look for them to pay you back. They may not even thank you, but rest assured that when you serve others, there is applause in Heaven. God sees your sacrifices. He sees your acts of kindness (Proverbs 15:3). When you serve others, inspired by the power of Christ in you, you'll be great in the Kingdom.

PRAY & DECLARE

Father, thank You that Jesus came to serve and gave His life for me. Thank You that You created me to serve others, to be truly fulfilled by living to give and not to receive. In Jesus' Name, Amen.

APRIL 20

Great Joy

Crowds listened intently to Philip because they were eager to hear his message and see the miraculous signs he did. Many evil spirits were cast out, screaming as they left their victims. And many who had been paralyzed or lame were healed. So there was great joy in that city.

ACTS 8:6–8, NLT

The great joy in the city was the result of miraculous healing. But it also came because of the preaching of the Gospel there by a believer named Philip. Persecution in Jerusalem scattered the believers. But they shared the Gospel wherever they went. Philip went from great distress and spread great joy, from great trouble to great miracles, from great rejection to people who loved him immeasurably.

You may have gone through things that have caused you great pain, great disappointment, or great loss. You could be bitter and live discouraged, but that is not how your story ends. As with Philip, you're going to come into new opportunities. Doors that weren't open before are going to open for you. What has been shaken in your life is leading to great joy, favor, relationships, and health.

PRAY & DECLARE

Father, thank You that the times of shaking and difficulty in my life are going to shift me to something greater. Thank You that You're giving me new desires and creativity and opening new doors of opportunity and abounding joy. In Jesus' Name, Amen.

Our God is
also the God
of the valleys.

APRIL 21

God of the Valleys

"This is what the Lord *says: 'Because the Arameans think the* Lord *is a god of the hills and not a god of the valleys, I will deliver this vast army into your hands, and you will know that I am the* Lord*.'"*

1 KINGS 20:28, NIV

The Israelites defeated the army of King Ben-Hadad on the top of a mountain. One of his assistants said to him, "Their gods are the gods of the hills. If we fight them in the valleys, we will certainly defeat them." So Ben-Hadad attacked the Israelites in the valley. God said to the Israelites, "They think I'm just the God of the mountains and not the valleys. I will help you defeat them to show them that I am the God of both."

When we're on the mountain and life is good, we know God is with us. But sometimes when we're in the valley, we think, "God, where are You? Why is this happening to me?" Be encouraged. Our God is also the God of the valleys.

PRAY & DECLARE

Father, thank You that You are God of both my mountains and my valleys. Thank You that when I am in the valleys, You are still my Lord. In Jesus' Name, Amen.

APRIL 22

Remember Your History

"He replied, 'The Lord, before whom I have walked faithfully, will send his angel with you and make your journey a success . . .'"

GENESIS 24:40, NIV

When Abraham was old, he told his assistant to travel back to his hometown to find his son Isaac a wife. The assistant asked him how he would know if it was the right girl, and Abraham was saying, "Don't worry, because I have a history with God. I've seen His faithfulness over and over down through the years. I have seen His goodness."

Instead of wondering if something's going to work out, worrying about your health, or over your finances, remember your history with God. As Abraham did, you'll see times when God brought a promise to pass that looked impossible; He provided when you didn't see a way; He showed you mercy and turned a situation around. Whatever you face, be confident that He will do it again and make your journey a success.

PRAY & DECLARE

Father, thank You that Your hand has been upon my life in so many ways. Thank You for the countless things You have made happen for my good that I could never make happen. I believe You will make my journey a success. In Jesus' Name, Amen.

APRIL 23

Controllers

The fear of human opinion disables;
trusting in God protects you from that.
PROVERBS 29:25, MSG

Some people always have problems, always want your help, and always are in crisis mode. They expect you to come running and keep them encouraged. And if you don't, they try to make you feel guilty. You love them, but you are not responsible for their happiness or to keep them fixed.

Protect your peace. You have a limited supply of emotional energy each day. If you're taking on their problems, you're not going to have the emotional energy for what you need. You're not their savior; they already have a Savior. A lot of times instead of helping them, we're simply enabling their dysfunction. If they get upset when you put up a boundary, they are controllers and manipulators. They like you for what you can do for them, not for who you are. You don't need "friends" like that.

PRAY & DECLARE

Father, thank You that You have called me to love and help others, but not to try to fix them or make them happy. Help me to protect my own emotional energy. I declare that I am not responsible for other people's happiness. In Jesus' Name, Amen.

APRIL 24

Come

"Come to me, all you who are weary and burdened, and I will give you rest. Take my yoke upon you and learn from me, for I am gentle and humble in heart, and you will find rest for your souls. For my yoke is easy and my burden is light."

MATTHEW 11:28–30, NIV

As we fight the good fight of faith daily, we all face weariness. When the battle is taking longer than expected, when we're working hard but not seeing increase, weariness can come. If the enemy can't take you out all at once, his next strategy is to wear you down. You may be suffering from battle fatigue. You've been standing a long time, trying to break an addiction or believing for a promotion, but it hasn't happened yet. Now you're tired.

God wants to breathe new life into your dreams. Jesus said to come to Him when you are weary and burdened, and He will give you rest. You don't have to do it on your own. Renewing your strength starts in your mind when you wait upon the Lord (Isaiah 40:31). The word "wait" is defined as "looking for God's goodness, expecting His favor, longing for His blessing."

PRAY & DECLARE

Father, thank You for Your promise that I can wait upon You to renew my strength. Thank You that You enable me to rise up with wings above the weariness that tries to wear me down. In Jesus' Name, Amen.

APRIL 25

Don't Hide

He heals the brokenhearted and binds up their wounds.

PSALM 147:3, NKJV

After Adam and Eve fell into sin, when God came looking for them in the garden, they hid in fear and shame. Sometimes when we make a mistake, we think, *I don't want God to find me. I'm ashamed of my weaknesses and failures. I already feel condemned enough.* This is where we fail to see who God really is. God is not coming to condemn you. He's coming to restore you. He wants to give you all that belongs to you as His child — the freedom, the joy, the peace, the victory, the abundance. Jesus said He came to set at liberty those who are bruised (Luke 4:18). When you're bruised by life, press into God. Remember, He is looking for you to set you free!

PRAY & DECLARE

Father, thank You that You didn't create me to hide my faults and weaknesses and hide from You. Thank You that I can come to You and unload all the weight of heaviness, regrets, and feelings of unworthiness. Thank You that I can trust You and draw close to You, even in my darkest moments. In Jesus' Name, Amen.

Protect
your peace.

APRIL 26

The Miracle in Your Mouth

Let us hold fast the confession of our hope without wavering, for He who promised is faithful.

HEBREWS 10:23, NKJV

There will be times when problems we face simply aren't changing. Today's scripture implies something is trying to take God's promises away. The enemy is trying to pull away what God put in your heart. If you're sick, keep speaking healing. If you're in debt, keep talking about abundance. If you have an addiction, keep talking about freedom.

The miracle is in your mouth. There is healing, there is freedom, and there are new levels in your mouth. Let me help you get started with this declaration: "I am blessed. I am prosperous. I am forgiven. I am healthy. I am free. I have the favor of God. Problems are turning around. New doors are opening. I will become all God created me to be."

PRAY & DECLARE

Father, thank You that when the enemy is trying to pull away what You have put in my heart, I can hold fast my confession. Thank You that there is a miracle in my mouth. By faith I declare that because I have Your favor, I am blessed, forgiven, and free. In Jesus' Name, Amen.

APRIL 27

Everything You Need

But to do this, you will need the strong belt of truth and the breastplate of God's approval.

EPHESIANS 6:14, TLB

Sometimes the reason people don't give you what you think you need in a relationship is because they didn't see it modeled growing up. If they didn't see family members giving love and approval and expressing their feelings, they don't have it to give. If you're trying to get it from them, you're going to be frustrated.

Let them off the hook and go to God for what they can't give. Here's the key: God has everything you need. When you learn the principle to not rely on people but to rely on Him for your approval, value, and encouragement, you won't live stressed out because somebody is not giving you what you expect. Remember this elevating truth: "Nobody owes me anything. God alone has everything I need."

PRAY & DECLARE

Father, thank You that You made me to be complete and content in You alone. Help me to realize when I'm looking to others to give me what only You can give and to let them off the hook. I believe and declare that I find everything I need in You. In Jesus' Name, Amen.

APRIL 28

Far More Exceeding

For our light affliction, which is but for a moment, is working for us a far more exceeding and eternal weight of glory.

2 CORINTHIANS 4:17, NKJV

There are times when life comes at us like a flood — a difficulty, opposition, a great loss. You can't choose when or where the flood comes. That's in God's hands. We may not understand it, but God said His plans for us are for good to give us a bright future. That doesn't mean bad things won't happen along the way, but God knows how to use them for good. He wouldn't allow it if it wasn't going to work to our advantage.

Remember that what you're going through is temporary, but what it works in you will bless you forever. By faith you can take hold of where God is taking you — the favor, the influence, the abundance, the health, the friends. Yes, He can create purpose through every challenge.

PRAY & DECLARE

Father, thank You that Your plans for me are for good to give me a bright future. Thank You that the difficulties I face are temporary and are working in me a far more exceeding and eternal weight of glory. In Jesus' Name, Amen.

APRIL 29

Soar

But those who wait on the LORD shall renew their strength; they shall mount up with wings like eagles, they shall run and not be weary, they shall walk and not faint.

ISAIAH 40:31, NKJV

You've never been closer than right now to those things you're believing for. When the prophet Isaiah says to "wait," he doesn't mean to passively sit around and ask, "God, when is this going to happen?" He means to wait with expectancy. Wait knowing that it's on the way. Say, "Thank You, Lord, that through Your strength I am indeed soaring in my spirit." You don't need to drag around, focusing on how long it's been, how it's never going to work out.

Come over to high-time expectancy. It could happen today or by this time tomorrow. Quit telling yourself that your breakthrough is way off in the distance. You're closer than you think. Today, you can soar, even as you wait for God's perfect timing.

PRAY & DECLARE

Father, thank You that I can wait upon You with a spirit of expectancy for those things in my life that I am believing You for. Thank You that I can soar today. I believe that this is my high time and the answer could come today. In Jesus' Name, Amen.

APRIL 30

Show Mercy

He is no longer like a slave to you. He is more than a slave, for he is a beloved brother, especially to me. Now he will mean much more to you, both as a man and as a brother in the Lord.

PHILEMON 1:16, NLT

Paul was in a predicament. A slave named Onesimus had run away from Philemon, and when he came to Paul, he gave his life to Christ. He had done something wrong (v. 18), but he became a brother in the faith to both Paul and Philemon. Paul wrote a letter to Philemon, asking him to forgive Onesimus and receive him back as a brother rather than as a slave whom he had the legal right to send to prison. Would Philemon forgive him, or would he hold on to the hurt and anger?

Sooner or later, someone who did you wrong is going to show up at your door. You could be bitter and angry . . . or through the power of Christ's forgiveness, you can show them mercy and even bless your enemies.

PRAY & DECLARE

Father, thank You for showing me Your mercy, Your kindness, and Your goodness over and over when I didn't begin to deserve it. Help me to have a heart that is free from being vindictive toward others who have done me wrong. Thank You for the blessing of blessing my enemies. In Jesus' Name, Amen.

May

MAY 1

The Only Approval That Matters

Even if my father and mother abandon me,
the Lord will hold me close.
PSALM 27:10, NLT

When the prophet Samuel came to Bethlehem to anoint one of Jesse's sons to be the next king, David was left out in the shepherds' fields. He didn't have his father's approval. For some reason Jesse saw David as being inferior to his other sons. He didn't see a king. People may leave you out, but God doesn't leave you out. If David had had to have his family's approval, he would never have taken the throne.

You may feel as though you've never received the approval from the people closest to you. But just keep being your best, knowing your Heavenly Father loves you just the way He made you. You don't have to have other people's approval to be happy. God's the only One who really matters.

PRAY & DECLARE

Father, thank You that You see the greatness that is in me, and You love me just the way You made me. When others don't give me their approval or affirm me, help me to let it go. In Jesus' Name, Amen.

MAY 2

Don't Write Someone Off

But the Lord said to Ananias, "Go! This man is my chosen instrument to proclaim my name to the Gentiles and their kings and to the people of Israel."

ACTS 9:15, NIV

We all have loved ones and friends we're hoping will change. We're praying and believing, but it's easy to get frustrated and think nothing will make any difference. But remember, you have the privilege of standing in the gap and covering them with mercy — not judging or condemning them but loving them into a relationship with a living God.

Before the apostle Paul was a follower of Christ, he was the biggest persecutor of the church. We would have thought he didn't have a chance of changing. Yet God told Ananias to go pray for Saul. We can face the same challenge. Some of the people we're tempted to write off are chosen vessels to do great things.

PRAY & DECLARE

Father, thank You for loving me when I've had a bad attitude and for never writing me off when I've been off course and failed. Thank You that You even saw a chosen instrument in Saul when he was persecuting the church. Help me to see people through Your eyes and with Your heart. In Jesus' Name, Amen.

MAY 3

What You Can't Control

The LORD will work out his plans for my life —
for your faithful love, O LORD, endures forever.
Don't abandon me, for you made me.

PSALM 138:8, NLT

Sometimes we're frustrated because we're trying to control things that only God can control. We're trying to figure something out that there is no answer to right now. The good news is, God doesn't ask us to figure everything out. We can rest knowing there is our job and there is God's job. Our job is to believe, thank God, walk in obedience, and live filled by His consuming love. God's job is to work things out that we can't work out, to open doors we can't open, to part Red Seas, to heal sick bodies.

Take the pressure off. You don't have to make everything happen. Live out the faith that He has already given you. Your time is coming. God always works out His plans.

PRAY & DECLARE

Father, thank You that what lies ahead and is unknown to me is well known to You. I trust that You are going before me with Your plan that is solely motivated by Your enduring love. In Jesus' Name, Amen.

MAY 4

Great Wrongs

Alexander the coppersmith did me great wrongs. The Lord will pay him back for his actions.

2 TIMOTHY 4:14, AMPC

While we don't know what wrongs Alexander did to the apostle Paul, God had it recorded in Scripture so we would know how to respond when we go through something that's unfair, when we've been wronged, when people take advantage of us. If you don't understand that God will settle your accounts, you'll get frustrated, try to get revenge, and manipulate things. Paul understood that you can rest and let God settle your accounts. His justice will eventually be served.

Don't have a victim mentality. Quit losing sleep over what someone did. Don't give it any more time or attention. Instead of focusing on who did you wrong or how unfair something was, keep moving forward and being your best right where you are. Thank God, knowing that He sees what's happened and will settle your account and right the wrongs.

PRAY & DECLARE

Father, thank You that You see everything that has happened to me, every unfair thing. Thank You that I can let go of the wrongs and forgive quickly before frustration sets in. I declare that You will right the wrongs. In Jesus' Name, Amen.

MAY 5

Deep Roots

If you faint in the day of adversity, your strength is small.

PROVERBS 24:10, NKJV

It's interesting that researchers have discovered that if trees grow up in an environment where they don't have to withstand any wind pressure, their roots don't develop properly and eventually can't withstand their own weight. They have a deficiency in what they call "stress wood," which is essentially the trees' reaction to wind. Stress wood helps the tree grow stronger and more solidly. Without it, the trees can't survive. The wind is essential for the tree to flourish and become what it was created to be.

In the same way, without the pressure of difficulties, we wouldn't develop properly. Stress is actually strengthening you. Your roots are going down deeper. You're developing courage, strength, and fortitude.

PRAY & DECLARE

Father, thank You that the difficulties and pressures I face are strengthening and are working in me a far more exceeding and eternal weight of glory. Thank You that they are developing the benefits of stress wood in the core of my life. I believe I am like a mighty tree, strong and deeply rooted. I'm going to stand tall and flourish. In Jesus' Name, Amen.

The miracle is in your mouth.

MAY 6

Glory to Glory

But we all, with unveiled face, beholding as in a mirror the glory of the Lord, are being transformed into the same image from glory to glory, just as by the Spirit of the Lord.

2 CORINTHIANS 3:18, NKJV

If you judge your life by something negative that is happening today, you may feel as though God has forgotten about you and get discouraged. But you can be transformed from glory to glory. The path of the righteous gets brighter and brighter. That means He already has a solution to the problem that's holding you back.

He's already arranged restoration for that loss, a new beginning for that setback, and promotion for that injustice. It's just a matter of time before you see the light break through to full day. When the lies come saying, "God has forgotten about you," just say, "No, thanks. This situation may be difficult, but I know that this is not how my story ends."

PRAY & DECLARE

Father, thank You for the promise that You are transforming me from glory to glory and making my path brighter and brighter. I believe that You are working right now to lift me to another level. In Jesus' Name, Amen.

MAY 7

Hot Winds of Persecution

"The stony ground represents those who enjoy listening to sermons, but somehow the message never really gets through to them and doesn't take root and grow. They know the message is true, and sort of believe for a while; but when the hot winds of persecution blow, they lose interest."

LUKE 8:13, TLB

In the parable of the sower, Jesus talks about the seed that falls on stony ground. The stony ground is like those who receive His word with joy, but their roots are shallow. They believe for a while, but they wilt when the hot winds of persecution blow. Persecution will come to every believer — times when you feel overwhelmed, when you're doing the right thing but it's not improving. Through the power of Christ, you can overcome in the most difficult times as you are rooted in Him. As those hot winds blow, keep doing the right thing, keep being good to people, keep letting God fight your battles. When you are rooted in God, He will not only turn it around, but He'll bring you out better.

PRAY & DECLARE

Father, thank You for the hot winds of persecution and using the pressure of challenges to make me stronger. Thank You that every test of my faith is preparing me to overcome and persevere, to go higher and increase me. I know through Your strength I am coming out better. In Jesus' Name, Amen.

MAY 8

Be Merciful

"But love your enemies, do good to them, and lend to them without expecting to get anything back. Then your reward will be great, and you will be children of the Most High, because he is kind to the ungrateful and wicked. Be merciful, just as your Father is merciful."

LUKE 6:35–36, NIV

No matter who we're in relationship with, no matter how good of a person they are, at times they're going to disappoint us, let us down, or hurt us. It's easy to let that press us down, and we become sour. It's easy to keep a list of all the things they've done wrong and all the things we don't like about them. The easy way out is to disconnect and stop spending time with them.

Praise be to God! This is a new day. God's mercy is fresh every morning. Through His grace, you can give that person room to be human. Yes, show them the mercy that God has shown you. Don't hold grudges. Forgive them and move forward. Be kind, encourage them, be generous, and help them reach their dreams.

PRAY & DECLARE

Father, thank You for freely giving me Your mercy that I might freely give it to others. Thank You that I can let the past go, that I can forgive and love, and that I can move forward. Help me give others the space to be human and not disconnect from them. In Jesus' Name, Amen.

MAY 9

Tell Yourself the Truth

I praise you because I am fearfully and wonderfully made;
your works are wonderful, I know that full well.
PSALM 139:14, NIV

Sometimes, we can let people label us, tell us what we're not, and what we can't do. We can allow circumstances, mistakes, and disappointments to define us as unforgiven, unworthy, washed up, having no future. If you let these voices play, it will keep you from your destiny.

Praise be to God! That we can say what He says about us. "I'm forgiven. I'm redeemed. I'm restored. My past is over, and my future is bright." As we reject the negative things people have said about us and get in agreement with what God says about us, we will experience what He has already put inside. You are a masterpiece. You've been fearfully and wonderfully made.

PRAY & DECLARE

Father, thank You that the truth is that I am fearfully and wonderfully made. Thank You that I am not all the negatives that I have been labeled with. I believe that nothing can hold me back from living out the masterpiece that You created me to be. In Jesus' Name, Amen.

MAY 10

Really?

Now the serpent was more crafty than any of the wild animals the LORD God had made. He said to the woman, "Did God really say, 'You must not eat from any tree in the garden'?"

GENESIS 3:1, NIV

The Scripture tells us to be aware of the enemy's schemes and strategies. Sometimes the temptation he brings is subtle. It's just a whisper of doubt. It's just enough to make you think that maybe a promise from God won't work out. In the garden of Eden, the serpent came to Eve and said, "Really? Did God really say . . . ?" It wasn't overwhelming. It was just a question: "Really?"

When God puts the promise in your heart that you're going to get well, don't be surprised if you hear the whisper, "You really think so, given the medical report?" "You really think you're going to have a good year . . . that that relationship is going to be restored?" Be aware of these subtle hints of doubt that might grow and counter the faith and promises God has placed within you.

PRAY & DECLARE

Father, thank You that the promises You have spoken always accomplish Your will and prosper. Thank You that You have made me aware of the enemy's subtle schemes to get me to doubt what You have said. In Jesus' Name, Amen.

He creates
purpose in every
challenge.

MAY 11

One Good Break

Boaz commanded his servants, saying,
"Let her glean even among the sheaves, and
do not insult her. Also you are to purposely slip
out for her some grain from the bundles and leave
it so that she may glean, and do not rebuke her."

RUTH 2:15–16, NASB

Ruth was a young widow, living in poverty and trying to provide for her elderly mother-in-law. To survive, she went into the fields to pick up the grain that the harvesters missed. But one day Boaz, the owner of the field, told his workers to purposely leave grain for Ruth. With that one good break, she had more than she needed. Then Boaz married Ruth, and she went from working the field to owning the field.

God is working behind the scenes in your life, speaking to the people you need to help you flourish in a time of setback and lining up the breaks you need. Get ready for what He's about to do. He's not going to just make the hard places easier; He's going to cause you to abound despite what you've been through.

PRAY & DECLARE

Father, thank You that You know every hardship and difficult situation I have faced and will face. I believe that You have more blessings and favor for me than I can dream. I believe that You are working behind the scenes to bring it all together. In Jesus' Name, Amen.

MAY 12

Welcome Forgiveness

Jesus replied, "I tell you the truth, Peter — this very night, before the rooster crows, you will deny three times that you even know me."

MATTHEW 26:34, NLT

When Jesus chose Peter as one of His disciples, He knew Peter's weaknesses and failures, including Peter's denial during His trial before Pilate. Why didn't He just pick someone else? God doesn't disqualify you because you have weaknesses and failures. If He did, none of us would have a chance. When Jesus rose from the dead, He even took Peter aside and assured him that he was forgiven. Peter could have lived defeated and condemned, but he received and welcomed Christ's forgiveness. He didn't live looking in the rearview mirror. Peter went on to give the inaugural address when the church was birthed on the day of Pentecost and three thousand people came to know the Lord.

PRAY & DECLARE

Father, thank You that there is no condemnation for those who are in Christ Jesus, and that includes me. Thank You that all the things that could have disqualified me and kept me undeserving were wiped away in Your mercy. I declare that I am forgiven, and I'm moving forward in victory. In Jesus' Name, Amen.

MAY 13

Fully Persuaded

Yet he did not waver through unbelief regarding the promise of God, but was strengthened in his faith and gave glory to God, being fully persuaded that God had power to do what he had promised. This is why "it was credited to him as righteousness."

ROMANS 4:20–23, NIV

Abraham was fully persuaded that God would do what He promised even when it seemed impossible for him and Sarah to have a baby. When you're fully persuaded, you're not going to change your mind. You're not going to let people talk you out of it. You're not going to let circumstances cause you to quit believing.

Often, before you see the promise, there's a waiting period. When you don't see anything happening, every thought will tell you, *You're wasting your time. Just accept that it's never going to happen.* Tap into the Spirit of God. Declare: "I'm not moved by what's not changing. I'm not discouraged because it's taking so long. I know God is a faithful God. I've seen Him do it in the past, and I know He'll do it again in the future."

PRAY & DECLARE

Father, thank You that my faith and trust are anchored in You and Your power at work in my life. Thank You that I don't have to be moved by the tests and troubles I face because I am fully persuaded You will do what You promised. In Jesus' Name, Amen.

MAY 14

Declare Victory

"All those gathered here will know that it is not by sword or spear that the LORD saves; for the battle is the LORD's, and he will give all of you into our hands."

1 SAMUEL 17:47, NIV

When David went out to face Goliath, before he slung that rock, he got his sword out. Not a physical sword, but the sword of the Spirit, the Word of God. He looked at Goliath and said, "This day I will prove to everyone here that the battle is the Lord's, that the victory is not by sword or spear." He declared victory.

He could have said, "God, why is this giant in my path? He's twice my size. I don't have the training in warfare. This is not a fair fight." However, David knew how to swing his sword — the Word of God. Before he slung that rock, he had already defeated Goliath. As you swing God's sword, He will direct the rock. As you declare victory, He'll bring down the giants.

PRAY & DECLARE

Father, thank You that no matter what I face, no matter how big it looks, the battle belongs to You. I declare words of victory. Through Your words, I release Your promises in my life. In Jesus' Name, Amen.

MAY 15

Resist It

"If you, then, though you are evil, know how to give good gifts to your children, how much more will your Father in heaven give good gifts to those who ask him!" So in everything, do to others what you would have them do to you, for this sums up the Law and the Prophets.

MATTHEW 7:11–12, NIV

Sometimes false religion tells us that God puts sickness on us to teach us something. Granted, you may learn something while you're sick, but God doesn't send sickness to teach you. Jesus said that if earthly fathers give their children good things, how much more will our Heavenly Father give good gifts to those who ask? What loving father would ever say, "I put this sickness on my child to teach them a lesson"?

Every sickness is the work of the enemy. Don't say, "My cancer . . . my diabetes . . . my arthritis." It's not yours. Your body is a temple of the Most High God. The Scripture says to resist the enemy, and he will flee from you. Stand firm. Resist it.

PRAY & DECLARE

Father, thank You that wherever Jesus went, He brought healing to every person who came to Him. Thank You that sickness does not come from You; it's not a teaching tool, but it is Your will to bring me healing. In Jesus' Name, Amen.

Stress is actually strengthening you.

MAY 16

Chain Breaker

O Lord, *I am your servant; yes, I am your servant, born into your household; you have freed me from my chains. I will offer you a sacrifice of thanksgiving and call on the name of the* Lord.

PSALM 116:16–17, NLT

Imagine your life with no chains holding you back. That's what the Lord has already done for you. It may not seem like it, but as His servant He has freed you from your chains. Take hold of that liberty that has already taken hold of you. Imagine all that you can accomplish without that chain of fear and insecurity . . . relationships without the chains of guilt and shame . . . freedom from that chain of negative words that were spoken over you.

You are, through Christ, released and unbound. The chain breaker, the Most High God, has and is working in your life right now. When you least expect it, things are going to shift in your favor. He is releasing you into increase, into favor, and into new levels. Yes, live out from a freedom mindset.

PRAY & DECLARE

Father, thank You that You are the Most High God, my chain breaker, who has released me into increase, favor, and new levels. Thank You that what has limited me in the past is not going to hinder me anymore. I believe my chains have been broken. In Jesus' Name, Amen.

MAY 17

One Act of Kindness

Naaman was general of the army under the king of Aram . . . a truly great man, but afflicted with a grievous skin disease. It so happened that Aram, on one of its raiding expeditions against Israel, captured a young girl who became a maid to Naaman's wife. One day she said to her mistress, "Oh, if only my master could meet the prophet of Samaria, he would be healed of his skin disease."

2 KINGS 5:1–3, MSG

Naaman had captured a young Israelite girl and brought her back as his wife's maid. You can imagine how her life was turned upside down, all because of Naaman. You would think she hated him. When she saw that he had leprosy, she could have thought, *I hope you die. You wrecked my life.* But instead, she offered the remedy through which he was completely healed. She showed kindness to someone who had done her wrong.

It's easy to hold a grudge, try to pay someone back, and make them suffer, but all that does is hold you down. Jesus said, "*Blessed are the merciful, for they will be shown mercy*" (Matthew 5:7, NIV).

PRAY & DECLARE

Father, thank You for showing me Your mercy over and over again when I didn't deserve it. Thank You for giving me a heart that is free from being vindictive toward others who have done me wrong. In Jesus' Name, Amen.

MAY 18

Who Is With You?

About midnight Paul and Silas were praying and singing hymns to God, and the other prisoners were listening to them.

ACTS 16:25, NIV

Paul and Silas had been beaten and put in jail for sharing the Good News. They had all kinds of questions with no answers. Would they have a fair trial . . . or be held there . . . or put to death? They could have been upset, worried, and losing sleep, but at midnight they were singing praises to God. Their attitude was, "We don't know what's coming, but we know that God is in control. Him being for us is more than the world being against us." About that time, there was a great earthquake and their chains fell off.

It's very powerful when you can say, "I don't know how this situation will work out, but God is fighting my battles, His plans for me are for good, and what He started in my life He will finish."

PRAY & DECLARE

Father, thank You that You, the all-powerful Creator of the universe, are with me, just as You were with Paul and Silas. In the difficult times, when I don't know how a situation is going to turn out, I offer You the sacrifice of praise. In Jesus' Name, Amen.

MAY 19

Windows of Grace

As Paul talked about righteousness, self-control and the judgment to come, Felix was afraid and said, "That's enough for now! You may leave. When I find it convenient, I will send for you."

ACTS 24:25, NIV

The apostle Paul had an opportunity to share his faith with the Roman governor of Judea, a man named Felix, and his wife. Felix was a ruthless, immoral governor. He knew he needed to change. This was a window of grace. God was speaking to his heart. But Felix put off dealing with the conviction. Two years later, he was out of office and gone.

Are you waiting for a more convenient time, putting off dealing with a conviction or a change of attitude, delaying taking a step of faith, or ignoring God's still, small voice? Don't keep making excuses. Today, when you hear His voice, step into the grace.

PRAY & DECLARE

Father, thank You for the ways You speak to my heart and open windows of grace for me to make changes in my life that need to be made. I declare I will not put off dealing with these heart issues for a more convenient time. In Jesus' Name, Amen.

MAY 20

No More Slavery

You say, "I am allowed to do anything" — but not everything is good for you. And even though "I am allowed to do anything," I must not become a slave to anything.

1 CORINTHIANS 6:12, NLT

There are a lot of things we can do and get away with. It's permissible to go around with a bad temper, a negative attitude, or a critical spirit, but it's not profitable. The apostle Paul said he wouldn't become a slave to anything. When we let our feelings rule us, we become a slave to anger, to lust, to self-pity.

But I believe it's a new day for us, and the flesh has been dethroned. No more living as slaves, no more being controlled by our feelings. We're rising up to say, "Feelings, you're not the boss of me. Flesh, you're not going to run my life. I thank God that Christ is on the throne of my life."

PRAY & DECLARE

Father, thank You that I can choose to be disciplined and say no to the flesh and its desires. Thank You that every day I can declare: My feelings are not on the throne; I am not a slave to anything. In Jesus' Name, Amen.

Don’t live
looking in
the rearview
mirror.

MAY 21

His Excellence Within

It is my prayer that your love may abound more and more, with knowledge and all discernment, so that you may approve what is excellent, and so be pure and blameless for the day of Christ, filled with the fruit of righteousness that comes through Jesus Christ, to the glory and praise of God.

PHILIPPIANS 1:9–11, ESV

God has called us to be His representatives, to be people of excellence and integrity. How you live, how you conduct your business, and how you do your work is all a reflection of your witness. When you have an excellent spirit, it shows up in the quality of everything you do and the attitude with which you do it. The Scripture says that whatever you do, you should give your best effort and do it as if you are doing it for God. But how do you go that extra mile to do what's right? It comes from God's love within you, not strife-filled self-effort. As you press into His love, you can't help but be excellent in all you do.

PRAY & DECLARE

Father, thank You for loving me and empowering me to live a life of excellence and integrity. Thank You that I have dedicated every area of my life to you and that excellence flows out of my heart of love for You. In Jesus' Name, Amen.

MAY 22

Feel the Burn

Never lag in zeal and in earnest endeavor; be aglow and burning with the Spirit, serving the Lord.

ROMANS 12:11, AMPC

The apostle Paul didn't say, "Never lag in faith, in confidence, or in experience." He said, *"Never lag in zeal."* He was saying that if you stay passionate about your dreams and what God promised, if you don't lag in zeal, then what you lack will eventually turn around. You may lag in resources, in friendships, or in good health, but as you stay aglow, burning with the Spirit, then the healing is coming, the confidence is coming, the abundance is coming, and the right people are coming.

You could go through the day sour, but you have to dig your heels in and say, "I am not going to let the enemy have my joy, my praise, or my expectancy. This day is a gift from God."

PRAY & DECLARE

Father, I worship You with all my heart because You are worthy, Almighty God. Thank You that I can keep my faith aglow and burning because You have given Your Spirit to dwell in me. I will not let the enemy steal my joy or my praise, and I will not lag in zeal. In Jesus' Name, Amen.

MAY 23

Sing to the Promise

Then Israel sang this song: "Spring up,
O well! All of you sing to it . . ."
NUMBERS 21:17, NKJV

All of us have dreams we want to accomplish and problems we're hoping will turn around. We know God has put a promise in our heart, but it seems impossible. This is how the Israelites felt. In the hot, barren desert and desperate for water, they came upon an old well where the Lord had said to Moses, *"Gather the people together, and I will give them water"* (v. 16, NKJV). Instead of complaining Israel sang this song, *"Spring up, O well!"* They were making a declaration of faith. They all sang to the well of promise over and over. That was the key. Suddenly, water began to flow. There are promises God has put in you. Your circumstances may say, "It's not going to happen." Let your praise, your thanksgiving, and your declaration of faith rise up. Believe for healing, abundance, and breakthroughs to spring forth.

PRAY & DECLARE

Father, thank You for the promises You have put in my heart and for the dreams I want to accomplish. I sing . . . sing . . . sing to the promises You have declared over me! I give You thanks that they are springing up even now. In Jesus' Name, Amen.

MAY 24

Planted and Flourishing

Those who are planted in the house of the LORD shall flourish in the courts of our God. They shall still bear fruit in old age; they shall be fresh and flourishing, to declare that the LORD is upright.

PSALM 92:13–15, NKJV

When you're plugged into a community of faith, there is a blessing on your life that will cause you to bloom, to blossom, and to flourish. This is true because Jesus said, "*Where two or three are gathered together in My Name, I am there in the midst of them*" (Matthew 18:20, NKJV). We each bring God with us. In His presence is healing and the fullness of joy. Together, our faith and strength are multiplied.

Given so much trouble in the world today, we need to plant ourselves in the house of the Lord to draw strength and encouragement from one another. David said, "*I love Your sanctuary, LORD, the place where your glorious presence dwells*" (Psalm 26:8, NLT). As you gather together with other believers, God's favor will shine down on you.

PRAY & DECLARE

Father, thank You for the promise that when I am plugged into a community of faith, I will flourish. When we gather in Jesus' Name, He is in our midst, and His glory shines upon us. I declare that I am flourishing in Your house. In Jesus' Name, Amen.

MAY 25

Foreshadowings

Then Pharaoh took his signet ring from his finger and put it on Joseph's finger. He dressed him in robes of fine linen and put a gold chain around his neck.

GENESIS 41:42, NIV

Joseph's father gave him a special robe of many colors that represented favor, but his jealous brothers bloodied that robe and sold Joseph into slavery in Egypt. I can imagine that he desperately wanted his robe back, wanted his old life back, but that would have kept him from God's purpose of putting on a robe of great honor, influence, and authority as prime minister of Egypt. The colorful robe simply foreshadowed what God was about to do.

Don't spend your life wishing you could go back to when you knew you were favored — before the setback, before the health issue, before the layoff. Here's the key: Not having the robe of many colors doesn't mean that you don't have favor; it means greater favor is coming. You had to lose that robe to step into the awesome future God has in store. You haven't seen, heard, or imagined the greater things God is about to do.

PRAY & DECLARE

Thank You that You are my way maker, my promise keeper, and my robe provider. I believe that greater favor is coming. In Jesus' Name, Amen.

As you declare victory, He'll bring down the giants.

MAY 26

Prevail

So the word of the Lord grew mightily and prevailed.

ACTS 19:20, NKJV

Jesus said God's Word is like a seed. When it's sown in your heart, it will grow and become what God promised. As you let His words grow, speak His promises, and thank Him for what He says, you'll see His Word prevail over sickness, addictions, fear, and depression.

In 1981, when my mother was diagnosed with terminal liver cancer and given a few weeks to live, she found about forty passages of Scripture that had to do with healing. Her voice was very weak, but she went around the house saying, "By His stripes I am healed. I will live and not die and declare the works of the Lord. With long life, God will satisfy me." My mother kept watering that seed, thanking God for what He promised. The seed kept growing, and week by week she got a little stronger. The Word of God grew mightily and finally prevailed to her full healing.

PRAY & DECLARE

Father, thank You for Your Word and precious promises that have been sown in my heart. Thank You that as I speak out Your promises, Your Word will prevail over whatever comes against me. In Jesus' Name, Amen.

MAY 27

Kiss It Goodbye

Then Naomi said to her two daughters-in-law, "Go back, each of you, to your mother's home. May the Lord *show you kindness, as you have shown kindness to your dead husbands and to me. May the* Lord *grant that each of you will find rest in the home of another husband." Then she kissed them goodbye and they wept aloud . . .*

RUTH 1:8–9, NIV

Naomi's husband unexpectedly died, and then ten years later both of her married sons died. Heartbroken and destitute, Naomi decided to move back to Bethlehem. Her daughter-in-law Ruth refused to leave her, but Orpah did. Naomi could have felt betrayed, but instead she kissed Orpah goodbye. Orpah represented Naomi's hurts, and broken dreams. Naomi was saying by her actions, "Life hasn't been fair, but God can turn this to my advantage," which is what happened later in Bethlehem.

People may walk away. It's tempting to get bitter, hold a grudge, lose your passion. When life doesn't turn out the way you thought, you have to kiss the bitterness goodbye, kiss the person that left you goodbye, kiss the dream that didn't work out goodbye.

PRAY & DECLARE

Father, You are able to make the most of unfair situations. You are directing my steps even through hurts and disappointments. Help me kiss the negatives goodbye and move on. In Jesus' Name, Amen.

MAY 28

Where Is Your Focus?

"For we are powerless against this great horde that is coming against us. We do not know what to do, but our eyes are on you."

2 CHRONICLES 20:12, ESV

King Jehoshaphat and the people of Judah were surrounded by three major armies. They could have panicked, but instead Jehoshaphat called people together to pray. He didn't deny the facts or act like the problem didn't exist. He admitted they were powerless, but he followed it up by declaring that their eyes were on God.

God told Jehoshaphat to march toward the enemy, and he appointed singers of praise to walk ahead of the army. The Lord worked a mighty victory, and they didn't even have to fight. Your problems may look too big, and you may feel powerless, but you have the most powerful force in the universe on your side. You may not know what to do, but when your eyes are upon Him, He'll make a way where you don't see a way.

PRAY & DECLARE

Father, thank You that You are in control of all the situations in my life, and You are fighting my battles. I choose to guard my mind from worrisome, anxious thoughts. Yes, my eyes are on You! In Jesus' Name, Amen.

MAY 29

Flooded With Light

I pray that your hearts will be flooded with light so that you can understand the confident hope he has given to those he called — his holy people who are his rich and glorious inheritance.

EPHESIANS 1:18, NLT

Many people get labeled as average or less than, and then they adapt to that environment and let their mind become conditioned to thinking they've reached their limit. Becoming a barrier breaker starts in your thinking — realizing that your heart can indeed be flooded with God's glorious light!

You were not created to live contained. Recondition your mind. Be bold and get rid of the thoughts that are holding you back. You may not see how you can do it in your own ability, but you're not on your own. You have the most powerful force in the universe breathing in your direction.

PRAY & DECLARE

Father, thank You that I am not on my own, and I am not limited by the times I've tried and failed. Flood my heart with Your light. I believe that I can rise to the next level, break through the barriers of the past, and overcome the things that have held me back. In Jesus' Name, Amen.

MAY 30

Sing a New Song

He has given me a new song to sing, a hymn of praise to our God. Many will see what he has done and be amazed. They will put their trust in the Lord.

PSALM 40:3, NLT

It's easy to complain about your boss, about the traffic, or about a relationship. We create much of our own unhappiness by how we respond to negative things and how we approach life. Here's the key: When you complain, you remain; but when you praise, you'll be raised.

David says that God gave him "a new song" of praise. Let it come out! When you develop a habit of always thinking about God's goodness, seeing the best, and singing a hymn of praise, you'll have joy despite what's happening around you.

You might have been through some difficulties, but receive the new melody He has placed in your heart. Start thanking God that new doors are opening and your best days are still ahead. As you sing His song, you'll start feeling the joy bubbling up, you'll get your passion back, and you'll see your dreams start coming to life.

PRAY & DECLARE

Father, thank You that You put a new song in my heart that lifts me up no matter what is happening around me. I choose to shut the door of complaining and sing praise to my God. In Jesus' Name, Amen.

MAY 31

Shame Be Gone

Then the Lord *said to Joshua, "Today I have rolled away the reproach of Egypt from you."*
JOSHUA 5:9, NIV

"Reproach" means "shame, blame, disgrace." For over four hundred years the Israelites had been in Egyptian slavery. They were not just physically beaten down, but over time they allowed the emotional abuse to steal their sense of value. As they were about to enter the Promised Land, they couldn't go in with a sense of shame, feeling unworthy and not valuable. God had to roll away the reproach.

You may be carrying a heavy load of guilt and shame due to past mistakes, failures, or even things that weren't your fault. Whatever your Egypt is — a divorce, a bad habit, someone you hurt, someone who abused you — today, let God roll away the reproach of the past. When thoughts come saying, *Shame on you*, answer right back, "Shame off me. I've been forgiven and restored. God doesn't remember it, so I'm not going to remember it."

PRAY & DECLARE

Father, thank You that You roll back the reproach of guilt and shame over my past. Thank You that the moment I ask You to forgive me, You not only forgive but You forget it. I declare, "Shame off me!" In Jesus' Name, Amen.

June

JUNE 1

Insider Trading

The secret of the LORD is with those who fear Him,
and He will show them His covenant.
PSALM 25:14, NKJV

As you honor God, He will tell you secrets. He'll whisper things in your inner ear and give insight into what you couldn't have known otherwise. You can't explain it; you don't know how you know it, but you just know it. It's like insider trading. That means somebody inside the company who has knowledge of what's going on is giving another person on the outside information about their stock that's going to cause it to go up or down before the public knows.

They have an advantage because they have inside information. That's what God does for us. He knows where the good breaks are, and He knows how to catapult you years ahead. As you are sensitive to His still small voice, God will give you inside information. You'll know things that you couldn't have known on your own that will thrust you into your destiny.

PRAY & DECLARE

Father, thank You that You whisper secrets in my inner ear and give me insight I couldn't know on my own. Help me to be sensitive to Your voice and to obey. In Jesus' Name, Amen.

JUNE 2

Supersized

You crown the year with Your goodness,
and Your paths drip with abundance.

PSALM 65:11, NKJV

In a fast-food restaurant, a supersized meal means you'll get bigger portions than expected. That's what God is going to do for you. His dream for your life is much bigger than your own. He's going to take you further than you're expecting. He's going to open doors that you could never open. He's going to give you more influence than you ever thought possible. God is going to supersize your life.

What you're dreaming about may seem big — to get out of debt, to pay off your house, for your child to get back on track — and you don't see how it can happen. God is going to make it bigger, better, and more rewarding than you have ever imagined. He is going to do exceedingly abundantly above all that you ask or think. He has a supersized life in front of you.

PRAY & DECLARE

Father, thank You for loving me and that Your goodness crowns Your plan for my life. Thank You for the abundant paths You have for me and how You will supersize my dreams. I believe that You are doing exceedingly abundantly above all that I ask or think. In Jesus' Name, Amen.

JUNE 3

God Celebrates You

Am I now trying to win the approval of human beings, or of God? Or am I trying to please people? If I were still trying to please people, I would not be a servant of Christ.

GALATIANS 1:10, NIV

When you base your value on what other people say or do to you, that's going to push you down. But when you base it on what God says about you, it's going to lift you up. You're going to have a smile on your face, a spring in your step. You're not going to be put off by what you didn't get or by who's not supporting you. What they say or do to you doesn't make you any less than the masterpiece God says you are.

God says you're amazing. He says He's proud of you. He says you're the apple of His eye. He says you're called, chosen, equipped, with seeds of greatness.

PRAY & DECLARE

Father, thank You that You created me just the way I am, and You chose me to be Yours long before I chose You. I celebrate the fact that You celebrate me, that You say that I am amazing and the apple of Your eye. In Jesus' Name, Amen.

JUNE 4

The Blessing Overrides All Else

And God said to Balaam, "You shall not go with them; you shall not curse the people, for they are blessed."

NUMBERS 22:12, NKJV

When the Israelites headed toward Jericho, the Moabite king saw how many Israelites there were, and he was afraid. So he hired a foreigner named Balaam to curse the people of Israel. But God told Balaam *"you shall not curse the people, for they are blessed."* Notice that when God's blessing is upon you, it doesn't matter what negative thing someone says or does to you. All that matters is that God put His blessing on you, and that blessing will always override any curse.

When you go through disappointments, when unfair things happen, it's easy to feel that's clouded your future. But remember, God's blessing is on you. You don't need to be upset because someone's talking about you. You won't be worried because of a setback. You know every force that's trying to stop you is powerless to change what He has put on your life.

PRAY & DECLARE

Father, thank You that Your blessing will override any curse or negative thing that is said or done against me. I believe that every force that is trying to stop me is powerless before You. In Jesus' Name, Amen.

JUNE 5

God's Gracious Humility

Moses was a very humble man, more humble than anyone else on the face of the earth.

NUMBERS 12:3, NIV

As a young man, Moses had the dream that he was supposed to deliver God's people from their slavery in Egypt, but he made a mistake that put him into a night season. After he spent forty years in a desert place, God said, "All right, Moses, now you're ready for Me to use you to deliver My people." Moses had learned to wait on God, to listen to His voice, and to walk in humility.

Moses couldn't handle it the first time, but God didn't write him off. He used the night season to refine him. In your night seasons, welcome change where you need to change, and deal with the areas that God is bringing to light. Then, as He did for Moses, God will bring you out of that night season and His dream within you will come to fruition.

PRAY & DECLARE

Father, thank You for loving me so much that at times You take me into a desert place to refine my character and fill me with Your divine humility. Thank You that You love me so much that You're getting me prepared to go where I've never gone. In Jesus' Name, Amen.

He'll make a
way where you
don't see a way.

JUNE 6

A Great Coming Together

He asked me, "Son of man, can these bones live?"
I said, "Sovereign Lord, *you alone know."*
EZEKIEL 37:3, NIV

God gave the prophet Ezekiel a vision of a valley filled with dry bones, which represented the people of Israel. Ezekiel could have said, "There's no way possible those bones can live." Instead he looked away from his circumstances and looked toward his God. He said, *"Sovereign Lord, You alone know."* He was saying, "God, You're the giver of life, the Sovereign One. I may not see a way, but You have a way." God said, "All right, Ezekiel, that's what I'm looking for — not somebody who's going to tell me all the reasons why it's not going to happen. Prophesy to those dead bones and watch it all come together."

Whatever looks dead in your life, prophesy victory, wholeness, and abundance. When you speak life, faith, favor, and health, you're going to see a great coming together.

PRAY & DECLARE

Father, thank You that I can speak to the things in my life that seem dead and You will breathe life into them. I believe that as I speak words of faith, You will make things happen — a great coming together. In Jesus' Name, Amen.

JUNE 7

Through the Fire

"But even if he does not, we want you to know, Your Majesty, that we will not serve your gods or worship the image of gold you have set up."

DANIEL 3:18, NIV

I love how the three Hebrew teenagers wouldn't bow down to the king's golden idol even when the king was going to have them thrown into a fiery furnace. They had the courage to stand in faith whether it worked out their way or not. They were not kept out of the fire, but God made them fireproof, allowed them to go through the fire, and they came out unharmed, without even the smell of smoke.

There are times in life when we all get thrown into the furnace. Remind yourself that the flames can't harm you, the trouble can't take you out, and those people can't stop what God has ordained. He will make things happen that you couldn't make happen.

PRAY & DECLARE

Father, thank You for Your promise to be with me through the fire and flames. Even when life doesn't make sense, I choose to trust in You and believe that You are working behind the scenes for my good. In Jesus' Name, Amen.

JUNE 8

Secure

So if God has given you the ability to prophesy, speak out with as much faith as God has given you. If your gift is serving others, serve them well. If you are a teacher, teach well. If your gift is to encourage others, be encouraging. If it is giving, give generously. If God has given you leadership ability, take the responsibility seriously. And if you have a gift for showing kindness to others, do it gladly.

ROMANS 12:6–8, NLT

When you're secure in who God made you to be, you don't feel less-than because you can't do what somebody else does. God has given us different gifts. You don't feel inferior because your friend is a doctor and you don't have a college degree. Your security is not in how you perform or your title. Your security is in the fact that you are a child of Almighty God. You realize you are His masterpiece, fearfully and wonderfully made, empowered, and anointed. Find your value in who you are and not what you do or you'll spend your whole life competing with others. Stay focused on what you're called to do and know that God knows you and has gifted you uniquely.

PRAY & DECLARE

Father, thank You for blessing me with gifts and talents to fulfill my destiny that are different from what others have been given. I am secure and content with who I am. In Jesus' Name, Amen.

JUNE 9

Your Time to Reign

"Here is the king's son! The time has come for him to reign! The Lord *has promised that a descendant of David will be our king."*

2 CHRONICLES 23:3, NLT

When King Ahaziah of Judah was killed, his mother, Athaliah, took the throne as queen. She killed the whole royal family of the house of Judah, except for Ahaziah's baby son, Joash, who was hidden by his aunt. When Joash was seven years old, Jehoiada, the high priest, declared that it was time for the king's son to reign and overthrew Athaliah. God's promise to David and his descendants was secured.

What God started in your life, He's going to finish. It's time for the King's children to reign! Whatever negative thing has been reigning over you is about to end. This is a new day. You are coming into destiny moments. God is about to take you where you can't go on your own. It's going to be unusual, it's not going to happen on a normal schedule, and it's going to be sooner than you think.

PRAY & DECLARE

Father, thank You that because I am Your child, I am going to reign in life. Thank You that the negative things that have been reigning over me are about to end. In Jesus' Name, Amen.

JUNE 10

Remember and Expect

Then I thought, "To this I will appeal: the years when the Most High stretched out his right hand. I will remember the deeds of the LORD; yes, I will remember your miracles of long ago. I will consider all your works and meditate on all your mighty deeds."

PSALM 77:10–12, NIV

Are you facing challenges today that look too big? The key to staying encouraged is to never forget what God has done. Every one of us can look back and see the hand of God on our lives. Start remembering how He helped you accomplish things you never could have accomplished on your own. He's brought you out of difficulties that you thought you'd never survive. Rehearse all the times He's protected you, given you promotions, healed your family members, and put you in the right places with the right people.

Expect breakthroughs. Expect problems to turn around. Expect to rise to new levels.

PRAY & DECLARE

Father, thank You for all the amazing things You've done in my life, for the victories You've helped me win, for the restoration, the vindication, and the favor You've shown. Thank You for the doors You've opened for me and for the times You've protected, promoted, and given me opportunities. In Jesus' Name, Amen.

He has a
supersized life
in front of you.

JUNE 11

His Love Empowers Our Love

For all the law is fulfilled in one word, even in this:
"You shall love your neighbor as yourself."
GALATIANS 5:14, NKJV

It's easy to dwell on what we think is negative about us, but it doesn't help us do or be better. Beating yourself up for past mistakes doesn't move you forward. If you're waiting to perform perfectly before you feel good about who you are, you'll be waiting your whole life.

Praise be to God that His love empowers us to not only love ourselves but to love others. When you live in the love that He has given us, through Christ, you can love yourself and love others. When you're kind to yourself, you can be kind to others. It all starts with embracing and living out His love for you.

PRAY & DECLARE

Father, thank You for loving me so much that You've blotted out all my sins and released me from condemnation through the incredible price that Jesus paid on the cross. Thank You for pouring out Your love for me and, through that great love, empowering me to love others. In Jesus' Name, Amen.

JUNE 12

Clothed With Power

Then the Spirit of the LORD clothed Gideon with power.

JUDGES 6:34, NLT

God chose a young man named Gideon to lead the army of Israel against the Midianites, but Gideon was afraid and hiding. When an angel came to him and said, *"Mighty hero, the LORD is with you"* (v. 12), he was saying, "Gideon, come out from under the fear, the insecurity, the defeated mindset." In this destiny moment for Gideon, he made the decision to take a step of faith and believe he was who God said he was. When he did, God breathed on his life in a new way and empowered him with a courage he'd never felt. He went on to be a mighty hero indeed and defeated the Midianites.

The enemy would love for you to live afraid, hiding with a defeated mindset. This can be a destiny moment for you. Today, believe that you too are a mighty hero. It's time to step up to who you were created to be.

PRAY & DECLARE

Father, thank You for Your calling upon my life and that You have an empowering of Your Spirit that enables me to accomplish my dreams. I declare that I am equipped and empowered to go where I've never been and do what I've never done. In Jesus' Name, Amen.

JUNE 13

Stand Your Ground

Therefore put on the full armor of God, so that when the day of evil comes, you may be able to stand your ground, and after you have done everything, to stand.

EPHESIANS 6:13, NIV

Being a person of faith doesn't exempt us from difficulty. The apostle Paul says you are going to have evil days when you must have on the full armor of God. You're going to have things in life that can knock the wind out of you, take your joy, and cause you to want to give up on your dreams. Paul says to stand in the face of the opposition, stand when the medical report is not changing, stand when your finances aren't improving, stand when your child is not making good decisions. To stand means you're not moved by what's not changing. You're not complaining because it's taking so long. You're not bitter because you had the setback. You're not frustrated because your plans didn't work out. You stand believing, trusting, hoping, expecting.

PRAY & DECLARE

Father, thank You that You have provided me with Your armor to be able to withstand the evil days. I declare and thank you that You give me the power to stand. In Jesus' Name, Amen.

JUNE 14

Trust His Plan

Your faithfulness extends to every generation,
like the earth you created; it endures by your decree,
for everything serves your plans.
PSALM 119:90–91, TLB

God's ways are not our ways. We think that it's just the good breaks and the great relationships that serve God's plan, but it's also the disappointments, the closed doors, and the people who do us wrong. Without that happening, we couldn't reach our destiny. We see the negative things as hindrances, but it is all necessary to become who we are created to be.

We all go through things that don't make sense, but God wouldn't have allowed it if it wasn't going to serve His plan. Just keep moving forward, doing the right thing, being faithful, serving others, and resting in His love. God is not going to waste anything you go through. What was meant for your harm, He will turn to your advantage.

PRAY & DECLARE

Father, thank You that You are able to make all things serve me for my good, even the negative things that stress me out and seem to be holding me back. Thank You that I can stay in peace and trust the process and Your plan for my life. In Jesus' Name, Amen.

JUNE 15

A Child of God

See what great love the Father has lavished on us, that we should be called children of God! And that is what we are! The reason the world does not know us is that it did not know him.

1 JOHN 3:1, NIV

Who told you that you can't accomplish your dreams, that you're less-than, not good enough, not smart enough, or that the obstacles are too big? That may be true if you were average or ordinary, but I know something about you. Your Father in Heaven loves you with great love. You have royal blood flowing through your veins. You have the spiritual DNA of Almighty God. You're the King's son, the King's daughter.

Maybe you've had some bad breaks, been overlooked, or been pushed down. Remember: You're a child of the King. You haven't made too many mistakes. Your obstacles are not too big. Live out His passion through you. Get your fire back. God is about to do something unusual, something unprecedented. You're on the verge of seeing favor you've never seen.

PRAY & DECLARE

Father, thank You for being my Heavenly Father and loving me with great love. I believe and declare that I am a child of the Most High God and that I'm going to reign over what has reigned over me. In Jesus' Name, Amen.

When you're
kind to yourself,
you can be kind
to others.

JUNE 16

Springs in the Desert

The lame will leap like a deer, and those who cannot speak will sing for joy! Springs will gush forth in the wilderness, and streams will water the wasteland.

ISAIAH 35:6, NLT

Isaiah's prophecies to the Israelites who had been in captivity in Babylon for decades was that God was about to suddenly make a way for them to return through the desert. Although they couldn't see anything happening, they needed to get prepared in their thinking and be expecting something brand new. God was coming to save them, and springs would gush forth in the wilderness to water their way. Today, God is turning your dry places into abundant places. You're going to see the new thing. He's going to bring you out of captivity. He's going to free you from limitations and negative things that have been passed down in your family line. There's about to be gushing springs in your desert. That barren land is about to be turned into fertile land, an abundant land, with dreams coming to pass.

PRAY & DECLARE

Father, thank You for the great things that You've done in my past, but I don't want to get stuck there and stagnate. Thank You that You are the God who is always doing something new. I declare that springs will gush forth in the wilderness areas of my life. In Jesus' Name, Amen.

JUNE 17

Trouble Can't Find You

For in the time of trouble He shall hide me in His pavilion;
in the secret place of His tabernacle He shall hide me;
He shall set me high upon a rock.

PSALM 27:5, NKJV

We all have things that come against us. It's easy to live worried, wondering how it's going to turn out. But in the time of trouble, God will hide us. It doesn't say we won't have trouble. Difficulties may come, but God's promise is that He's going to make you invisible to the enemy.

You don't know how many times trouble has come, but it couldn't find you. Sickness had your name on it, but you were invisible. That accident was sent to take you out, but you were nowhere to be found. You were just going about your day and forces that should have stopped you didn't have any effect on you. Why? You were safe, hidden, and secure in His tabernacle.

PRAY & DECLARE

Father, thank You for Your promise of protecting me when troubles come. Thank You that I am invisible to the enemy. Thank You that my children, my health, my finances, my marriage, and my dreams are all hidden in your secret place. In Jesus' Name, Amen.

JUNE 18

Overwhelming Victory

No, despite all these things, overwhelming victory is ours through Christ, who loved us.

ROMANS 8:37, NLT

During the thirteen years between when Joseph was sold into slavery to when he was made prime minister of Egypt, practically every day he suffered and had to fight having a victim mentality. Thoughts would whisper, *You keep doing the right thing and yet you're the victim of others' wrongs.* But Joseph's attitude was: "I refuse to be a victim of my brothers, of the slave traders, of Potiphar's wife whose lie sent me to prison, or of the cupbearer who forgot about me after I helped him. They tried to harm me, but I know God means it for my good."

Nobody can force you to have a victim mentality. You have to give permission to become a victim. Don't say, "I'm going to feel sorry for myself. This bad break has stopped my future." Rather, declare, "No, thanks. Despite what's been done, I am going to see an overwhelming victory through Christ Jesus."

PRAY & DECLARE

Father, thank You for the promise of an overwhelming victory through Jesus. Thank You for Your love and that I am a victor and not a victim of circumstances. I'm going to stay in peace knowing that no obstacle can stop Your plan. In Jesus' Name, Amen.

JUNE 19

When You Don't Know

Trust God from the bottom of your heart; don't try to figure out everything on your own. Listen for God's voice in everything you do, everywhere you go; he's the one who will keep you on track.

PROVERBS 3:5–6, MSG

We all have situations that we don't see how they're going to work out. We do our best to find a solution, but there are some things God doesn't want us to know. He has the solution, but we can only imagine it by faith.

Sometimes there is no logical solution. The more we try to reason it out, the more discouraged we get. This is what faith is all about. You don't have to come up with a plan. We can actually be comfortable not knowing the details, yet "knowing" in our heart. Sometimes we think it's a lack of faith to say, "I don't know." Take the pressure off. God knows. And it's a joy to listen to His voice. He will direct your steps.

PRAY & DECLARE

Father, thank You that You will keep my life on track. Thank You that I can be free from trying to figure everything out. Thank you for Your divine whisper and voice in everything I do. In Jesus' Name, Amen.

JUNE 20

Empowered for Good Works

For we are His workmanship, created in Christ Jesus for good works, which God prepared beforehand that we should walk in them.

EPHESIANS 2:10, NKJV

Jesus chose Peter to be one of His disciples even though he knew he was hot-tempered, impatient, and would fail many times. He didn't choose him because he was perfect; He chose him because He had the blueprint for Peter's life. The messes didn't disqualify Peter. He knew that Peter would become one of the most respected, influential leaders in the church.

We all have some messy areas we need to improve in. The point is that the Master Workman is at work within you. He knows the hot temper, the addiction, and the negative attitude are not who you are. Know that you have been empowered to grow, to resist temptation. Every time you do the right thing, it makes it a little easier the next time. The power of His workmanship will result in good works.

PRAY & DECLARE

Father, thank You that You, indeed, have prepared me to walk in Your goodness. I thank You and praise You that You have empowered me to do Your good works. In Jesus' Name, Amen.

What was meant
for your harm,
He will turn to
your advantage.

JUNE 21

Don't Discount Your Gift

"The master said, 'Well done, my good and faithful servant.
You have been faithful in handling this small amount,
so now I will give you many more responsibilities.
Let's celebrate together!'"

MATTHEW 25:23, NLT

In the parable of the talents, the owner gave one man one talent, another two talents, and another five talents. It seems like if God were fair, He would've given them all the same number, but God is sovereign. He might give you five talents and give me two talents. He's God. I can complain about the two and try to compete with you, but you still have five and I have two. Better to say, "God, I'm going to take these two talents and be the best I can be."

Don't discount the gift God has put in you. Compared to others, there is nothing ordinary about you. God has put greatness in you. As you faithfully develop the gift you have, that gift will open doors to places you've never dreamed.

PRAY & DECLARE

Father, thank You that You are sovereign in the gift and the calling You have given me. Thank You that the gift and creativity and dreams You have given me are all I need. I will celebrate and develop all that You have given me. In Jesus' Name, Amen.

JUNE 22

Remember What God Said

"He is not here; he has risen! Remember how he told you, while he was still with you in Galilee: 'The Son of Man must be delivered over to the hands of sinners, be crucified and on the third day be raised again.'"

LUKE 24:6–7, NIV

The three women who went to the tomb on Sunday morning to care for Jesus' body were met by the angel's words, *"Remember how He told you . . ."* They came to the tomb discouraged, depressed, and defeated, and they left excited, passionate, and full of faith and hope.

When we're under pressure, too often we forget what God has said and go by what we see. We let negative thoughts drown out what God has promised. The enemy would love for you to get so caught up in your circumstances that you forget what God told you. But you have the power through the risen Christ to say, "Yes, I remember what You told me and declared over me."

PRAY & DECLARE

Father, thank You for the strength that rises within me whenever I remember what You have promised me. Thank You that I can stay focused on what You have said and walk by faith and not by sight. Negative thoughts cannot drown out Your voice and hold me back. In Jesus' Name, Amen.

JUNE 23

Storms

His wife said, "Still holding on to your precious integrity, are you? Curse God and be done with it!"

JOB 2:9, MSG

When Job and his wife went through a series of very painful losses, and then Job suffered a crushing illness, instead of encouraging Job, she said, "Job, you've always done the right thing, and see what it got you. Just curse God and give up." Fortunately, even though he didn't understand why it had happened, Job declared that God's favor had been on his life. By faith, Job eventually came out of it with double and lived a long, blessed life.

Every person has unfair, painful seasons. But you have to remind yourself that it's just a season. Don't make a judgment based on a betrayal or a setback that's temporary. Don't give up on your dreams, lose your passion, or live bitter. The storm may be difficult, but what God is about to do is going to supersede anything you've ever seen.

PRAY & DECLARE

Father, thank You that the unfair, painful seasons are only for a season of my life. Thank You that the storms are temporary. I believe that Your favor will shine again, and You will supersede anything I've seen You do before. In Jesus' Name, Amen.

JUNE 24

Put on God's Labels

"Do not be afraid; you will not be put to shame. Do not fear disgrace; you will not be humiliated. You will forget the shame of your youth and remember no more the reproach of your widowhood. For your Maker is your husband — the LORD *Almighty is his name — the Holy One of Israel is your Redeemer; he is called the God of all the earth."*

ISAIAH 54:4–5, NIV

Perhaps you are living with a sense of shame because of something that happened to you that wasn't even your fault. The enemy will twist things and try to convince you that it was your fault. Don't believe those lies. If someone did you wrong, the problem wasn't with you; the problem was with them. God saw what happened, and He's going to make your life so blessed, so rewarding, and so fulfilling that you won't remember the shame or reproach.

Through Christ, forgive the people who did you wrong. And let it go. What they have done to you did not change your identity. Take off the label that says "Damaged" and put on some of God's labels, such as "Accepted," "Approved," "Valuable," and "Masterpiece." God will take your scars and turn them into stars.

PRAY & DECLARE

Father, thank You for the freedom from any sense of shame I have about what happened to me in my past. I declare that I am putting on the new labels of what You call me. In Jesus' Name, Amen.

JUNE 25

The Only Praise That Matters

Yet at the same time many even among the leaders believed in him. But because of the Pharisees they would not openly acknowledge their faith for fear they would be put out of the synagogue; for they loved human praise more than praise from God.

JOHN 12:42–43, NIV

Jesus talks about those who love the praise of people more than the praise of God. When someone whom we respect or like wants us to go one direction, we can say "no" because God is prompting us in our heart to take another path. Remember His favor, His anointing, and His blessing will cause you to excel. As you quit worrying about what others think, you'll see new opportunities and relationships. People will tell you how to run your life. If you try to please everyone, you'll be confused, frustrated, and miserable. Don't let people control you and go around feeling guilty because you don't fit into their boxes. They may not understand why you don't take their advice, but look straight ahead, and, as the apostle Paul says, *"Run with purpose in every step"* (1 Corinthians 9:26, NLT). Praise God and go where you're celebrated!

PRAY & DECLARE

Father, thank You for the way You guide me with Your peace and joy. Thank You that I can be free from living for the approval of others because I have Your approval. In Jesus' Name, Amen.

Live out
His passion
through you.

JUNE 26

Greater Honor

You will restore me to even greater honor
and comfort me once again.
PSALM 71:21, NLT

Joseph was sold into slavery in Egypt, where he ended up in prison for thirteen years. But when he interpreted Pharaoh's dream, Pharaoh was so impressed that he put Joseph in charge of the whole country. Raised as a shepherd, Joseph was made prime minister. I'm sure that when people saw Joseph, they thought he was raised in royalty. They didn't know he was a former slave and prisoner. There was no sign of the injustice, the betrayals, the suffering. All they saw was a man who had great influence and honor.

You may be in an unfair situation like Joseph's. You're doing the right thing, but the wrong thing is happening. Don't worry. God is a God of justice. He sees the wrongs, and He knows how to make up for what you've been through and how to restore you to greater honor.

PRAY & DECLARE

Father, thank You that You are a God of justice, and You have seen everything I've gone through. Thank You that You know how to make up for all the negative things that I've faced. I am comforted knowing You will bestow even greater honor. In Jesus' Name, Amen.

JUNE 27

Equipping

Now may the God of peace — who brought up from the dead our Lord Jesus, the great Shepherd of the sheep, and ratified an eternal covenant with his blood — may he equip you with all you need for doing his will.

HEBREWS 13:20–21, NLT

We all have dreams God has put in our heart, but too often we get discouraged by the equipping process. We've had setbacks; somebody did us wrong. But every struggle, disappointment, and delay is depositing something in you. It's making you stronger, developing your character, equipping you for what God wants you to do.

God knows what's in your future. He knows what it's going to take to keep you there. You may not understand why you're in a lonely season, a frustrated season, a stagnant season, but everything you go through is that you might know His love and power. God wouldn't have allowed it if it wasn't a part of the process. Without it, you couldn't give birth to what He put in you. Praise God. For what He promised you will come to pass.

PRAY & DECLARE

Father, thank You for the dreams You put in my heart. Thank You that You are equipping me. I believe that even in the downturns, I have the privilege and joy of experiencing the power of Jesus Christ. In Jesus' Name, Amen.

JUNE 28

Speak the Truth About Yourself

Does anyone want to live a life that is long and prosperous? Then keep your tongue from evil and your lips from telling lies.

PSALM 34:12–13, NLT

In today's scripture, we think it only means that we should never lie to other people. But it also means to not tell lies about yourself. Don't go around saying things that contradict what God says about you. "I'm just average. I'm not good enough. I'll never do anything great." That's telling lies. God didn't create anyone average. When He breathed life into you, He put greatness inside. Be careful what you say about yourself. No more speaking defeat. Get in agreement with God. All through the day, bless yourself by saying, "I am strong. I am talented. I am healthy. I am well able." Speak life, speak favor, speak victory, and watch God pour out life, long and prosperous.

PRAY & DECLARE

Father, thank You for creating me in Your image and breathing life and greatness into me. Thank You that my words have the power to bless my life and lift me to live out what You've created me to be. Thank You that You have empowered me to speak what You say about me. In Jesus' Name, Amen.

JUNE 29

What Is God Saying About You?

Then the Lord said to Satan, "Have you considered my servant Job? There is no one on earth like him; he is blameless and upright, a man who fears God and shuns evil."

JOB 1:8, NIV

I love the fact that God was bragging on Job. If you could hear what God is saying about you, you'd be amazed. We think God is focused on our shortcomings, but God sees the good things in you. He sees your heart to help others, your sincerity, your kindness, your courage. I can hear Him telling the angels, "Have you seen My children, Jim and Rachel? There's no one like them." God made you in His own image. He calls you a masterpiece.

Remember that just because you're having difficulty, as Job did, doesn't mean you've done something wrong. We all go through seasons we don't understand. Dark seasons are not permanent. He will bring you out promoted, increased, and at a new level of your destiny.

PRAY & DECLARE

Father, thank You that You made me in Your image and call me a masterpiece. Thank You that You brag on me before the angels. Thank You that I can live victoriously knowing what You have declared over me. In Jesus' Name, Amen.

JUNE 30

Unexpected Sunshine

"If your eye is pure, there will be sunshine in your soul."

MATTHEW 6:22, TLB

When we have an attitude of faith — we're positive, hopeful, expecting good things — that pure eye is letting sunshine into our life. But when we go around stressed out, worried, or thinking the clouds over our health or finances are never going to change, that's stopping the sun. It's causing more clouds to roll in, more defeat, and more mediocrity. Through Christ, we have the pathway already opened to let sunshine into our life.

Instead of being discouraged by the dark clouds, we can declare: "Any moment this can change. Healing is coming, promotion is coming, the right person is coming, breakthroughs are coming." Yes, we can shake off the negativity and turn our situation around. Say, "God, I know You're in control of these clouds. They will pass. I believe at any moment I'm going to see that unexpected sunshine."

PRAY & DECLARE

Father, thank You that I walk by faith and not by sight. Thank You that Your power can turn clouded situations around and open the right door. I am living with a sense of expectancy that You are about to bring some unexpected sunshine. In Jesus' Name, Amen.

July

JULY 1

Be Merciful

Do not judge and criticize and condemn others, so that you may not be judged and criticized and condemned yourselves.

MATTHEW 7:1, AMP

All around us are broken, hurting people whom God has put in our lives so we can help restore them. It's easy to criticize them for not making better decisions. But you don't know where you would be if you had walked in their shoes. Life is not a level playing field. When you're tempted to judge, remind yourself that they probably didn't receive everything you did growing up. God has freely given you His mercy that you might freely give it to others. God is counting on us to lift the fallen, restore the broken, and heal the hurting.

God wants us to run to help the hurting rather than turning away. God put them in your life so you could be the one to love them, to see the best in them, and to help them get free.

PRAY & DECLARE

Father, thank You for freely giving me Your mercy that I might freely give it to others. Thank You that I can help lift the fallen, restore the broken, and heal the hurting. In Jesus' Name, Amen.

JULY 2

Mighty Hero

The angel of the LORD appeared to him and said,
"Mighty hero, the LORD is with you!"

JUDGES 6:12, NLT

Gideon was hiding in the winepress, afraid of his enemies, when God said he was to deliver the people of Israel from the Midianites. He was feeling inadequate, weak, and intimidated, yet God called him a mighty hero. Gideon said, "God, not me. I come from the poorest family, and I am the least one in my father's house." Yet God gave Gideon favor, and he went out with three hundred men and defeated an army of over a hundred thousand. Gideon became a great leader and is now listed as one of the heroes of faith.

Your gift may seem small, you may feel unqualified, and the obstacles may look too big, but like Gideon, you are a mighty hero. Stir up what God has already placed in your heart and come out of hiding. God wouldn't have put it there if He weren't going to bring it to pass.

PRAY & DECLARE

Father, thank You that You know me. Thank You that You have equipped and empowered me to be strong where I feel weak and less than. I declare: I am a mighty warrior! In Jesus' Name, Amen.

JULY 3

Live Connected

You will show me the path of life; in Your presence is fullness of joy; at Your right hand are pleasures forevermore.

PSALM 16:11, NKJV

God promises that joy is found in His presence. When you don't have joy, you're in some way disconnected from God's presence. In the tough times, the joy of the Lord is what gives you the strength to make it through.

God wants you to experience His supernatural joy at all times. Joy manifests as you tap into the heart of Jesus. Praise your Heavenly Father for who He is and what He's done in your life. The Scripture says that He inhabits the praises of His people (Psalm 22:3). Anytime you feel depleted or overwhelmed, just begin to praise and thank God. Draw near to Him and He'll draw near to you (James 4:8). In His presence you'll be refreshed and restored to His full joy.

PRAY & DECLARE

Father, thank You that though I face challenges and obstacles today, I can still walk in the fullness of joy. Thank You that no matter what happens to me, You inhabit my praises with Your presence. I receive Your joy as my strength to rise up and overcome the tough times. In Jesus' Name, Amen.

JULY 4

Take the First Step

"Blessed are the peacemakers, for they will be called children of God."

MATTHEW 5:9, NIV

A lot of times we think, *When he or she changes, I'll change.* But here's the key: God has empowered you to put your ego down and take the first step. Pride will tell you, "When they're acting wrong, don't treat them right. They don't deserve it." But you're not doing it for them; you're doing it unto God. You're not saying, "I approve of how you treat me." You're saying, "God, I'm going to be a peacemaker, even though I don't like this."

Human nature says to treat people like they're treating us. All that does is make matters worse. God brought the people into your life on purpose. It was all part of His plan. We all have weaknesses and shortcomings. If you make the first move, that seed you're sowing will be what God uses to bring a harvest of peace.

PRAY & DECLARE

Father, thank You that You have made me a peacemaker even when I don't like how someone else is treating me. I look forward to the harvest of peace You are bringing to me and those around me. In Jesus' Name, Amen.

JULY 5

Light Will Break for You

"Is it not to share your food with the hungry and to provide the poor wanderer with shelter — when you see the naked, to clothe them, and not to turn away from your own flesh and blood? Then your light will break forth like the dawn, and your healing will quickly appear; then your righteousness will go before you, and the glory of the Lord will be your rear guard."

ISAIAH 58:7–8, NIV

Too often we're waiting for the light to break forth — the promotion, the healing, the new level — but we've pushed serving others to the side. When you focus on not just accomplishing your dreams but on being a blessing to others, you're going to experience joy abounding. When you make it your business to serve, you're going to see breakthroughs, promotion, and doors open that you couldn't open.

Take a break from what's bothering you. Take a break from what you want, from what you're believing for, and go be a blessing to somebody else. When you serve others, that's a seed you're sowing. God will make sure that you're blessed in all that concerns you.

PRAY & DECLARE

Father, thank You that as I move out joyfully to serve others, You come bursting in with light and direction. I believe that You, the Creator of the universe, will make sure that I am blessed as I bless others. In Jesus' Name, Amen.

There's about
to be gushing
springs in your
desert.

JULY 6

Labor to Rest

So then, there remains a Sabbath rest for the people of God, for whoever has entered God's rest has also rested from his works as God did from his. Let us therefore strive to enter that rest, so that no one may fall by the same sort of disobedience.

HEBREWS 4:9–11, ESV

"Strive" or "labor" to enter God's rest. It sounds like a contradiction. God used that word because He knew it would take work to stay seated. It's easy to stand up and worry over problems and try to fix everything in our own strength. That's why it says to labor to enter His rest. It's going to take effort. It doesn't say work to make that problem go away or work to break that addiction. He says work to stay seated. Work to live from a place of resting in God's grace and strength.

If you're trying to break a bad habit, remember, you're not working to get the victory; you are working from the place of His victory. Stay in peace, and let God make things happen that you couldn't make happen.

PRAY & DECLARE

Father, thank You for providing a place where I can rest in Your grace and strength to fight my battles. Thank You that I can stay in peace and know that You can make things happen that I never could. I praise You for Your gift of rest. In Jesus' Name, Amen.

JULY 7

Power in Vulnerability

No, dear brothers, I am still not all I should be, but I am bringing all my energies to bear on this one thing: Forgetting the past and looking forward to what lies ahead, I strain to reach the end of the race and receive the prize for which God is calling us up to heaven because of what Christ Jesus did for us.

PHILIPPIANS 3:13–14, TLB

Paul was one of the church's greatest apostles. He wrote nearly half the books in the New Testament. He was a scholar, theologian, and preacher. He was enormously effective. But he had the humility to admit, "I don't have it all together. I welcome just being real before My God." He could have let pride hide his weaknesses. He could have masked his shortcomings, but he was vulnerable. He was real. There's power in vulnerability.

Too often we try to impress people by putting on masks and performing to make them think we're this or that. Take off the mask. Be real. God is not looking for the ideal you, the pretend you, or the future you. He's looking for the real you, the vulnerable you.

PRAY & DECLARE

Father, thank You that You know the real me, for me to be honest about my struggles, my doubts, my weaknesses, and my fears. Thank You that You love me just as I am and that there is true power in being vulnerable. I have nothing to hide. In Jesus' Name, Amen.

JULY 8

Serve Faithfully

"Well done, good and faithful servant.
You have been faithful over a little; I will set you
over much. Enter into the joy of your master."
MATTHEW 25:21, ESV

There are times in life when we feel like we're doing the right thing but not making progress. It's easy to get discouraged, lose our passion, or feel like we're just going in circles.

When you're faithful in the routine, something is happening that you can't see. Your character is being developed. Your spiritual muscles are getting stronger. The routineness of life is not exciting, but it's necessary. Those "little things" are every bit as important as the "big things" in life. When you're living out His goodness within you month after month, you're being prepared for where God is taking you. God has empowered you to be faithful in the ordinary, and as you live out that faith, He will take you into the extraordinary. When you're faithful in average days, you will overcome on exceptional days.

PRAY & DECLARE

Father, thank You for calling me to be faithful in the routine, knowing that You are preparing me for the new things You have in store. Thank You that You will take me from the ordinary to the extraordinary. In Jesus' Name, Amen.

JULY 9

Worth the Wait

Be still before the Lord and wait patiently for him;
do not fret when people succeed in their ways,
when they carry out their wicked schemes.

PSALM 37:7, NIV

One reason we get in a hurry and make bad decisions is that we think we're falling behind. Our friend is getting married, our coworker got promoted, our neighbor moved into a new house. We feel we're being left out and need to make things happen.

What God has put your name on is not going to go to anyone else. What belongs to you will not go to another person. Don't be impatient for God to act. Keep abounding in His limitless love. What God has for you is on the way. You're being prepared for what God has prepared for you. The reason it's taken so long is that it's going to be much bigger and more fulfilling than you thought. When you see what God does, you're going to say it was worth the wait.

PRAY & DECLARE

Father, thank You that everything You have for me will be released in my life at the right time. Thank You that You are working behind the scenes and preparing me for whatever is next. Help me to be patient and know that You are always on schedule. In Jesus' Name, Amen.

JULY 10

Feeling Stuck?

"What do you think? If a man has a hundred sheep, and one of them goes astray, does he not leave the ninety-nine and go to the mountains to seek the one that is straying?"

MATTHEW 18:12, NKJV

Jesus told a parable about a shepherd who will leave the ninety-nine sheep to go find the one that's gone astray. He'll search night and day until he finds that one lost sheep. When life has pushed you down, somebody did you wrong, or you made mistakes and now you're off course, you may feel that you're stuck, as though you can never reach your destiny. The good news is that the Good Shepherd is looking for you. He's coming after you. Why? Because He's not in the condemning business. He's in the restoration business. The God who created the universe is about to pick you up, breathe new life into your dreams, and propel you toward your destiny.

PRAY & DECLARE

Father, thank You for loving me and looking for me because You want me to have all that belongs to me as Your child. Thank You that I am never stuck, no matter where I am or how stuck I feel. I believe that You will find, rescue, and restore me. In Jesus' Name, Amen.

What belongs to you will not go to another person.

JULY 11

Fill This Prescription

"These things I have spoken to you, that in Me you may have peace. In the world you will have tribulation; but be of good cheer, I have overcome the world."

JOHN 16:33, NKJV

Jesus acknowledged that we're going to have challenges in this life. Nevertheless, He added, *"But be of good cheer."* He didn't say to be discouraged, to be upset, to be sad, or to be offended. In the tough times, the joy of the Lord is what gives you strength. If the enemy can deceive you into living weighed down, discouraged, and somber, he'll be able to defeat you at every turn. Don't fall into that trap. Your circumstances may not change, but you can change. Make the choice that right in the midst of difficulties you're going to be of good cheer.

I have a prescription for you: Stay cheerful, be good-natured, laugh every day, find the humor in life, and keep a joyful atmosphere in your home. As you live, empowered by this prescription, you'll have the strength to make it through the tough times.

PRAY & DECLARE

Father, thank You that though I have challenges and tribulations, I can still be of good cheer. I receive Your joy as my strength to rise up and overcome the tough times. In Jesus' Name, Amen.

JULY 12

Get Ready for an Explosion

"Ah, Lord God! Behold, You have made the heavens and the earth by Your great power and outstretched arm. There is nothing too hard for You."

JEREMIAH 32:17, NKJV

In the Scripture, the original Greek word used for God's power is "dunamis" (Acts 1:8). That's where we get the word "dynamite." Dynamite is used to level buildings and clear out whatever's in the way. God can level your mountains — those obstacles that look permanent to you — not make a tunnel through them, not make a path around them, not give you the strength to go over them.

God can do the extraordinary. He can place the dynamite and light the fuse. Get ready for an explosion of good breaks, an explosion of healing, joy, freedom. Those obstacles that have been holding you back are about to be blown away.

PRAY & DECLARE

Father, thank You that You are the all-powerful God who goes before me to level my mountains and the obstacles before me. Thank You that nothing is too hard for You. I declare that I am expecting an explosion of blessing in my life that will be a testimony to Your glory. In Jesus' Name, Amen.

JULY 13

Beginnings and Endings

"I am the Alpha and the Omega — the beginning and the end," says the Lord God. "I am the one who is, who always was, and who is still to come — the Almighty One."

REVELATION 1:8, NLT

We get excited about new beginnings. We talk a lot about God being the Alpha and doing new things, but we don't hear much about how He, the Omega, brings things to an end. It could be a relationship, a broken dream, a business that didn't make it, or a loved one who passes away. This is hard for us because an ending can feel like a setback and even a failure. But just as God opens a door, He brings things to an end. The reason He closes a door is because He has something better. Instead of being sour and losing your joy, the best thing you can do is to just say goodbye to the questions, the disappointment, and the self-pity. Accept it as part of God's plan, be at peace with what's behind you and move on.

PRAY & DECLARE

Father, thank You that You are the Alpha and Omega, the Beginning and the End. Thank You that just as I can trust You with new beginnings, so I can trust You with what comes to an end and the wonderful, new opportunities You have in store. In Jesus' Name, Amen.

JULY 14

Always Green

They are like trees along a riverbank bearing luscious fruit each season without fail. Their leaves shall never wither, and all they do shall prosper.

PSALM 1:3, TLB

Because your hope is in the Lord, the psalmist says you're not going to be bothered by the drought. While others are drying up, you're going to flourish. When they're going under, you're going over. Why? Your hope is in the Lord. You may be in a barren place, but your roots go deep in God's provision.

God is not limited by the economy, your job, or the stock market. He owns it all. Keep your hope in Him, and you're not going to just make it, you're going to keep producing luscious fruit — not shriveled up or mediocre. You're going to see abundance, overflow, pressed down, shaken together, and running over. Not after the drought, but in the drought.

PRAY & DECLARE

Father, thank You that Your plan for my life is that I am always bearing luscious fruit. Thank You that You are not limited by seasons or for the right conditions to be in place in order for You to do what You want. I declare, in the Lord, my life is always green. In Jesus' Name, Amen.

JULY 15

Thrown Mercy

Then Jesus stood up again and said to the woman, "Where are your accusers? Didn't even one of them condemn you?" "No, Lord," she said. And Jesus said, "Neither do I. Go and sin no more."

JOHN 8:10–11, NLT

Jesus was teaching in the temple when the religious leaders dragged a woman caught in adultery in front of the crowd and said, "The law of Moses says to stone her. What do You say?" She was guilty, deeply shamed, without a defense. Rather than answer, Jesus stooped to the ground and wrote in the dust with his finger.

They may have thought He was stooping down to pick up a rock to throw, but He stooped down to throw mercy. He said, "You who are without sin, go ahead and throw the first stone." It was dead silence until one man walked out, then another and another.

Jesus is a God who stoops in the dirt to restore someone caught in sin, shame, and disgrace. His way is to free you from guilt and release you from condemnation.

PRAY & DECLARE

Father, thank You that Your love is real. Thank You that You sent Jesus to stoop into the dirt in my life and free me from all condemnation for my sins. I declare: Because of what Jesus accomplished on the cross, I am now free from all guilt. In Jesus' Name, Amen.

God didn't
create anyone
average.

JULY 16

Rest

For we who have believed do enter that rest . . .

HEBREWS 4:3, NKJV

Whenever you're waiting for something to change, perhaps for your health or finances to improve, once you've believed, you don't have to figure everything out. When you don't see anything changing, you'll be tempted to worry, but stay at rest. When you're at rest, you show God that you trust Him. Maybe you're thinking it would have happened by now. You could be worried and complaining, but instead you're thanking God, you're declaring His promises, you're being your best each day. When you're at rest, you're in faith.

But if you're upset over what's not changing, worried about your finances, and can't sleep because your child is off course, come back to a place of peace. When you believe and know God is in control, you're at rest, you know all things are going to work for your good, and you know what He started He's going to finish.

PRAY & DECLARE

Father, thank You for providing a place where I can rest in Your grace and strength to fight my battles. Thank You that I can stay in peace and know that You will make things happen that I never could. In Jesus' Name, Amen.

JULY 17

The Way of Endurance

We do this by keeping our eyes on Jesus, the champion who initiates and perfects our faith. Because of the joy awaiting him, he endured the cross, disregarding its shame. Now he is seated in the place of honor beside God's throne.

HEBREWS 12:2, NLT

On the night before Jesus was crucified, He was in such distress in the garden of Gethsemane that His sweat was like drops of blood. He prayed three times, "Father, if it's possible, let this cup pass from Me." All of His emotions said give up. The victory was won right there. In the darkest time, He determined to endure the cross, looking forward to the joy that was coming.

In those difficult times when you're trying to keep your marriage together, trying to take your family to a new level, trying to help a friend who is depressed, remember, there is a joy awaiting you; breakthrough is coming. It's worth it.

PRAY & DECLARE

Father, thank You that Jesus endured the pain of the cross for the joy of redeeming us. Thank You that in the difficult times that feel like a garden of Gethsemane, I can focus on the fact that the cause is worth it and endure. I look forward to the joy that awaits. In Jesus' Name, Amen.

JULY 18

Don't Expect a Straight Path

Show me the path where I should go, O Lord;
point out the right road for me to walk.
PSALM 25:4, TLB

God doesn't always take us down a straight path. There will be detours, delays, and curves. There will be times when you feel like you're going the wrong way. You may say, "God, I'm believing for promotion, healing, or freedom, but I'm seeing just the opposite." Don't get set on the method. The way you think it's going to happen may not be the way God's going to do it. What you can't see is that on the path that seems to be going the wrong way, there's a turn that leads to a shortcut that will catapult you ahead. That's the way our God is. Where He's leading you is going to be better than you've imagined. The reason it's taking longer is because it's going to be bigger than you thought — more rewarding, more fulfilling.

PRAY & DECLARE

Father, thank You that You are the Most High God and that You have a way of making all the detours and seeming wrong ways in my life work to my advantage. Show me Your path. I believe that where You lead is better than I've imagined. In Jesus' Name, Amen.

JULY 19

Be a Lifter

Encourage the hearts of your fellow believers and support one another, just as you have already been doing.

1 THESSALONIANS 5:11, TPT

There are times when people need you to stand in the gap when they're down, even if they're off course, not making good decisions. It's easy to criticize and find fault. "Why did they do that? They should have known better." They don't need your judgment; they need your faith. Try a different approach. Pray for them. Ask God to show them mercy to get them back on course. You can be the one who pushes them past the discouragement and lifts them back on their feet.

God is counting on you to be a friend with faith. Be a lifter, be an encourager. Tell them that you're praying for them, that you love them, that you believe in them. Your faith can be what lights their passion.

PRAY & DECLARE

Father, thank You for all the people You have placed in my life. Thank You that I can stand in the gap for the ones who are down and need my faith, my prayers, my encouragement. Help me to have a heart of compassion and to be a lifter of others. In Jesus' Name, Amen.

JULY 20

Grass in the Desert

Then Jesus directed them to have all the people sit down in groups on the green grass.

MARK 6:39, NIV

Jesus spent an entire day teaching thousands of people in a deserted place. Late in the day, Jesus directed His disciples to have the hot, tired, and hungry crowd sit in groups on the green grass. Before Jesus multiplied the food miraculously, God gave them grass in the desert. He made the hard place easier for them.

We all go through deserted places in life — problems that should overwhelm us. But somehow in the midst of the challenges, we feel strength that we didn't have — courage to keep moving forward, grace to endure. We look back and think, *How did I make it through that loss, that sickness, that difficulty?* It was God giving you grass in the desert, God making the hard places easier. He didn't stop the trouble, but He kept the trouble from stopping you.

PRAY & DECLARE

Father, thank You for loving me so much that even when I am in a deserted place, You provide me with green grass. Thank You that no matter where I go or what I go through, You are always here with me. In Jesus' Name, Amen.

Laugh every day, find the humor in life, and keep a joyful atmosphere in your home.

JULY 21

Expect His Favor

The women said to Naomi: "Praise be to the LORD, who this day has not left you without a guardian-redeemer. May he become famous throughout Israel! He will renew your life and sustain you in your old age."

RUTH 4:14–15, NIV

After the deaths of her husband and two sons, Naomi felt heartbroken, empty, and bitter. But when her daughter-in-law Ruth fell in love and married Boaz and had a baby named Obed, Naomi's life was renewed. She took care of that baby like he was her own son and was happier than she'd ever dreamed. What's significant is that Obed became the grandfather of David, and out of David's family line, Jesus came. Naomi couldn't see it, but through her heartbreak she became instrumental in our Savior being born.

You may be at an empty place. If Naomi were here, she would tell you that's not how your story ends. God has things in your future exceedingly, abundantly, beyond what you've imagined.

PRAY & DECLARE

Father, thank You that You are all about transforming the difficulties in my life. Thank You that Your plans are always so much more fulfilling and bigger than my understanding and plan. I declare that You will restore, redeem, and renew my life. In Jesus' Name, Amen.

JULY 22

Joy in His Presence

You make known to me the path of life; you will fill me with joy in your presence, with eternal pleasures at your right hand.

PSALM 16:11, NIV

It's good to be passionate about our dreams, passionate about healing, freedom, and promotion. But don't be so consumed that you're not going to be happy while you're waiting for God to make His path known to you. Don't put your happiness on hold until everything works out. This day is a gift. Enjoy your life while God is working. Don't be uptight, stressed out, and saying, "When is it going to change?" Rather, enter His presence and say, "I am going to enjoy this day. This crisis, these challenges, or this bad break is not going to stop me. God, Your presence in my life is my joy. I trust Your timing, and I trust Your ways."

PRAY & DECLARE

Father, thank You that this day is a gift from You. Thank You that my happiness is not dependent on my situations but upon Your presence in my life. I've made up my mind that I'm going to rejoice in You and be glad. In Jesus' Name, Amen.

JULY 23

Sweet Waters

After leaving Marah, the Israelites traveled on to the oasis of Elim, where they found twelve springs and seventy palm trees. They camped there beside the water.

EXODUS 15:27, NLT

The Israelites traveled into the desert and desperately needed water. They finally came to a pool or well at Marah and rushed to it, but the water was bitter. They couldn't drink it. Their excitement turned to great disappointment. Then God showed Moses a certain piece of wood to throw into the water, and the bitter waters became sweet. Now the people could drink all the water they wanted. God knows how to take a bitter loss, breakup, or difficult childhood and make it sweet.

When God touches that bitter situation, it will turn sweet. The relationship will be restored, the child will come home, the dream will come to pass. God is going to bring you out of the bitter places into an oasis, to springs of abundance, joy, health, and fulfillment like you've never seen. From the bitter to the sweet.

PRAY & DECLARE

Father, thank You that I can trust You to transform the bitter situations in my life and make them sweet. Thank You that You are supernatural, and You can lead me into an oasis of refreshing and restoration. In Jesus' Name, Amen.

JULY 24

Fully Restored

"The father said, 'Quick, bring me the best robe, my very own robe, and I will place it on his shoulders. Bring the ring, the seal of sonship, and I will put it on his finger. And bring out the best shoes you can find for my son.'"

LUKE 15:22, TPT

The prodigal son wasted all of his father's inheritance on partying and returned home dirty, broken, desperate, and feeling worthless. But when the father, who represents God, saw his son, he ran to him and embraced him. He immediately fully restored his son with the best robe, the family ring, and new shoes.

When God restores us, we come out fully restored, full of joy, with gifts coming out, healthy, blessed, and prosperous. Don't settle for less than. Put on the Father's robe of righteousness and favor. Put on the ring of authority. He's bringing you the best, new shoes to take you to a place of destiny.

PRAY & DECLARE

Father, thank You that You forgive me and that every mistake I've made has already been paid for by Jesus on the cross. Thank You for Your heart of compassion, love, and restoring mercy. I believe that You robe me in Your righteousness and favor. In Jesus' Name, Amen.

JULY 25

Name Your Future

She named the child Ichabod (which means "Where is the glory?"), for she said, "Israel's glory is gone." She named him this because the Ark of God had been captured and because her father-in-law and husband were dead. Then she said, "The glory has departed from Israel, for the Ark of God has been captured."

1 SAMUEL 4:21–22, NLT

An Israelite woman was about to give birth when she heard that the ark of the covenant had been stolen. The ark signified the presence of God with the Israelites. When she gave birth, she was so distraught that she named her son Ichabod, which means "no glory," or "where is the glory?" She named her future based on her past. She could have just as easily named him "the glory will return." But she was so caught up in the disappointment and heartache that it soured her future.

Don't name your future based on hurtful things from your past. Get that Ichabod spirit off you. Name your future "blessed, prosperous, victorious, healthy, strong, wise, and talented."

PRAY & DECLARE

Father, thank You that Your plans for me are for good to give me a bright future and hope. Thank You that the difficulties I face are temporary and pale in comparison to the weight of glory that is coming. I declare that I will not name my future based upon my past. In Jesus' Name, Amen.

Be a lifter,
be an
encourager.

JULY 26

Keep Traveling Steadily

Don't be impatient for the Lord to act! Keep traveling steadily along his pathway and in due season he will honor you with every blessing, and you will see the wicked destroyed.

PSALM 37:34, TLB

Most of us don't like times of waiting. We're interested in the destination, but God is interested in the journey. When we understand that He's working in us along the way, waiting and patience become part of the process. You won't have to make it happen in your own strength or try to force the door open. God will give you the position, give you the spouse, give you the influence. You're not falling behind. God has already lined up the blessings He's going to give you. He's already put your name on things bigger and better than you've imagined. Now keep traveling steadily; keep trusting Him when you don't see anything happening.

PRAY & DECLARE

Father, thank You that there is a purpose for times of waiting, whether I understand it or not. Help me to be patient and to rest in the fact that it's all part of Your process. I believe that I am right where You want me and that You have every blessing already lined up for me. In Jesus' Name, Amen.

JULY 27

Where Have You Pitched Your Tent?

"David said it all: I saw God before me for all time. Nothing can shake me; he's right by my side. I'm glad from the inside out, ecstatic; I've pitched my tent in the land of hope."

ACTS 2:25–26, MSG

David said he pitched his tent in the land of hope. Where have you pitched your tent? "Well, I've had a lot of disappointments." "I'll never get well." "I can't accomplish my dreams." Move out of the land of "It can't happen." Through Christ you can pick up your tent and pitch it in the land of "With God all things are possible," the land of "Goodness and mercy are chasing me down," the land of "What was meant for my harm, God is turning to my advantage." Just one touch of God's goodness and you'll beat the cancer or the addiction. Get up every morning expecting God to surprise you.

PRAY & DECLARE

Father, thank You that I can pitch my tent in the land of hope where all things are possible through You. I look forward to what You're bringing my way. In Jesus' Name, Amen.

JULY 28

God's Big Picture

This is the confidence we have in approaching God: that if we ask anything according to his will, he hears us.

1 JOHN 5:14, NIV

It would have made sense that when Joseph's brothers were about to sell him into slavery, he would have prayed, "God, stop them from betraying me." But his prayer, which seems like it would have been God's will, wouldn't have been answered. That's not because God didn't love him, but because God could see the big picture. He knew the betrayal was a step that was leading Joseph down a difficult path to something amazing — saving his family from famine. Had God kept him from the betrayal, it would have kept him from his destiny.

When we pray and it's not answered in our way, it's tempting to ask, "God, why not?" But praise be to God! God loves you too much to answer a prayer that is going to keep you from His purpose in you.

PRAY & DECLARE

Father, thank You that just as You hear my prayers and are faithful to bring Your will to pass, so You're faithful not to answer what is not Your will. Thank You that You see the big picture and know what I need to face to reach my destiny. In Jesus' Name, Amen.

JULY 29

Pearls

"Don't waste what is holy on people who are unholy. Don't throw your pearls to pigs! They will trample the pearls, then turn and attack you."

MATTHEW 7:6, NLT

Jesus says to overcome evil with good and to bless our enemies, but He also says not to cast your pearls among swine. Some people won't value the calling on your life. They will reject and trample over who God made you to be. They will not respect what you have to offer. Your time is too valuable to waste it with people who discount your pearls. Don't hang around people who try to lessen you and who make you feel like you have to prove to them who you are. You don't need their approval; you have Almighty God's approval. He created you in His own image. He calls you a masterpiece. Hang around people who recognize your gifts, who inspire you, who bring out the best in you, and who cause your pearls to shine.

PRAY & DECLARE

Father, thank You that when others don't value Your calling on my life, I can let them go. Thank You that I don't need their approval, because I know I have Your approval. I will not throw my pearls before those who will trample them. In Jesus' Name, Amen.

JULY 30

Clothed in Humility

All of you, clothe yourselves with humility toward one another, because, "God opposes the proud but shows favor to the humble."

1 PETER 5:5, NIV

King Nebuchadnezzar looked out over his magnificent city and said, "*Is not this the great Babylon I have built as the royal residence, by my mighty power and for the glory of my majesty?*" (Daniel 4:30, NIV). His attitude was, "Look at me. It is my power, my might, my majesty." However, we aren't created to take the glory; we're created to give God the glory. The moment Nebuchadnezzar kept the glory, it left.

Through Christ, we have been clothed in humility. He empowers us to say, "God, it was Your goodness that got me to where I am, that delivered me from the mistakes I made, that kept the opposition from defeating me, and that opened the doors of opportunity. Thank You."

PRAY & DECLARE

Father, thank You that You are the Most High God. I recognize Your goodness in my life and where I am at today. You chose to bless me, to have mercy on me, and to take me where I couldn't go on my own. Thank You for Your robes of righteousness and humility. I welcome giving You all the glory. In Jesus' Name, Amen.

JULY 31

The Father of Lights

Every good gift and every perfect gift is from above, coming down from the Father of lights, with whom there is no variation or shadow due to change.

JAMES 1:17, ESV

God has gifts in store for you that are more than you can ask or think. Don't be frustrated if you find yourself waiting for what you know He wants you to have. Sometimes God shows His love for us not by what He gives us but by what He withholds. If He provided you with that job, that house, or that baby before you're ready, it would limit your future. He knows what you can handle and when.

He not only knows what you're going to need, He knows who you're going to need. Sometimes God is saying not yet because He's still getting somebody else ready who's going to be instrumental in your life. Trust His timing and go through the waiting period knowing that the Father of Lights is shining in all things.

PRAY & DECLARE

Father, thank You that You are not just good, but You are my great Heavenly Father — the Father of Lights. Thank You for giving me the patience to know that when it seems You are withholding a gift, everything is still on Your schedule. In Jesus' Name, Amen.

August

AUGUST 1

Blossoms Overnight

Now it came to pass on the next day that Moses went into the tabernacle of witness, and behold, the rod of Aaron, of the house of Levi, had sprouted and put forth buds, had produced blossoms and yielded ripe almonds.

NUMBERS 17:8, NKJV

When the people were questioning Moses' and Aaron's authority as leaders, God instructed Moses to take the staffs from the leaders of each of the tribes of Israel and place them in the tabernacle, where God's presence was manifest. These staffs were old walking sticks, dead pieces of wood. The next morning the staff of Aaron had sprouted, blossomed, and even produced almonds. This dead wood that blossomed was proof of who God's leaders were.

God can change what looks dead overnight, whether it's a marriage, a dream, or a financial situation. You may think it's going to take years to get well or to restore a relationship. Suddenly, unexpectedly, God can change it overnight. What you might think is dead, can still cause it to blossom.

PRAY & DECLARE

Father, thank You for the dreams and desires You put in my heart. Thank You that You can resurrect overnight what I may have thought was dead and sprout forth new buds, blossoms, and ripe almonds! In Jesus' Name, Amen.

AUGUST 2

Powerless

Therefore, since the children share in flesh and blood, He Himself likewise also partook of the same, so that through death He might destroy the one who has the power of death, that is, the devil, and free those who through fear of death were subject to slavery all their lives.

HEBREWS 2:14–15, NASB

Two thousand years ago, Jesus defeated the enemy once and for all. The enemy tried his best, but his best could not keep Jesus in the grave. Jesus rendered the devil powerless. Jesus is alive forevermore and holds the keys to death and hell. The enemy has no power over you. He can't keep you from your purpose. Therefore, don't listen to his lies: "Look at all the mistakes you've made. God can't bless you. You'll never accomplish your dreams."

When the enemy's trying to stop you with fear, depression, or anxiety, just say, "No, thanks. I know the blood of the sinless, spotless Lamb of God is more powerful than any of these lies. I know that God's mercy is bigger than my mistakes."

PRAY & DECLARE

Father, thank You that Jesus rendered the enemy powerless on the cross. Thank You that His blood is more powerful than any of the devil's lies. I'm going to stay in peace knowing that nothing can keep me from the awesome future You have for me. In Jesus' Name, Amen.

AUGUST 3

Catching the Little Foxes

Catch all the foxes, those little foxes, before they ruin the vineyard of love, for the grapevines are blossoming!

SONG OF SOLOMON 2:15, NLT

Through Jesus, God has made us people of integrity. A person of honor is open and honest and true to their word. He says what he means and means what he says. She doesn't have any hidden agendas or ulterior motives. He doesn't need a legal contract to force him to fulfill his word. People of integrity are the same in private as they are in public. They do what's right whether anybody is watching or not. Integrity is the foundation on which truly successful relationships are built.

Even though God has richly given us all things, the "little foxes" can come in and try to steal it and ruin the beautiful vineyard that is our life. However, He has given us the ability to "catch" those foxes — to be on guard and thwart their efforts. We can declare: His integrity is my integrity.

PRAY & DECLARE

Father, thank You that You made my heart — the vineyard of my soul — pure, productive, and capable of bearing much fruit. Thank You that I have the power to catch and stop the little foxes that are powerless in light of Your great integrity within me. In Jesus' Name, Amen.

AUGUST 4

Choose Your Battles Wisely

Take control of what I say, O Lord, and guard my lips.

PSALM 141:3, NLT

When David heard the giant Goliath taunting the army of the Israelites, his oldest brother, Eliab, heard him ask some soldiers what the reward would be for the man who killed Goliath. He tried to embarrass David by saying, "You're just a little shepherd boy who's conceited and has a wicked heart." Now, David had killed a lion and a bear, but it says David just walked away. If he had gotten into an argument with Eliab, trying to prove he was a champion, he may have never faced Goliath and gained immediate prominence.

Learn to walk away from petty arguments, from disrespect, from jealous people, from battles that don't matter. If the thing that comes against you is not between you and your destiny, ignore it. Avoid making the mistake of engaging in every conflict. Choose your battles wisely.

PRAY & DECLARE

Father, give me wisdom to know when something that is coming against me is simply a distraction that will get me off course. Help me to guard my lips and not get involved in battles that don't matter. In Jesus' Name, Amen.

AUGUST 5

The Best Path

This time God said, "Don't attack them head-on. Instead, circle around behind them and ambush them from the grove of sacred trees."

2 SAMUEL 5:23, MSG

A few months prior to today's scripture, the Philistines had come up the same valley, and when David inquired of the Lord as to what to do, the Lord said to attack them. When the Philistines came again, David could have assumed, "No need to ask God this time. I know what to do." But David realized that yesterday's information may not be appropriate for today's challenge. So, he inquired of the Lord again. It was the same enemy, the same valley, but this time God said, "I have a different strategy for you."

God's ways are not our ways. He doesn't want you to get hooked on a formula; He wants you to be hooked on Him. Just ask, "God, how do You want me to respond to this challenge?" Watch His wisdom come in new and expanded ways.

PRAY & DECLARE

Father, thank You for Your promise that You will lead me down the best path for my life. Help me not to assume that I know what to do. Thank You for always providing fresh insights. In Jesus' Name, Amen.

God, Your presence in my life is my joy.

AUGUST 6

Kill the Giant

The priest replied, "The sword of Goliath the Philistine, whom you killed in the Valley of Elah, is here; it is wrapped in a cloth behind the ephod. If you want it, take it; there is no sword here but that one."

1 SAMUEL 21:9, NIV

Every day for forty days, Goliath stood on the side of the mountain and shouted insults across the valley at the Israelite army. When King Saul and the Israelites heard him, they were terrified and ran away. David heard those same intimidating threats, but he refused to let Goliath keep them trapped in the valley. He ran at Goliath and said, *"You come against me with a sword and spear and javelin, but I come against you in the name of the LORD Almighty, the God of the armies of Israel, whom you have defied"* (1 Samuel 17:45, NIV).

It's the same today. In your thoughts the enemy will shout discouragement, worry, and fear. Be a David and talk back to the enemy. Start declaring what God says about you. There's nothing more powerful against these negative threats than God's Word coming out of your mouth.

PRAY & DECLARE

Father, You are the Most High God and no giant is too great for You. The valleys I find myself in are not going to stop me, but You will turn my valley of trouble into a gateway of victory. In Jesus' Name, Amen.

AUGUST 7

Speak Words of Power

Oh, give thanks to the Lord, for He is good! For His mercy endures forever. Let the redeemed of the Lord say so, whom He has redeemed from the hand of the enemy.

PSALM 107:1–2, NKJV

When an angel told Zechariah that his wife, Elizabeth, was going to have a baby, he said, "How can I be sure of this? We're too old now." The angel said, "It's going to happen, but now you will be silent and not able to speak until the day this happens." That's how powerful words are. God knew that if Zechariah went around speaking words of defeat, he would be speaking the impossible over the possible.

God has spoken promises to your spirit that may seem impossible. Don't talk yourself out of the miracle. Your words have creative power. When you speak something out, you're agreeing with THE Word of God. Yes, believe that you have favor, healing, and dreams fulfilled. Now, speak out His Word. Dare to declare what He put in your heart.

PRAY & DECLARE

Father, thank You for the promises You have spoken to my spirit. Thank You that I can speak words of faith that agree with Your promises. I will "say it's so" to Your words of power in my life. In Jesus' Name, Amen.

AUGUST 8

Do Not Be Deceived

Then the LORD God said to the woman,
"What is this you have done?" The woman said,
"The serpent deceived me, and I ate."
GENESIS 3:13, NIV

The enemy's main tool is deception. God put a crown of glory and honor on your head (Psalm 8:5). There's nothing the enemy would love more than for you to go through life not wearing your crown, letting people and circumstances convince you that "You don't deserve to be blessed. You don't have what it takes. You're not good enough."

Don't give away your crown! It was put there by your Creator. It has nothing to do with how you feel, how you look, or what other people say. It's based solely on the fact that you are a child of the Almighty God.

You don't need other people's approval; you have Almighty God's approval. Declare: "You can celebrate me or criticize me, but one thing is for certain: I'm not giving you my crown. I know who I am. I am royalty. I am accepted. I am valuable."

PRAY & DECLARE

Father, thank You that You put a crown of glory and honor on my head by Your grace. Thank You that I am not deceived. I declare: You have made me royalty, and the enemy does not have the power to change that. In Jesus' Name, Amen.

AUGUST 9

Don't Be Squeezed into a Mold

Do not conform to the pattern of this world,
but be transformed by the renewing of your mind.
Then you will be able to test and approve what
God's will is — his good, pleasing and perfect will.
ROMANS 12:2, NIV

It's easy to fit in and do what everybody else is doing, go where everybody else goes, think like everyone else thinks. But God didn't breathe His life into you so you would do what everybody else does. You were created to be uncommon, to live by a higher standard, to do what others are not willing to do, and to believe for things that others think are too big. He created you to be a cut above.

To be uncommon means you're passionate about your future. You ask God for increase, you're expecting new levels, and you won't compromise your integrity. You do the right thing when no one is looking, and you keep your word when it costs you something. You are unmolded by the world and molded into His unique shape for you.

PRAY & DECLARE

Father, thank You that I don't have to let society squeeze me into its mold. Thank You that my life stands out as uncommon for You. I'm not going to be pressured into compromising, and I'm not going to live like everyone else. In Jesus' Name, Amen.

AUGUST 10

Destiny Calling

Delight yourself also in the Lord, and He will give you the desires and secret petitions of your heart.

PSALM 37:4, AMPC

God called Abraham "the father of many nations" (Genesis 17:4). At that time, Abraham didn't have any children. He and his wife, Sarah, were too old to have kids. Abraham could have thought, *God, my wife is barren. I'm childless. What are You talking about?* Here's the principle: God calls you what you are before you become it; people call you what you are after it happens.

There are promises, goals, and dreams that God has placed in your heart. Those aren't just your desires; God put them there. The *"secret petitions of your heart"* are the things you dream about that you haven't told anyone. They seem too big, too far out. That's your destiny calling. That's God telling you what you will become. Don't talk yourself out of it. God has spoken it. He will give you the desires of your heart.

PRAY & DECLARE

Father, thank You that You put desires and secret petitions in my heart. Thank You that You're calling me to my destiny. I know that You being for me is everything, and I can delight in You and the desires You have placed within me. In Jesus' Name, Amen.

Keep trusting
Him when you
don’t see anything
happening.

AUGUST 11

Remember His Power

They did not remember his power and how he rescued them from their enemies. They did not remember his miraculous signs in Egypt, his wonders on the plain of Zoan.

PSALM 78:42–43, NLT

What has God done for you? Don't be like the Israelites who had seen amazing miracles and yet didn't remember them when they needed faith to move forward into the Promised Land. Those victories you experienced weren't just to protect you, to promote you, or to heal you. They're fuel. When you face new challenges, obstacles that look too big, as you remember what God has done, that will give you the faith, the confidence, the knowing that He's in control, to silence whatever is trying to stop you. The forces for you are greater than the forces against you. Don't be worried and afraid. Go back over your history. Thank God for what He's done, and watch the fuel of faith rise in your heart.

PRAY & DECLARE

Father, thank You for the history I have with You and for every time You have not allowed the enemy to triumph over me. Thank You for all the times when You've rescued me. Your goodness is fuel indeed for every challenge I face today. In Jesus' Name, Amen.

AUGUST 12

It's Already Established

Job answered God: "I'm convinced: You can do anything and everything. Nothing and no one can upset your plans."

JOB 42:1–2, MSG

Job went through a time of severe testing of his faith. His life was shattered by great personal losses and covered in a season of darkness. The Scripture talks about how Satan had to ask for permission to test Job. The enemy can't do anything he wants; he has to get God's permission to touch you. God is not only in control of your life; He's in control of your enemies. You have nothing to worry about. He has a hedge of protection around you that cannot be penetrated.

Perhaps you hear thoughts whispering, *You'll never be as happy again. You've seen your best days.* Don't believe those lies. You will laugh a new laugh, dance a fantastic dance, sing a beautiful new melody. God has already established your expected end.

PRAY & DECLARE

Father, thank You that nothing and no one can upset Your plans for my life. Thank You for watching over me. I believe there is a hedge about me and that as I move forward, You will bring me to my expected end. In Jesus' Name, Amen.

AUGUST 13

Crooked Places Straight

"I will go before you and make the crooked places straight . . ."

ISAIAH 45:2, NKJV

You may have big obstacles in your path that you can't overcome on your own. The good news is that you're not on your own. You have the most powerful force in the universe breathing in your direction. When He speaks, Red Seas part, blind eyes open, and dreams come back to life. We look at our circumstances in the natural, but He's a supernatural God. He goes before you, makes your crooked places straight, and fights your battles. No person can stop you — no bad break, no sickness, no failure.

Maybe at one time you believed, you were passionate and excited about life, but things haven't turned out the way you hoped. God is saying, "It's time to believe again." You haven't seen your best days. What God promised you is still going to come to pass. He will make every crooked path straight.

PRAY & DECLARE

Father, thank You that You go before me and make the crooked places straight and level the mountains of opposition. Thank You that no bad break, no sickness, and no failure can stop me because You fight my battles. In Jesus' Name, Amen.

AUGUST 14

Look Straight Ahead

Keep your eyes straight ahead; ignore all sideshow distractions. Watch your step, and the road will stretch out smooth before you.

PROVERBS 4:25–26, MSG

The Scripture says to ignore sideshow distractions. Focusing on your weaknesses will distract you from your purpose. Always thinking about how you don't measure up will distract you from the good things God has in store.

It's sometimes tempting to stay negative toward yourself, to go through the day reliving your failures, beating yourself up for past mistakes, or letting a negative recording condemn you for everything that you're not. But when you accept what God has said about you, declare, "God, I'm going to keep looking straight ahead to Jesus, knowing that He is my change-maker, my world-changer. How beautiful is the road that You have stretched out before me."

PRAY & DECLARE

Father, thank You that my life is in Your hands — not just my dreams and goals, but my weaknesses and shortcomings. Thank You for where I am right now and that any faults are overcome by Your goodness. Thank you for keeping my eyes fixed straight ahead and not on sideshow distractions. In Jesus' Name, Amen.

AUGUST 15

Wipe the Slate Clean

And be constantly renewed in the spirit of your mind . . .

EPHESIANS 4:23, AMPC

The apostle Paul says that every day, Jesus is constantly renewing your mind. The Scripture says, *"We have the mind of Christ,"* (1 Corinthians 2:16, NIV). By that power, we can let go of the negative from yesterday and not bring it into today.

We wake up each morning, declaring, "Father, thank You that this day is a gift. Everything may not be perfect, but I'm grateful to be alive, grateful for my family, grateful for today's opportunities. I'm going to make the most of this day." That's not just being positive; that's renewing the spirit of your mind by the power of Christ's spirit within you. You are wiping the slate clean. Let go of the disappointments; let go of what didn't work out. His Spirit will overcome any worldly downturn.

PRAY & DECLARE

Father, thank You that You've given me this day as a gift to live for You. Thank You that through the power of the mind of Jesus within me, I can wipe yesterday's slate clean. In Jesus' Name, Amen.

Get up every
morning
expecting God
to surprise you.

AUGUST 16

Surely

Surely, Lord, you bless the righteous; you surround them with your favor as with a shield.

PSALM 5:12, NIV

David could have just said, "Lord, You will bless the righteous." But he added the word "surely." He was saying, "I'm absolutely convinced that You will bless me. I'm fully persuaded that what You promised is on the way." You need to have some "surely"s. "Surely, I'll get well. Surely, I'll pay my house off. Surely, I'll meet the right person. Surely, this problem is turning around. Surely, new doors are opening. Surely, I'll come through this crisis better than I was before." It's not, "Maybe . . . there's a good chance, if the medicine works, if I get the promotion, or if these people like me." No, you need to add the surely; you have to be convinced.

If you have the "if"s, you're going to talk yourself out of it. "Surely" means giving up is not an option; not believing is not something you even consider. Your face is set. You know what God promised is on the way.

PRAY & DECLARE

Father, thank You that You have put Your favor upon me and that it surrounds me as with a shield at all times. Thank You that You are surely going to bless me. In Jesus' Name, Amen.

AUGUST 17

You Can't Pay God Back

Therefore, there is now no condemnation for those who are in Christ Jesus, because through Christ Jesus the law of the Spirit who gives life has set you free from the law of sin and death.

ROMANS 8:1–2, NIV

Sometimes we think we have to pay God back for our mistakes and sins, and we try to do it by staying down and discouraged to show Him that we're sorry, that we're remorseful. Granted, there should be conviction and genuine remorse when we do something wrong. My point is that once you ask God for forgiveness, you don't have to pay Him back.

The price has already been paid on the cross. But when you live feeling guilty, you're saying, in effect, the sacrifice Christ made wasn't enough. You're saying, "Let me add something to it. Let me do my part by paying some kind of penalty for the wrongs I've done." Living under guilt and condemnation negates what He has done. There is no condemnation for those who are in Christ Jesus — none.

PRAY & DECLARE

Father, thank You that I am forgiven. Thank You that I am redeemed by the blood of Your Son. Thank You that the price for my sins has been paid once and for all. I receive Your love and forgiveness and refuse to live under guilt and condemnation. In Jesus' Name, Amen.

AUGUST 18

Standstill Prayers

The smoke of the incense, together with the prayers of God's people, went up before God from the angel's hand.

REVELATION 8:4, NIV

The apostle John describes how the angels around the Heavenly throne are constantly worshiping God, but he also wrote that there was silence in Heaven for about half an hour. During that time an angel came to the altar with a golden censer that represents the prayers of God's people. Notice how powerful prayer is. What could be so important that all of Heaven came to a standstill? Heaven heard the prayers of God's people. It makes a difference when you pray. Your prayers go up like incense before the throne of God.

It may feel like nobody's listening to your prayers. No, just remember that when you pray, something powerful happens, and the Creator of the universe hears. That's when supernatural things take place. When you pray, Red Seas part, Goliaths are defeated, and blessings rain down.

PRAY & DECLARE

Father, thank You for this powerful vision of the worship and praise that surrounds Your throne at all times. Thank You that You are listening to my every prayer, and my prayers are like the smoke of incense before You. In Jesus' Name, Amen.

AUGUST 19

The Anchor of Hope

We must pay the most careful attention, therefore, to what we have heard, so that we do not drift away.

HEBREWS 2:1, NIV

The Scripture describes hope as the anchor of our soul (Hebrews 6:19). It wouldn't say "anchor" unless there was a possibility of drifting. The waves of life can make us feel storm-tossed. Yet, the fact is we are anchored in Christ. Thoughts try to set us adrift to a dark place: *I don't think I'll ever get out of debt. I'll never get well. It's been so long. I'll never meet the right person.*

But then we remember and can declare: "I am anchored in hope!" You may have had some bad breaks, but that doesn't mean you're not going to fulfill your destiny. That anchor is like being in the eye of a hurricane. The wind and tempest may be swirling all around you, but you're in His calm, anchored by His hope. What God promised you, He's still going to bring to pass.

PRAY & DECLARE

Father, thank You that You've given me hope as the anchor of my soul to keep me from drifting into doubt and worry. I believe that what You have promised me, You will bring to pass. In Jesus' Name, Amen.

AUGUST 20

Crowned with Favor

Bless the Lord, my soul, and all that is within me, bless His holy name. Bless the Lord, my soul, and do not forget any of His benefits; who pardons all your guilt, who heals all your diseases; who redeems your life from the pit, who crowns you with favor and compassion.

PSALM 103:1–4, NASB

We weren't created to go through life overcome by problems, stuck in mediocrity. God didn't create you to live defeated, burdened down by fear or addictions. He created you to reign, to be the victor not the victim. He's lined up moments of favor when He's going to make things happen that you couldn't make happen.

God has crowned you with favor. You are crowned to defeat enemies, to take your family to a new level, to succeed, to leave your mark. Anything negative that's been reigning over you — guilt, bad breaks, insecurity, people trying to pull you down — there's about to be a shift, a change in authority. You're about to reign over what's been reigning over you. Even now chains are being broken. Things that have held you back are coming down. It's your time to be free.

PRAY & DECLARE

Father, thank You that You put a crown of favor on my head by Your grace. Thank You that You created me to reign in life with You, to be the victor and not the victim. In Jesus' Name, Amen.

God has gifts
in store for you
that are more
than you can
ask or think.

AUGUST 21

Power Up

"For by you I can run against a troop,
and by my God I can leap over a wall."
2 SAMUEL 22:30, ESV

Today's scripture is one of the declarations David made on the day when God had delivered him from all his enemies and from King Saul. You can't run through a troop of hundreds of soldiers or leap over city walls on your own. God will never let you face a challenge that you can't overcome. He'll never put a dream in your heart that you can't accomplish. You may not have the size, the skill, or the experience. That's okay, because when God breathes on your life, you will accomplish things that seem impossible. You'll outlast opposition that should have overwhelmed you. You'll discover talent and ability that you hadn't known you had. Don't believe the lies that the problem is too big, the dream is too great. That may be true if you stayed like you are, but God is about to power you up.

PRAY & DECLARE

Father, thank You that other people and circumstances cannot keep me from what You have purposed for me. Thank You that You are empowering my life. I believe that You will take me through or over or around whatever stands in my way. In Jesus' Name, Amen.

AUGUST 22

Absolutely Convinced

Yet I am confident I will see the Lord*'s goodness while I am here in the land of the living. Wait patiently for the* Lord*. Be brave and courageous. Yes, wait patiently for the* Lord*.*

PSALM 27:13–14, NLT

David had every opportunity to live defeated and discouraged. He said enemies were waiting to attack him, accusing him of things he'd never done. People were lying about him, being mean and violent. But just when you thought he was defeated, he says, "Yet I am confident I will see the goodness of God." He was saying, "All these negative things have come against me, but the one thing I am confident of is that God will deliver and vindicate me. I am confident I will see His favor." He didn't deny negative things were happening; he just didn't let it get inside. He could have overflowed with discouragement, but instead he turned it around and overflowed with hope. He said, "I am confident. I am absolutely convinced that I will see the goodness of God."

PRAY & DECLARE

Father, thank You that You are my deliverer and vindicator when negative things come against me. Thank You for the absolute confidence I have that I will see Your goodness. I believe that You will amaze me with Your goodness. In Jesus' Name, Amen.

AUGUST 23

Restoration and Healing

"For I will restore health to you and heal you of your wounds," says the Lord, *"Because they called you an outcast saying: 'This is Zion; No one seeks her.'"*

JEREMIAH 30:17, NKJV

We all go through disappointments — things we didn't see coming — a breakup, a setback in our finances, an illness. God didn't say we wouldn't go through challenges, but He did promise that He will restore and heal. He's a God of restoration. You may have experienced a loss, but that's not how your story ends. Don't judge your situation too soon. You're going to get it all back — the joy, the peace, the health, the strength, the family, the dreams.

The beauty of our God is that even when we make mistakes, even when we bring trouble upon ourselves, God doesn't say, "Too bad for you. I would restore you if you had performed better. I would help you if you had been more committed." God is full of mercy, and when He says it's time to restore, all the forces of darkness cannot stop Him.

PRAY & DECLARE

Father, thank You that in times of disappointment when I don't see the way out, I have Your promise that You will restore me. Thank You that in Your goodness You will turn it around and pour out health and healing. In Jesus' Name, Amen.

AUGUST 24

Take the Throne

Jehoiada and his sons brought out the king's son and put the crown on him; they presented him with a copy of the covenant and proclaimed him king. They anointed him and shouted, "Long live the king!"

2 CHRONICLES 23:11, NIV

Joash, the son of King Ahaziah, was only seven years old and would be killed if he were brought out of hiding. He was helpless to take the throne in his own strength, his own ability. But God used the high priest Jehoiada and other patriots to take back young Joash's throne, place the crown upon him, and anoint him as their king.

Notice that Joash didn't go after the crown; the crown came to him. God has blessings that are going to chase you down; increase that's going to come looking for you because you are a son or a daughter of the King. Suddenly there's an unexpected phone call, a divine connection, or a good break that takes you from the background to the foreground — something you didn't see coming. Yes, believe that it's your time to reign!

PRAY & DECLARE

Father, thank You that You are the Most High God, and because I am Your child, I have royalty in my blood. Thank You that You have put a crown of honor on my head and anointed me with Your grace. In Jesus' Name, Amen.

AUGUST 25

Get Outside Your Tent

And He brought him outside [his tent into the starlight] and said, Look now toward the heavens and count the stars — if you are able to number them. Then He said to him, So shall your descendants be.

GENESIS 15:5, AMPC

When God promised Abraham that he was going to be the father of many nations, he was seventy-five years old. There was no way in the natural that he and Sarah could have a baby. It looked impossible, but God was saying, "Abraham, as long as you're in your tent, all you see is you and Sarah. You're only focused on what you can accomplish. Go outside your tent and look up."

When you're in your tent, you can be tempted to just look at your limitations, what you can't do. Follow the Lord, who graciously will bring you out of your tent to show you a bigger vision. He makes ways when you don't see ways. He will take you further than you ever dreamed.

PRAY & DECLARE

Father, thank You for calling me to come out of my tent and get a bigger vision of what You can do. Thank You for the new perspectives You give that remind me of the promises You have spoken over me. In Jesus' Name, Amen.

I know that
God's mercy is
bigger than my
mistakes.

AUGUST 26

Overflow With Hope

May the God of hope fill you with all joy and peace as you trust in him, so that you may overflow with hope by the power of the Holy Spirit.

ROMANS 15:13, NIV

We all have situations that don't look as though they're going to work out. We don't see how we can get well, how we can accomplish a dream, or how our family will be restored. It's one thing to have hope in these times, but the apostle Paul prayed that we would overflow with hope. When you overflow with hope, you're not moved by what the circumstances look like, and you're not worried because you don't see a way. You know that God is ordering your steps and His plans for you are for good.

We can be tempted to overflow with doubt, fear, or discouragement. But praise be to God that through the power of the Holy Spirit, we overflow with hope, even in the darkest moments.

PRAY & DECLARE

Father, thank You that You are the God of hope and You have purposed that my life does overflow with hope by the power of the Holy Spirit. Thank You that along with hope, you are also filling me with joy and peace. In Jesus' Name, Amen.

AUGUST 27

Guard Your Thoughts

"Don't call me Naomi," she told them. "Call me Mara, because the Almighty has made my life very bitter."

RUTH 1:20, NIV

After Naomi's husband and two sons died, she was so discouraged that she tried to change her name from Naomi, which means "pleasantness," to Mara, which means "bitter." One reason Naomi got bitter is that she kept repeating her pain and telling herself, "I'm broken and empty. I've seen my best days." She was focused on what she lost, what didn't work out, how it wasn't fair.

Her own thoughts were defeating her. In difficult times, you may feel empty, but telling others that you're broken, defeated, addicted, or lonely only reinforces it in your spirit. That's why Joel 3:10 says, *"Let the weak say, 'I am strong'"* (NKJV). You don't have to deny the facts; just don't let the facts have the last word. Say what God says about you.

PRAY & DECLARE

Father, thank You that I can call myself "pleasant" and not "bitter." Thank You that You will bring good out of the unfair things that I've gone through. I will not allow my thoughts to defeat me or change my name from what You call me. In Jesus' Name, Amen.

AUGUST 28

Is God Listening?

"The son started his speech: 'Father, I've sinned against God, I've sinned before you; I don't deserve to be called your son ever again.' But the father wasn't listening."

LUKE 15:21–22, MSG

When the prodigal son returned home after having wasted his father's inheritance on wild living and partying, he passionately started pouring out his genuine remorse, but his father wasn't listening. He was calling his staff to kill the fatted calf for a party and declaring, "My son was lost and now he's found!"

Are you doing what this son did, telling your Father everything you've done wrong and how unworthy you are of His love? Can I tell you that God is not listening? The moment you asked God to forgive you, He forgave you and then He forgot your sins. You're not worthy because of what you did or didn't do. You're worthy only because of what Jesus did for you on the cross.

PRAY & DECLARE

Father, thank You that Your mercy is bigger than my mistakes. Thank You that You are not holding my past against me. Thank You that I am forgiven. Thank You that I'm redeemed because of what Jesus did on the cross. In Jesus' Name, Amen.

AUGUST 29

The Power of Your Words

Death and life are in the power of the tongue, and those who love it and indulge it will eat its fruit and bear the consequences of their words.

PROVERBS 18:21, AMP

Did you know that the words you speak today are setting the direction for your life? If you want to know what you're going to be like five years from now, listen to what you're saying about yourself. "I'll never get well. I'll never break this addiction. I'll never recover from this setback." You're prophesying your future. You can't speak defeat and have victory. You can't talk sickness and have health. You can't speak lack and have abundance.

Pay attention to what you're saying about yourself, your family, your finances, and your health. All through the day say what God says about you: "I am blessed. I am strong. I am healthy. I'm surrounded by favor. Something good is going to happen to me." The fruit of those words is blessing, favor, and abundance.

PRAY & DECLARE

Father, thank You that my words have the power to help set the direction of my life. Thank You that through Christ I give my faith a voice by speaking words of life and blessing over myself and my future. In Jesus' Name, Amen.

AUGUST 30

Abide

"Abide in Me, and I in you. As the branch cannot bear fruit of itself, unless it abides in the vine, neither can you, unless you abide in Me."

JOHN 15:4, NKJV

To abide in Christ means you're connected to Him and trusting in Him for all you need. When you're abiding, it takes the pressure off. Instead of focusing on what you can do, you're focused on what God can do. You're depending on His goodness, His favor, His power. The problem is that we all face difficulties and situations that are too big. No matter how hard we try, our strength, our effort, and our talent will not be enough.

That's why God said you can't bear fruit by yourself. You can't overcome that challenge just with your own willpower and hard work. You need power from on high. As you abide, there is a force that breathes in your direction, a favor that opens doors that you can't open, breaks chains that are holding you back, releases healing, creativity, and increase that will catapult you into your destiny.

PRAY & DECLARE

Father, thank You that I abide in You. Thank You that I can be free from striving to accomplish things and move by Your strength within me. In Jesus' Name, Amen.

AUGUST 31

Life's Puzzle

Turn my eyes from worthless things, and give me life through your word. Reassure me of your promise, made to those who fear you.

PSALM 119:37-38, NLT

When you isolate a negative experience and focus on it, it may not make sense. It's like when you have a piece to a jigsaw puzzle that doesn't look like it fits anywhere. You're sure the manufacturer made a mistake. It's an odd shape, not the right color, too blurry. It looks random, like it's unnecessary. But when the other pieces come together, it makes sense. There will be a perfect fit where the colors match and the edges line up. Without it, the puzzle wouldn't be complete.

You may have a piece to your life puzzle that doesn't make sense. You could think, "God didn't ordain this setback or loss. This piece doesn't fit." But God isn't finished. Nothing is random. That piece is instrumental in getting you to your destiny.

PRAY & DECLARE

Father, thank You that Your plans for me are good. Thank You that the pieces of my life puzzle that I don't understand now are going to come together and be a perfect fit. Through Christ, life's "puzzles" work out beautifully in all that You've designed for me. In Jesus' Name, Amen.

September

SEPTEMBER 1

Completely Astonished

But overhearing what they said, Jesus said to the ruler of the synagogue, "Do not fear, only believe."

MARK 5:36, ESV

After Jesus told a synagogue leader named Jairus that He would come to his house and heal his dying daughter, He was delayed with the healing of a woman who had been sick for twelve years. While I'm sure that Jairus was amazed by the healing and happy for the woman, his daughter died in the meantime, dashing his hopes. But Jesus reassured him that He would do what He had promised. This man came to Jesus asking for healing, but because of the delay, he received a greater miracle, a resurrection that left everyone completely astonished.

When you have to wait a long time, don't get discouraged. God hasn't forgotten about you. The circumstances may tell you it's never going to happen, but God has something bigger, something better, something you weren't expecting.

PRAY & DECLARE

Father, thank You that no matter what happens in my life, no matter what seems delayed, You will do what You have promised. Thank You that I can know that You have something bigger and better than I've expected. I will not be afraid. I will believe. In Jesus' Name, Amen.

SEPTEMBER 2

The God of Jacob

Then he said, "I am the God of your father, the God of Abraham, the God of Isaac and the God of Jacob." At this, Moses hid his face, because he was afraid to look at God.

EXODUS 3:6, NIV

Scripture talks about the God of Abraham, the God of Isaac, and the God of Jacob. I can understand how He is the God of Abraham, the father of our faith. I can understand how He is the God of Isaac, who was the miracle child of God's promise. But when it says He is the God of Jacob, that doesn't make a lot of sense. Jacob was a cheater. He went around deceiving people. He stole his brother's birthright. Jacob was known for making poor choices.

What was God saying? "I'm not just the God of perfect people, of those who never make a mistake. I'm the God of people who have failed." You may have made mistakes, but be encouraged. He is the God of Jacob. He is your God, too.

PRAY & DECLARE

Father, thank You that Your love and forgiveness are not based on my performance but upon the fact that I am Your child. Thank You that You love me, imperfect as I am, and that every mistake I've made has already been paid for in full. In Jesus' Name, Amen.

SEPTEMBER 3

You Are More Than You Think

I praise you because I am fearfully and wonderfully made;
your works are wonderful, I know that full well.
PSALM 139:14, NIV

When David praised God that He had made him wonderfully, he wasn't just talking about his looks, personality, and talents. He was also talking about the way God designed things in him that he couldn't see.

God has a plan for the challenges you will face as well. Out of nowhere, a strength rises up, with faith to overcome it and a determination to stand strong and outlast the opposition. Because God designed you, you're stronger than you think. You have more endurance, more stamina, and more capacity for grace and forgiveness than you can imagine.

When something feels overwhelming — a loss, a setback, a disappointment — that's exactly when you discover what's in you. You'll discover what Jesus has placed there: perseverance, courage, and faith like you've never seen.

PRAY & DECLARE

Father, thank You that You made me fearfully and wonderfully and in ways that are a joy to discover. Thank You that You designed me with all that I need to withstand whatever challenges I am facing and will face. In Jesus' Name, Amen.

SEPTEMBER 4

Vulnerability

I do not sit with false persons,
nor fellowship with pretenders.
PSALM 26:4, AMPC

If you read the stories of the heroes of faith, whether it's Abraham, David, John the Baptist, or the apostle Paul, they were not pretenders. They had doubts, they had fears, they had questions, and they didn't pretend like they had it all together. They refused to wear religious masks. They knew the power of vulnerability and honesty. They knew that in our weaknesses, God's strength shows up the greatest.

Are you down on yourself because you have doubts and fears, weaknesses you don't understand? Are you trying to hide what you're struggling with, thinking God or someone else would not be pleased with you? Are you trying to perform just right, to keep up your image, to impress your friends and family? Why don't you take the pressure off and be at peace with not being perfect? There's amazing strength when you go to God and others with transparency.

PRAY & DECLARE

Father, thank You that I don't have to pretend to have no shortcomings or mask my doubts and fears. Thank You that I can be vulnerable with You and that Your strength comes out in my weakness. In Jesus' Name, Amen.

SEPTEMBER 5

Difficulties Bring a Push

"I thought, 'Surely I shall die quietly in my nest after a long, good life.'"

JOB 29:18, TLB

Job had his nest all fixed up, had his house just as he wanted it, and had a successful business. Things were going great. He was finally comfortable, but what happened? God stirred up his nest. God doesn't bring the trouble, but He will allow difficulties to push us into our destiny. Almost overnight Job lost his health, his children, and his business. If the story stopped there, it would be a sad ending. But Job understood this principle. In spite of great difficulties, he said, "I know my Redeemer lives" (Job 19:25). He was saying, "I know God is still on the throne. This trouble is not going to defeat me; it's going to push me." In the end Job came out with twice what he'd had before. God's dream for his life was greater than he could imagine.

PRAY & DECLARE

Father, thank You that no difficulty and no one can upset Your plans for my life. Thank You that You order my steps in the way that is pushing me to new levels of my destiny. I declare: This trouble is not going to defeat me! In Jesus' Name, Amen.

Your prayers go up like incense before the throne of God.

SEPTEMBER 6

Your Inner Circle

Then Jesus halted the crowd and wouldn't let anyone go on with him to Jairus's home except Peter and James and John.

MARK 5:37, TLB

Jesus went to pray for a little girl who had died. When He arrived at the home, He didn't allow anyone to go in with him except for His inner circle. Why? Jesus wanted to show those three who He was in a greater measure. If you have people close to you who are constantly pulling you down, understand that it is scriptural to keep them at a distance. It may be difficult, but when you're in the heat of the battle, when you need a breakthrough, you need people who are joined in spirit with you. You need people who will say, "If you're bold enough to believe it, count on me. I'm bold enough to agree with you."

PRAY & DECLARE

Father, thank You that Jesus made it so clear that I need to be careful about whom I allow into the inner circle of my life. Thank You for the people who are truly joined in spirit with me and who I can count upon. In Jesus' Name, Amen.

SEPTEMBER 7

Mountains to Molehills

"So, big mountain, who do you think you are? Next to Zerubbabel you're nothing but a molehill. He'll proceed to set the Cornerstone in place, accompanied by cheers: Yes! Yes! Do it!"

ZECHARIAH 4:7, MSG

God put a dream in Zerubbabel to rebuild the destroyed temple in Jerusalem, but people were against him and got a decree from the Persian king that forced him to stop. For years it looked like it would never happen, but then he heard the prophecy. He was saying, "I have this big mountain in front of me, but it's about to become a molehill." How would it happen? Other translations say by shouting "Grace to it." Another word for "grace" is "favor." He was saying, "Yes, this obstacle is big, but I have the favor of God to overcome and finish this project." He didn't talk about how daunting the mountain was. He talked about how small and insignificant the molehill was.

When you face challenges, speak favor and grace over them.

PRAY & DECLARE

Father, thank You that no matter how big the mountain of obstacles is, I have Your favor to overcome it. I will speak grace to my mountains and see them turn into molehills. In Jesus' Name, Amen.

SEPTEMBER 8

Overcoming Weariness

But those who wait on the Lord *shall renew their strength; they shall mount up with wings like eagles, they shall run and not be weary, they shall walk and not faint.*

ISAIAH 40:31, NKJV

Weariness comes to all of us. Weariness is overcome by simply waiting on the Lord. You can let go of your weariness by not being focused on your problems, thinking about how impossible something is. What causes your strength to be renewed is when you live with the expectancy that God is in control.

You may be facing a situation that is wearing you down, but God has given you strength for that battle. He says you will never face something you can't handle. Quit telling yourself it's too much, and rest, taking hold of His strength. That cancer, that legal problem, or that situation in your finances is no match for you. God will not only renew whatever strength you need, but you will soar like an eagle.

PRAY & DECLARE

Father, thank You for Your promise that as I wait upon You, You will renew my strength and enable me to rise up with wings like an eagle. Thank you for turning my weariness into Your strength. In Jesus' Name, Amen.

SEPTEMBER 9

All Things New

And he who was seated on the throne said, "Behold, I am making all things new." Also he said, "Write this down, for these words are trustworthy and true."

REVELATION 21:5, ESV

Sometimes we get stuck in old mindsets and limitations that have been passed down to us. That's why it's important to stop and reevaluate our lives at times. Why are you doing what you are doing? Do you feel limited?

God is always doing something new. It's a marvel to simply behold who is seated on the throne and what He is doing. As He inspires you, watch Him reveal fresh insights. Be willing to try something new. Don't stay stuck in your ways. Through His power, you can walk away from a bad attitude, from that person who's poisoning your future, from compromise, from doing things that are holding you back. Seek His new vision and creativity, and watch Him open new doors for an amazing future.

PRAY & DECLARE

Father, thank You that I am so drawn to simply stand in awe of who is on the throne. Thank you for making the old things new and for Your fresh vision that causes me to break free from any earthly limitations. In Jesus' Name, Amen.

SEPTEMBER 10

Power to Endure

An angel from heaven appeared to him
and strengthened him.

LUKE 22:43, NIV

The night before Jesus was crucified, He went to the garden of Gethsemane to pray. He knew the suffering He would face. He felt weary, lonely, and so overcome with emotion that His sweat became drops of blood. Remember that even though Jesus is fully God, He is fully man. He felt everything we have felt. He felt overwhelmed. In that moment when it seemed as though He couldn't go on, God sent an angel to strengthen Him.

God knows the weight of what you are carrying. He sees you being your best as you raise the children, fight an addiction, be successful in your business, or face the illness. When you run out of strength, don't worry, for angels are coming. You're going to feel strength that you didn't have, joy when you could be discouraged, hope when you should be depressed. It's not because of your own efforts; it's the angels ministering to you.

PRAY & DECLARE

Father, thank You that You make provisions of special strength for me all along the way. Thank You that You even send angels to minister to my needs. In Jesus' Name, Amen.

If you have the “if”’s, you’re going to talk yourself out of it.

SEPTEMBER 11

Shame Removal

"You will forget the shame of your youth and remember no more the reproach of your widowhood."

ISAIAH 54:4, NIV

Isaac named his son Jacob, which means "trickster, deceiver, swindler," and he became exactly that. Later in life, Jacob decided to confront his shameful past and change his life. One night the Angel of the Lord told Jacob, "God is giving you a new name. You will be called Israel," which means "a prince with God." Instead of saying, "Jacob, shame on you," He said, "Jacob, shame off you. I've called you to be a prince and reign in life."

As with Jacob, you may be wearing negative labels that say "addicted, washed up, undisciplined, not valuable, made too many mistakes, poor spouse, or bad parent." No, this is what grace is all about. God says, "I'm removing the shame. I know who you are. I'm changing your name to redeemed, forgiven, prince, princess, highly favored."

PRAY & DECLARE

Father, thank You that because of what Jesus has done on the cross, You remove the shame from my life. Thank You that You have made me into royalty and crowned me as highly favored, redeemed, and forgiven. I believe You have given me a new name and called me to reign in life. In Jesus' Name, Amen.

SEPTEMBER 12

Don't Go by Your Circumstances

Abraham fell facedown; he laughed and said to himself, "Will a son be born to a man a hundred years old? Will Sarah bear a child at the age of ninety?"

GENESIS 17:17, NIV

Sarah was ninety years old when she gave birth to Isaac. This is way too old in the natural, but we serve a supernatural God. He can make a way where you don't see a way. Don't give up on what God promised you. You can still give birth. You can still meet the right person, start your own business, go to college, or break the addiction.

Here's the key: You can't judge what's in you by what's around you. All of Sarah's circumstances said, "You'll be barren your whole life. You're too old. No woman your age has babies. It's impossible." If she had believed that lie and let that seed take root, the miracle birth would never have happened. Don't let what you see around you cause you to give up on your dreams.

PRAY & DECLARE

Father, thank You that I am not limited by my circumstances. Thank You that what surrounds me does not determine the seeds of greatness You have placed within me. In Jesus' Name, Amen.

SEPTEMBER 13

Your Rough Edges

You are to live clean, innocent lives as children of God in a dark world full of people who are crooked and stubborn. Shine out among them like beacon lights, holding out to them the Word of Life.

PHILIPPIANS 2:15–16, TLB

Some of the things that God has in your future you wouldn't be able to handle if He gave them to you right now. He loves you too much to let that happen. He's developing your character. That boss who doesn't treat you right — you keep trying to pray him away. The reason he's not going away is that God is using him like sandpaper to rub the rough edges off you. As you keep doing the right thing, being faithful to your responsibilities, that's doing a work in you. You couldn't develop your character without him.

You may not like it, but God can use difficulties for your good. This includes the closed doors you face, the delays, and the loan that didn't go through. Everything that happens in life, God can use to reveal Himself in a greater measure.

PRAY & DECLARE

Father, thank You that You never allow anything out of which You can't bring good to me. Thank You that You are growing my character through the difficulties I face. I believe that You have me right where You want me. In Jesus' Name, Amen.

SEPTEMBER 14

Be the Original You

You made all the delicate, inner parts of my body
and knit me together in my mother's womb.

PSALM 139:13, NLT

When God created you, He made sure you were completely equipped for the race that's been designed for you. You didn't get shortchanged. You don't need to wish you were something different: "If I was just . . ." Don't get distracted by what someone else has. As long as you want what they have, you'll be frustrated. If you didn't get what somebody else has, that means you don't need it. You are equipped for your destiny.

You have the right looks, talents, and personality. If you needed to be taller, God would've made you taller. If you needed a different personality, He would've given you one. If you needed to be another nationality, you would be another nationality. God doesn't make mistakes. You have been fearfully and wonderfully made. Be confident in what you have and who you are.

PRAY & DECLARE

Father, thank You that I can stop wishing I had what other people have because You have given me all that I need. Thank You that I am fully outfitted and supplied for the race You have designed for me. I declare that I am going to be the original me. In Jesus' Name, Amen.

SEPTEMBER 15

Get Rid of the Coat

When Jesus heard him, he stopped and said, "Tell him to come here." So they called the blind man. "Cheer up," they said. "Come on, he's calling you!" Bartimaeus threw aside his coat, jumped up, and came to Jesus.

MARK 10:49–50, NLT

When the blind beggar, Bartimaeus, heard Jesus say "come," the first thing he did was throw off his coat. This was significant because people who had a legitimate disability in those days were given an official coat from the government that gave them the legal right to beg. It qualified them to make their living but also marked their dependency. When Bartimaeus threw this coat aside, he was making the declaration, "I no longer need this coat for my dependency. Jesus has come, and I *am* going to be healed."

Praise be to God! Jesus is calling us to cast off any beggar's coat that we might be wearing and jump into a world of strength, healing, courage, and new possibility.

PRAY & DECLARE

Father, thank You for Your call to come to You and leave the past behind. I let go of all my excuses and refuse to settle for less and receive freely Your best for me. I declare that I will have a victor's mindset and live out all You created me to be. In Jesus' Name, Amen.

In our weaknesses, God's strength shows up the greatest.

SEPTEMBER 16

Much Fruit

"I am the vine, you are the branches. He who abides in Me, and I in him, bears much fruit; for without Me you can do nothing."

JOHN 15:5, NKJV

Jesus says that He is the vine, we are the branches, and His Father is the gardener who prunes our lives. He mentions "fruit," "more fruit," and "much fruit." He provides increase as we abide in Him. He was saying, "When things happen that you don't understand, know that you abide in Me. Believe that I'm still directing your steps. Yes, release your praise. Rekindle your faithfulness." You can rest even as you keep doing the right thing — serving, giving, expecting favor, going the extra mile. Even when you go through cutback seasons, He is and will release you into much fruit. New doors are about to open, new relationships are on the way, and negative situations are about to turn around. Because it is an eternal fact that you abide in Him, abundance, healing, and breakthroughs are coming.

PRAY & DECLARE

Father, thank You that every day I can draw my life from the true vine, Christ Jesus. Thank You that I abide in You, the source of everything good, abounding and overflowing. Thank You that through You I am bearing much fruit. In Jesus' Name, Amen.

SEPTEMBER 17

Friends Pull You Up

Then Peter said, "Silver or gold I do not have, but what I do have I give you. In the name of Jesus Christ of Nazareth, walk." Taking him by the right hand, he helped him up, and instantly the man's feet and ankles became strong.

ACTS 3:6–7, NIV

After Peter spoke a word of faith to the crippled beggar, Peter wouldn't let him stay down. He didn't give him a choice. He prayed and then pulled him up. You need people who love You so much they won't let you stay discouraged or give up on your dream. They not only pray but pull you up.

You may need to get away from a negative environment and people who are enabling your dysfunction and holding you back. Get away from people who tell you that where you are is where you'll always be. Stay in an environment of empowering, life-giving faith.

PRAY & DECLARE

Father, thank You for friends who won't let me stay down but are there to help pull me up when I need them. Thank you for opening and developing relationships with encouraging, life-asserting people who will strengthen me through Your power. In Jesus' Name, Amen.

SEPTEMBER 18

Change the Channel

Summing it all up, friends, I'd say you'll do best by filling your minds and meditating on things true, noble, reputable, authentic, compelling, gracious — the best, not the worst; the beautiful, not the ugly; things to praise, not things to curse.

PHILIPPIANS 4:8, MSG

The Scripture tells us that we can't dwell on every imagination because our minds can often gravitate toward the negative. If you're not disciplined and you let those images play, you're going to live worried, stressed out, and have no joy. If you're dealing with an illness, a downturn in your business, or a difficult relationship, negative imaginations can multiply and show you going downhill fast. When you dwell on those negative images, it's going to cause you to live in fear and discouragement, which only makes you weaker.

Change the channel. You can create new pictures in your mind. Start seeing your business taking off, health and healing, and vibrant relationships. As you fill your mind with these uplifting, transforming, Heaven-sent thoughts, you'll be filled with newfound hope.

PRAY & DECLARE

Father, thank You for giving me the power to control the imaginations and thoughts playing in my mind. Thank You that I can change the channel from negative imaginations that come against me to positive eternal truths that keep me moving forward. In Jesus' Name, Amen.

SEPTEMBER 19

The Final Word

Jesus answered them, "Destroy this temple, and I will raise it again in three days."

JOHN 2:19, NIV

Satan and all the forces of darkness thought they had finally defeated Jesus on the cross. They didn't realize that Jesus had prophesied not only His death but His resurrection three days later. While the enemy celebrated, Jesus rose up, took away the keys of death and hell, and said, "I am He that lives. I was dead, but I am alive forevermore."

Whatever you face, God has the final word. Your story doesn't end in defeat but in victory. Along the way there may be some setbacks, times when it looks impossible, but you're about to see God show out. There's a sudden change coming — healing, opportunities, promotion, breakthroughs. What you thought was permanent is about to change in your favor. You're going to rise higher, accomplish dreams, and reach the fullness of your destiny.

PRAY & DECLARE

Father, thank You that no matter what challenges and setbacks I face, You have the final word over all things. Thank You that it's never over until You say it's over. I believe that You are breaking the powers of darkness and victory is on the way. In Jesus' Name, Amen.

SEPTEMBER 20

Out of Deep Waters

"He reached down from on high and took hold of me;
he drew me out of deep waters. He rescued me from my
powerful enemy, from my foes, who were too strong for me."
2 SAMUEL 22:17–18, NIV

We all face things that are too powerful for us to stop or overcome, but they're not too powerful for our God. You may not be able to escape the accident, beat the cancer, or overcome the bad break on your own, but you're not on your own; the Most High God is with you. The enemy is not in control of your life. He can't stop your purpose. God has the final say. He's going to draw you out of deep waters.

God rules over that addiction, people who talk against you at work, that consuming illness. Instead of dwelling on how powerful your enemies are, know that Your God overrules and will overcome the forces too strong for you.

PRAY & DECLARE

Father, thank You for Your promise to draw me out of the deep waters and rescue me from my enemies. Even when life seems to be out of control, I choose to trust in You and believe that You have the final say. I declare that You are with me, and You overrule. In Jesus' Name, Amen.

When you face challenges, speak favor and grace over them.

SEPTEMBER 21

Standing Guard Over You

"I will rebuke the devourer for you, so that it will not destroy the fruits of your soil, and your vine in the field shall not fail to bear," says the LORD *of hosts.*

MALACHI 3:11, ESV

God has promised that when you're a giver and planted in the house of the Lord, He will open the windows of Heaven for you and pour out blessings you can't contain. It goes on to say that He will rebuke the devourer for your sake. That means what was going to harm your family and relationships, devour your finances and opportunities, and cause breakdowns, God will rebuke. It's always good to pray and stand against the forces of darkness, but when you're under the open windows of Heaven, you have the Creator of the universe as your protector and defender.

The Most High God is standing guard over your life. You don't have to live worried, on edge, or in fear.

PRAY & DECLARE

Father, thank You that I am under the open windows of Heaven, and You are standing over me and guarding me from the devourer. Thank You for all the times You have protected me. Thank You that my vines will bear much fruit. In Jesus' Name, Amen.

SEPTEMBER 22

The Blessing and the Burden

The angel said to her, "Rejoice, highly favored one, the Lord is with you; blessed are you among women!"

LUKE 1:28, NKJV

Mary was told she would give birth to the Savior of the world. You can't get any more favored than that. But with that blessing came a burden. She was favored but misunderstood, ridiculed, and controversial. People whispered, "She got pregnant before her wedding." On one hand, she's excited and can hardly believe the blessing. On the other hand, she must tell Joseph and face having her heart broken.

Sometimes God will ask us to do things that are difficult. It would be much easier to stay in our comfort zone and not rock the boat. But God loves you too much to let you miss your destiny. Believe that you've been highly favored. He can take you where you've never dreamed and open doors that you couldn't open. In your own life, do as God empowered Mary to do — focus on the blessing not the burden.

PRAY & DECLARE

Father, thank You for the favor You have put on my life and every blessing you have poured out. Thank You that You are taking me on a journey of faith that surpasses every burden. In Jesus' Name, Amen.

SEPTEMBER 23

While You Wait for Change

"I make known the end from the beginning,
from ancient times, what is still to come. I say,
'My purpose will stand, and I will do all that I please.'"

ISAIAH 46:10, NIV

What's upsetting you? God already has it figured out. He knows the end from the beginning. But here's the key: He doesn't give us the details. If you knew how everything was going to work out, it wouldn't take faith. If He told you that three months from now a big door is going to open and there's a shortcut that's going to put you ahead, you would relax and say, "Okay, it's all going to work out."

Why don't you do that now? God has it all planned out. He's doing things you can't see. There are good breaks coming — healing, favor, the right people. They're already on your schedule. God is saying, "Release it to Me. I'm in control. I'm ordering your steps. I'm working behind the scenes. I can turn it for your good."

PRAY & DECLARE

Father, thank You that in the midst of a very insecure world I can rest in the security of knowing that my end has been set. I release control of what is bothering me and believe You always cause me to triumph. In Jesus' Name, Amen.

SEPTEMBER 24

Ignore the Roar

Be sober, be vigilant; because your adversary the devil walks about like a roaring lion, seeking whom he may devour.

1 PETER 5:8, NKJV

Anytime we try to move forward, thoughts will come telling us what we can't do and how the problem is too big. We know what God promised; we believe it in our heart, but the enemy comes like a roaring lion, bombarding our mind with doubts. The purpose of a lion's roar is to intimidate any opponent, so much so that it will paralyze the other animal and get it to back down. The enemy goes about "like" a roaring lion — he's not a lion. He loves to roar in our thoughts: *You'll never get well, break the addiction. You don't have any talent.* But Jesus empowers us to ignore the roar.

PRAY & DECLARE

Father, thank You that when the enemy is roaring, bombarding my thoughts with doubts and fears, I can resist him, firm in the faith. Thank You that he does not have any power over me. I declare that I will not be intimidated into backing down. In Jesus' Name, Amen.

SEPTEMBER 25

Know Who You Are

David said to the Philistine, "You come against me with sword and spear and javelin, but I come against you in the name of the Lord *Almighty, the God of the armies of Israel, whom you have defied."*

1 SAMUEL 17:45, NIV

Overlooking the Valley of Elah, David heard the giant Goliath taunting the Israelite army. Goliath was twice David's size, the Philistine's most skilled warrior, wearing a full set of armor. David had no military experience, no armor, no sword, just a slingshot. The HOW seemed impossible. But David understood that the HOW wasn't up to him. He said, in effect, "Goliath, the odds look against me, but I have an advantage. I know who I am. I belong to the Most High." He didn't focus on the HOW; he focused on the WHO, and he brought Goliath down.

When you face situations that you don't see how they can work out, shift your perspective from the HOW to the WHO. There's no giant too big for God.

PRAY & DECLARE

Father, thank You that when the challenges in my way look bigger, stronger, and more powerful than I can handle, I can focus on how great You are. I believe You being for me is more than anything that comes against me. In Jesus' Name, Amen.

When you run out of strength, don't worry, for angels are coming.

SEPTEMBER 26

To the Depths

"He is not here; he has risen, just as he said. Come and see the place where he lay."

MATTHEW 28:6, NIV

Jesus stooped down from the glory of Heaven and the worship of angels and came to be born in a lowly manger on earth. He stooped to be betrayed, mocked, beaten, and crucified on the cross for our sins. He said, "Father, I'll stoop down. I'll go low, so low I'll be buried in a grave." But the good news is that He didn't stay there. He defeated sin, death, and hell for you and me. That's how He's not only the all-powerful, resurrected Savior, but He is the God who stoops. He comes to your messy places, meets you where you are, rescues and restores you even when it was your fault, and sets you in a place of honor as His child.

PRAY & DECLARE

Father, thank You that Jesus stooped so low to pay the incredible price to blot out all my sins and set me free. Thank You that He defends me and drowns out the accusing voices all around me. In Jesus' Name, Amen.

SEPTEMBER 27

Our Father

So He said to them, "When you pray, say:
Our Father in heaven, hallowed be Your name."

LUKE 11:2, NKJV

When Jesus' disciples asked Him how to pray, He taught them what we know now as the Lord's Prayer. He started off saying, "*Our Father in Heaven.*" The prayer goes on to talk about our daily bread, protection from evil, and forgiving others. But it's significant that before we ask for our needs, before we ask for protection and guidance, God says, "I want you to acknowledge who you are. I want you to see yourself as My child." We're saying, "God, I know who I am. I belong to you. You're my Heavenly Father. You created me. You love me. You care for me. You protect me. You favor me." Because of who you are, you can stay in peace, knowing that your Father in Heaven can do for you more than you can ask, think, or imagine.

PRAY & DECLARE

Father, thank You for Your promise that I am Your child, and You really are my Heavenly Father. Thank You that I don't have to worry about if or how You're going to work things out in my life. I declare, "Hallowed be Your name." Yes, I belong to You. In Jesus' Name, Amen.

SEPTEMBER 28

What's Trying to Stop You?

But be assured today that the Lord *your God is the one who goes across ahead of you like a devouring fire. He will destroy them; he will subdue them before you. And you will drive them out and annihilate them quickly, as the* Lord *has promised you.*

DEUTERONOMY 9:3, NIV

The Israelites were standing at the Jordan River, contemplating whether to go into the Promised Land. Their parents had the same decision before them forty years earlier, but they talked themselves out of it for fear of the Anakites, who were descendants of giants. This was a critical moment. As they debated what to do, God gave them the promise in today's scripture. When they heard that, they changed their mindset. "This is not going to be difficult because God will go before us to take care of what's trying to stop us." They went in with boldness and defeated the Anakites.

You may be facing challenges that look overwhelming, but God is going to do for you what He did for them. He's crossing over ahead of you right now so you can easily conquer.

PRAY & DECLARE

Father, thank You for the great promise that You are crossing over before me to subdue challenges that seem impossible. Thank You that I can have the boldness to move forward and conquer. In Jesus' Name, Amen.

SEPTEMBER 29

Never Late

"For still the vision awaits its appointed time; it hastens to the end — it will not lie. If it seems slow, wait for it; it will surely come; it will not delay."

HABAKKUK 2:3, ESV

Sometimes we want something so badly that we get out of balance. We feel like we're falling behind and start to panic. Through the power of Christ Jesus, you can release control of how and when God is going to bring it to pass. Hold tightly to your dreams but hold loosely to how God is going to do it.

There is a set time for God to favor you, to heal you, to turn the problem around. If there's a right time, that means there's a wrong time. Instead of fighting where you are, embrace where you are. "God, I know You're ordering my steps. I am right where I'm supposed to be. Thank You that my set times are coming." God is not going to be one second late.

PRAY & DECLARE

Father, thank You that this is my appointed time for favor and You are never late. Thank You that You are ordering my steps and helping me do what I could not do on my own. I believe that my set time is established, and You will make it happen. In Jesus' Name, Amen.

SEPTEMBER 30

This Present Step

The steps of a good man are ordered by the LORD,
and He delights in his way.

PSALM 37:23, NKJV

Most of us are very focused on the destination for our life, on our dream coming to pass, on our problems turning around. Life is not about the destination; it's about the journey — with all the bumps in the road, the disappointments, the things you don't understand. Too often we rush through the day, trying to force our way through the challenges and setbacks to the destination when we should slow down and enjoy the journey.

God is ordering your steps. Oftentimes the journey He leads us on is not comfortable, but all the difficulties, delays, and betrayals are a part of His plan to get us to our destiny. He will work all these things for your good. Stay in the present. Take it one day at a time. Welcome His love and grace for this present step.

PRAY & DECLARE

Father, thank You that You have a destination for my life as well as a journey to enjoy while I'm getting there. Thank You that You purposefully order my steps in the way that is best for me. In Jesus' Name, Amen.

October

OCTOBER 1

Stay in the Moment

"Give your entire attention to what God is doing right now, and don't get worked up about what may or may not happen tomorrow. God will help you deal with whatever hard things come up when the time comes."

MATTHEW 6:34, MSG

So often our mind is either in the past, focused on what didn't work out, who did us wrong, mistakes we've made, or it's in the future, thinking about our goals, worried about our finances, anxious about our health. The problem with being in the past or being in the future is that you miss the present. The reason some relationships are not healthy is that your mind is somewhere else. You're thinking about how you are going to accomplish something tomorrow. Or your mind is in yesterday, thinking about what you should have done better.

Make the most of each moment, loving your family, appreciating the simple things in life. Don't get worked up about yesterday or tomorrow. Psalm 118:24 says, *"This is the day that the Lord has made; let us rejoice and be glad in it"* (ESV).

PRAY & DECLARE

Father, thank You for this day that You have made and given to me as a gift. Help me to give my entire attention to the present and not be focused on the past or on the future. In Jesus' Name, Amen.

OCTOBER 2

The Fish's Mouth

"But so that we may not cause offense, go to the lake and throw out your line. Take the first fish you catch; open its mouth and you will find a four-drachma coin. Take it and give it to them for my tax and yours."

MATTHEW 17:27, NIV

When the tax collectors came asking Peter if Jesus paid the temple tax, Jesus told Peter to go to the lake, and the first fish he caught would have a silver coin in its mouth to pay their taxes. God is not going to allow those finances to take you down. He controls the economy and your finances. God knows what's happening, and He will make a way. Quit worrying. God has you in the palms of His hands. He never asked you to figure out how to work your life out. In fact, Proverbs 3:5–6 says, *"Trust in the Lord with all your heart and lean not to your own understanding; in all your ways submit to him, and he will make your paths straight"* (NIV). We serve a supernatural God. Suddenly just the right fish is caught and things fall into place.

PRAY & DECLARE

Father, thank You that You are in no way limited to what my circumstances look like and have been. Thank You that I am in the palms of Your hands and You have supernatural ways of providing for my needs. In Jesus' Name, Amen.

OCTOBER 3

Now Is the Time

"Now therefore, give me this mountain of which the LORD spoke in that day; for you heard in that day how the Anakim were there, and that the cities were great and fortified. It may be that the LORD will be with me, and I shall be able to drive them out as the LORD said."

JOSHUA 14:12, NKJV

Sometimes we think that we're running out of time to accomplish a dream. You might think you've made too many mistakes, missed your chance, or you're too old. For forty years, Caleb had been kept out of the Promised Land because of the negative report of the other ten spies. But what God promised, He brought to pass. When Caleb was eighty-five years old, God said, "I haven't forgotten about you. I said you'd go into the Promised Land, and now's the time."

God has not forgotten about the dreams He put in your heart. You're not running out of time; you're running into time. You haven't missed out on what is best. You're about to come in to some bests — best opportunities, relationships, and health.

PRAY & DECLARE

Father, thank You that whether Your promise is fulfilled in my life today or years from now, You will bring it to pass in Your time. I can say, "God, give me this mountain." I declare that every giant that stands in the way, will be conquered. In Jesus' Name, Amen.

OCTOBER 4

By Faith

By an act of faith, Rahab, the Jericho harlot,
welcomed the spies and escaped the destruction
that came on those who refused to trust God.
HEBREWS 11:31, MSG

By an act of faith, the prostitute Rahab hid the Israelite spies in the city of Jericho. Imagine one of those spies telling her, "What you've just done is going to make such an impact that thousands of years from now people are going to be talking about you. You're going to marry an Israelite and one day be in the family line of Jesus Christ." She would have said, "You have the wrong person. Don't you see the way I've lived?"

God doesn't judge or write people off the way people do. God calls you a masterpiece. He put royal blood in your veins. He's crowned you with favor. Nothing you've done has lessened your value or made Him love you any less. He's leading you to an amazing future, to something better than you've imagined.

PRAY & DECLARE

Father, thank You that You see me as a masterpiece of Yours. Thank You that when others try to write me off, You have already written me in. I believe that You are leading me into an amazing future. In Jesus' Name, Amen.

OCTOBER 5

Keep Getting Back Up

Though a righteous person falls seven times, he will get up, but the wicked will stumble into ruin.

PROVERBS 24:16, CSB

When life knocks you down, steps on you, takes your health, or squashes your dreams, you just have to get back up again. The way you win some battles is not by defeating them but by outlasting the opposition. You have comeback power. Some enemies are stubborn. You can't be weak and give up because it's not happening on your timetable. You have to outlast the trouble at work, the slow season in your finances, the difficulty in your marriage. We all want God to deliver us from attacks, but if He's not changing it, then it's really simple — you have to keep getting back up and outlast the attacks.

Sometimes we think God has forgotten about us. We've seen Him turn situations around in the past, but this problem won't seem to go away. God empowers us to say: "Staying down is not an option. I'm going to outlast this sickness, this addiction, this injustice, these critics."

PRAY & DECLARE

Father, thank You that You have given me comeback power to tap into in order to outlast whatever is coming against me. I will keep getting back up until the victory is mine. In Jesus' Name, Amen.

I'm removing the shame. I know who you are.

OCTOBER 6

Applause

"Your approval means nothing to me."

JOHN 5:41, NLT

Other than His Father in Heaven, Jesus Christ never looked to anyone — not to the religious leaders, not to His family, not to His disciples, or the crowds — for His approval. He would not allow what others said or thought about Him to determine who He was or to stop His purpose.

Living to gain other people's approval, trying to impress them and win their praise, may feed our ego, but it's a dead-end street. Don't get baited into being competitive, trying to outperform, thinking that's going to give you more worth. Proving to others that you're talented and successful may make you feel good, but what people think about you doesn't determine your destiny. Promotion is not going to come from the person you impress. They don't open doors, they don't part Red Seas, and they don't line up favor and divine connections. Live for God's applause, not people's.

PRAY & DECLARE

Father, thank You for the people You've placed in my life to help me move to my destiny. Help me to not become dependent upon their approval or try to get my value from them. I declare that I have Your applause and love and that's all I need. In Jesus' Name, Amen.

OCTOBER 7

Tender Mercies

Who redeems your life from destruction, who crowns you with lovingkindness and tender mercies, who satisfies your mouth with good things, so that your youth is renewed like the eagle's.

PSALM 103:4–5, NKJV

Where would you be if God had not redeemed you from your wrong choices? Perhaps some of the things in your past — the group of friends, the drugs and alcohol, the reckless driving, a freak accident — could have taken you out. You were headed down the wrong path, but you encountered the God who overrules. He loves you too much to let you miss your purpose. Today's scripture talks about the tender mercies of God — not "mercy" but "mercies." Again and again, God shows you mercy. His mercies are new and available to you every morning.

You may have made a lot of mistakes, but the good news is, you don't have to carry that around with you. Come to His throne of grace and receive His tender mercy. Ask for His forgiveness for every failure. Don't carry around yesterday's mistakes any longer. Let Him refresh and restore your soul right now.

PRAY & DECLARE

Father, thank You for the countless ways You've shown me Your tender mercies, protecting me from accidents and delivering me from mistakes I've made. Thank You that Your mercies are new for me. In Jesus' Name, Amen.

OCTOBER 8

Immeasurable

. . . so that in the coming ages he might show the immeasurable riches of his grace in kindness toward us in Christ Jesus.

EPHESIANS 2:7, ESV

In another translation of today's scripture, the apostle Paul said that we would see *"the immeasurable (limitless, surpassing) riches of His free grace (His unmerited favor)" in [His] kindness and goodness of heart toward us in Christ Jesus* (AMPC). That's favor as we've never seen it before. That's how the word "explosion" is defined. It means a "sudden, widespread increase." That's what God wants to do for us. Suddenly. You won't expect it. It's out of the ordinary, and it's not small. It's so amazing you know it had to be the hand of God.

You may think your situation is permanent. All the calculations are telling you that you'll never get out of debt, but God is saying, "You need to get ready. You haven't seen My explosive blessings. You haven't seen the immeasurable, limitless, surpassing greatness of My favor. I have blessings that will catapult you years ahead. I have increase that goes beyond your calculations."

PRAY & DECLARE

Father, thank You for Your unlimited, immeasurable favor and supply of everything I need in this life. Thank You that I can take the limits off because I know all things are possible for You. In Jesus' Name, Amen.

OCTOBER 9

Humanly Speaking

Jesus looked at them intently and said, "Humanly speaking, it is impossible. But not with God. Everything is possible with God."

MARK 10:27, NLT

When we say that God is sovereign, that means He reigns over everything you face. Not only does He reign over the universe, but He reigns over your life, your finances, your career, your marriage, and your children. He has the final word over it all. When thoughts tell you that you're never going to get well, just say, "No, thanks. My God has the final say over my health. It may not have happened yet, but healing is coming."

Are you spending more time thinking about problems or God's promises? Are you talking more about how big the challenge is or how big your God is? Don't dwell on what seems impossible. God overrides whatever is trying to stop you. Everything is possible with God.

PRAY & DECLARE

Father, thank You for being on Your throne, for reigning as sovereign over my health, my finances, my family, and my circumstances. There are things in my life that I want to see changed that seem unchangeable, but I trust You to override them. In Jesus' Name, Amen.

OCTOBER 10

Great Character

Do not be overcome by evil, but overcome evil with good.

ROMANS 12:21, NIV

You don't overcome evil that has been done to you by repaying the person with the same evil they did to you — they hurt you, so you hurt them. Not only will you make the problem worse and multiply the conflict, but you'll get stuck where you are.

When unfair things happen to you, the apostle Paul says to not take revenge but to leave it in God's hands to repay. That takes a big person; that takes great character. But through Jesus' life within you, you can not only access but activate God's great love. You have the power to take the high road, to rise above, to not be bitter but be better than the evil that may have come into your life. Yes, you have been purposed through God's grace to do good to those who may have done anything but good to you.

PRAY & DECLARE

Father, thank You that in every way possible, Jesus overcame evil by doing good. Thank You for giving me the grace to overcome evil by doing good as well. Help me to bless those who have done me wrong, to leave them in Your hands. In Jesus' Name, Amen.

You can't judge what's in you by what's around you.

OCTOBER 11

Sharper or Duller

As iron sharpens iron, so a friend sharpens a friend.

PROVERBS 27:17, NLT

Your friends should be sharpening you, making you better. Is that true of your circle of friends? Whatever qualities your friends have — either good or bad — eventually will either dull you or sharpen you. If you hang out with people who gossip, who compromise, or who are stingy, that's what you'll be tempted to do. But if you hang around excellent people, generous people, and motivated, successful people, those good qualities will sharpen your life. This is why it's so important that you are selective with whom you spend your time.

Don't worry about being in the right group, having the most friends, or being the most popular. The quantity of friends is not important; it's the quality of your friends that really matters. Seek to engage with eagles in your life — people who inspire you to reach your dreams, who motivate you to go further, who make you better.

PRAY & DECLARE

Father, thank You for the friends in my life who sharpen me, inspire me, encourage me, and make me better. Help me to know if there are relationships that are having a negative impact on me and dulling me. In Jesus' Name, Amen.

OCTOBER 12

Did I Not Tell You?

Then Jesus said, "Did I not tell you that if you believe, you will see the glory of God?"
JOHN 11:40, NIV

Even after Lazarus had died, Jesus said to his grieving sisters, *"Did I not tell you that if you believe, you will see the glory of God?"* They soon saw a resurrection. You may be facing a sickness, and you're worried. Remember that by His stripes you are healed. Thank God for what He told you instead of focusing on what you see.

When you're under pressure, it's so important to dwell on God's promises. Maybe you're discouraged over how long your dream is taking. Philippians 1:6 says, *"Being confident of this, that he who began a good work in you will carry it on to completion until the day of Christ Jesus"* (NIV). When you remember what the Word of God says, fear, doubt, and worry cannot stay, and faith will rise in your heart.

PRAY & DECLARE

Father, thank You for the power that comes when I remember the promises in Your Word, when I remember what You have said. Thank You for what You have whispered to me in the night. I declare that, through the power of Christ within me, I will walk by faith in You and not focus on what I see. In Jesus' Name, Amen.

OCTOBER 13

That Day

That day the Lord made Joshua a great leader in the eyes of all the Israelites, and for the rest of his life they revered him as much as they had revered Moses.

JOSHUA 4:14, NLT

As the Israelites were about to cross the Jordan River into the Promised Land, God told Joshua, "Today, I will begin to make you great in the eyes of all the Israelites." God was saying, "Joshua, this is your moment. I'm about to endorse you. People are going to see the greatness I've put in you. You've been in the background serving Moses, being faithful, but today you're coming into the foreground." Not long after that, Joshua led the Israelites into the Promised Land, and "that day" the Lord established Joshua as their leader.

God has a "that day" for you, a time when He will cause you to stand out, where you will accomplish things you never dreamed you could accomplish. You will know it, and the people around you will see the talent, creativity, ability, courage, strength, and greatness in you.

PRAY & DECLARE

Father, thank You for setting me apart as Your child to be favored. Thank You that You will do great things in my life that will bring You glory. In Jesus' Name, Amen.

OCTOBER 14

All Along the Way

"Praise be to the Lord, who has given rest to his people Israel just as he promised. Not one word has failed of all the good promises he gave through his servant Moses."

1 KINGS 8:56, NIV

When God brought the Israelites out of slavery, God showed them their destination, the Promised Land, but in the middle God didn't say, "I gave you the promise, and now you're on your own. Good luck." All along the way, God supernaturally provided them with blessings — parting the Red Sea, provisions in the desert, protection from enemy nations. He was showing them and us, "I'm not just the God of the start and the finish. I'm the God of the middle who will bring you through the adversity."

When you're in the middle, God has given you the promise, and you know the destination. But you're en route. Along the way, you'll face situations that look impossible. Be encouraged, knowing that the God of the middle is right there with you. Keep moving forward, knowing that God is in control.

PRAY & DECLARE

Father, thank You that not one word of Your promises will fail. I believe that what You have purposed for me will come to pass and nothing can stop it. In Jesus' Name, Amen.

OCTOBER 15

Hold Them Up

When Moses' hands grew tired, they took a stone and put it under him and he sat on it. Aaron and Hur held his hands up — one on one side, one on the other — so that his hands remained steady till sunset.

EXODUS 17:12, NIV

Moses was watching a battle. As long as he held his rod up in the air, the Israelites were winning. But whenever he put his hands down, the Amalekites started to win. Finally, Moses was too tired and would have needed miraculous strength to continue, so Aaron and Hur helped hold his hands in the air. The Israelites won the victory.

There are people God puts in our paths that need your encouragement. Your kind words can put people back on their feet. A phone call, giving someone a ride, taking them out to dinner, encouraging them in their dreams — there are miracles in you waiting to happen. That may seem simple to you, but to the other person it can be life-giving.

PRAY & DECLARE

Father, thank You that You bring people across my path so I can help them win. Thank You that I can speak a kind word, lift them up when they're hurting, and encourage them to follow their dreams. In Jesus' Name, Amen.

There’s a sudden change coming — sudden healing, opportunities, promotion, breakthroughs.

OCTOBER 16

Mustard Seed Faith

He replied, "If you have faith as small as a mustard seed, you can say to this mulberry tree, 'Be uprooted and planted in the sea,' and it will obey you."

LUKE 17:6, NIV

When the odds are against you and what you're up against seems impossible, don't believe the lie that you don't have enough faith. God says when you have faith the size of a mustard seed, nothing is impossible. A mustard seed is one of the smallest seeds. A little faith is like a little match that can ignite a huge fire. A little faith can start a huge blessing. Little faith can open big doors. Little faith can heal you from a terminal illness. Little faith can defeat great giants.

You have the faith you need to get you to your destiny. Agree with what God promised. "Lord, thank You that I can do all things through Christ."

PRAY & DECLARE

Father, thank You that You don't expect me to have a great faith that never doubts. Thank You that even if I only have mustard seed faith, that it is enough to make anything impossible. In Jesus' Name, Amen.

OCTOBER 17

Take a Break From You

After Job had prayed for his friends, the LORD restored his fortunes and gave him twice as much as he had before.

JOB 42:10, NIV

We all want to accomplish dreams, but as long as we're only focused on ourselves, we'll be stuck. God brings people and opportunities across our path so we can be a blessing. It might mean bringing an elderly neighbor food, cleaning up someone else's mess, or mentoring a young person. We think we have to work our way to the top, but the truth is that you serve your way to the top.

If Job had stayed focused on himself and all the troubles he'd gone through, he wouldn't have prayed for his friends. The reason some people are not happy is because all they think about is their dreams, their problems, their family. It's actually a joy to take a break from you. Something powerful happens when you are good to somebody else.

PRAY & DECLARE

Father, thank You that Jesus came not to be served but to serve others and give His life as a ransom for many. Thank you for keeping my eyes open to the people and opportunities You bring me to serve and bless. In Jesus' Name, Amen.

OCTOBER 18

Rise Again

Though the righteous fall seven times, they rise again . . .

PROVERBS 24:16, NIV

So often you might be tempted to look in the mirror and say, "I am good." But when you say, "I am good," it's not because of who you are; it's because of whose you are. You are a child of the Most High God. He handpicked you, breathed life into you, and crowned you with favor. Don't go around intimidated and insecure, feeling as though you don't measure up. Your performance doesn't determine who you are; your Heavenly Father determines who you are.

When you fall down and make mistakes, thoughts will whisper, *Look at you! You're a hypocrite.* Don't live with that heaviness. Just answer back, "I may have fallen, but I got back up again." Hold your head up and feel good about who you are. Celebrate where you are.

PRAY & DECLARE

Father, thnk You that You are the Most High God, and because I am Your child, I have royalty in my blood. Thank You that when I fall, You empower me to never stay down in discouragement and condemnation. I declare that I am righteous because of who You are. In Jesus' Name, Amen.

OCTOBER 19

People Are Contagious

Do not be misled: "Bad company corrupts good character."

1 CORINTHIANS 15:33, NIV

People are contagious. You're going to catch what they have. If your friends are prejudiced, you're going to be tempted to act in prejudiced ways. If they compromise, you might compromise. If they have no goals and little motivation, that narrow-minded thinking may hold you back. If they're not making you better, inspiring you, and causing you to grow, you need to make changes. Be nice to everyone, but remember, negative, critical, jealous, small-minded, bitter people can negatively influence your thinking.

God has given you a gift that will flourish and grow in the soil of good character. As you give to people of integrity and they to you, you will not just avoid being pulled down, you'll see exponential, positive growth in your own life.

PRAY & DECLARE

Father, thank You for the gifts and potential You put in me. Thank You for making it so plain that I need to be selective about whom I surround myself with. Thank You for giving me the discernment to engage with friends and people who inspire me and cause me to grow in my faith. In Jesus' Name, Amen.

OCTOBER 20

Recalculating Your Route

The steps of good men are directed by the Lord.
He delights in each step they take. If they fall,
it isn't fatal, for the Lord holds them with his hand.
PSALM 37:23–24, TLB

Even though God is directing our steps, there are times when we make mistakes and go the wrong way. But God doesn't say, "That's it. I'm done with you." He holds us in His hands and helps us get back on the right course. It's like a GPS system in your car. It tells you precisely where to go, but if you miss a turn, it doesn't say, "You loser! I'm done helping you." It says, "Recalculating route." The GPS system just keeps recalculating your route no matter how many mistakes you make.

How much more can the Creator of the universe recalculate your route when you make mistakes? God isn't mad at you. He's saying, "Recalculating route to your destiny. The mistakes didn't stop My plan." So quit beating yourself up over your failures. God has already calculated a new route.

PRAY & DECLARE

Father, thank You that You hold me in Your hands, and You delight to direct my steps. Thank You that You are always there to recalculate my route when I make mistakes. In Jesus' Name, Amen.

Jesus
empowers us
to ignore the
roar.

OCTOBER 21

The Blessing Stands

The Lord greatly blessed Joseph there in the home of his master, so that everything he did succeeded.

GENESIS 39:2, TLB

As a teenager, God gave Joseph a dream that one day people would bow down before him. But he was betrayed by his brothers, taken to Egypt, and sold as a slave. Joseph could have been bitter and complained, "God, I thought Your blessing was on my life. I thought You said I would do great things." Instead he kept being his best, and he was greatly blessed in everything he did.

God was with Joseph in the unfair situation. The blessing was still on his life. Sometimes we think we're not blessed when something goes wrong. That didn't stop the blessing. People can't take away the favor God put on you. The setbacks are not the end; they are a setup for what God is about to do.

PRAY & DECLARE

Father, thank You for Your presence and favor in my life that no situation or person can take away. Thank You for the blessing that is on my career, on my property, and on my health. I believe that I am blessed because I am Your child. In Jesus' Name, Amen.

OCTOBER 22

Become a Nathanael

Jesus saw Nathanael coming toward Him, and said of him,
"Here is an Israelite indeed [a true descendant of Jacob],
in whom there is no guile nor deceit nor duplicity!"
JOHN 1:47, AMP

Because of Christ living out through us, we are so honest, so above board, so full of integrity that Jesus can describe us as He did Nathanael. "That's not me," you say. Maybe not in some of your actions. But look deeply in your heart and lean into Jesus. The grace of Christ within you can empower you to do the right thing when no one is watching.

It starts in the home — as you continually abide in Jesus, you can act the same in private as you do in public. Remember: Your heart's desire is to treat your family with abounding love. Don't be kinder and more considerate to coworkers than you are to your spouse and children. You can be real and love others with the love of Jesus because of the hope of glory, Christ in you.

PRAY & DECLARE

Father, thank You for Jesus living His life out through me, especially at home. Thank you for making me a person of integrity. Thank You for compelling me to express Your love to my family in new and abounding ways. In Jesus' Name, Amen.

OCTOBER 23

Fireproof

"When you pass through the waters, I will be with you; and when you pass through the rivers, they will not sweep over you. When you walk through the fire, you will not be burned; the flames will not set you ablaze."

ISAIAH 43:2, NIV

Maybe you prayed for God to turn a situation around, but it didn't happen. Now thoughts tell you, *He must not care about me.* Shadrach, Meshach, and Abednego would tell you, "We know how you feel. We prayed and asked God to deliver us from going into the fiery furnace, but God didn't answer our prayer the way we wanted. We were tempted to panic and complain, but instead we decided to trust Him. We told the king that even if God didn't deliver us, we would not bow to his idol. When he threw us in the furnace, amazingly, the fire didn't burn us. Then all of a sudden, in the middle of the fire, the Son of God showed up!"

You may be in the fire, but stay in faith. You are fireproof. God is right there with you. Keep believing, keep praying. You're even going to come out without the smell of smoke.

PRAY & DECLARE

Father, thank You that no matter what the situation is, You have made me fireproof. Though there may be flames all around . . . I declare that You will deliver me. In Jesus' Name, Amen.

OCTOBER 24

Doubters

For even [Jesus'] own brothers did not believe in him.

JOHN 7:5, NIV

Jesus' own brothers did not believe in Him until after He rose from the dead. He was performing miracle after miracle, but they didn't see Him as the Messiah. They only saw Him as their brother and thought, *Oh, it's just Jesus. We grew up with Him.* Even when Jesus began to gain popularity, His brothers scoffed at Him. They tried to discount Him and talk Him out of His destiny. Jesus let it go in one ear and out the other.

Sometimes the people who have known you the longest will try to keep you in the same box that you grew up in, but people don't determine your destiny. What they say about you cannot stop what God has ordained for your life.

PRAY & DECLARE

Father, thank You that You have called me to be a unique being in the world, whether the people around me recognize it or not. Thank You that I am not limited by where I come from or by what others say or think about me. I will not allow others to put a limitation on what You have put in my heart. In Jesus' Name, Amen.

OCTOBER 25

Who's Your Architect?

And my God shall supply all your need according to His riches in glory by Christ Jesus.

PHILIPPIANS 4:19, NKJV

When an architect designs a skyscraper, he or she calculates all the loads, how much each floor will weigh, and how much wind stress it will face so it can withstand all the pressures it will bear. The good news is that your architect is the Most High God. He not only designed solar systems and mountain ranges, He designed you. When He laid out the plan for your life, He calculated everything you would face — all the pressure, the weight, the elements. He took into account every hurt, injustice, loss, and mistake. He designed your beams thick enough and your foundation deep enough. He put in you the strength, the fortitude, and the tenacity that no matter what comes against you, it will not be too much to bear. When you're tempted to think, *I can't handle this*, tell yourself, "I am well able. My God shall supply all my needs in Christ Jesus."

PRAY & DECLARE

Father, thank You that You are my architect and that You have designed me to withstand whatever comes against me. I believe that You are supplying all my needs, pouring them out according to Your riches. In Jesus' Name, Amen.

The way you win
some battles is not
by defeating them
but by outlasting
the opposition.

OCTOBER 26

In His Hands

But I am trusting you, O Lord. I said, "You alone are my God; my times are in your hands."

PSALM 31:14–15, TLB

It's good to be honest with God and tell Him your dreams. "God, this is what I want. Open these new doors." Pray, believe, and then leave it in His hands. Don't get so focused on what you want that you miss the beauty of this day. Everything may not be perfect. There may be things that need to change. But God has given you the grace to be happy today. It's very freeing when you can say, "God, it's in Your hands. I trust You unconditionally, whether it works out my way or not. I trust You unconditionally, even when I don't understand it."

PRAY & DECLARE

Father, thank You that You know best when it comes to the things I want and ask You for. Thank You that You are directing my steps, and You take me through the things I don't understand. I declare that You alone are my God, and my times are in Your hands. In Jesus' Name, Amen.

OCTOBER 27

Bigger, Greater, and More Powerful

You, dear children, are from God and have overcome them, because the one who is in you is greater than the one who is in the world.

1 JOHN 4:4, NIV

We all have times when we feel like we're surrounded by difficulties, by a sickness, or by debt. When you're in a difficult time, the enemy will tell you, "I have you surrounded. You're never going to get well, overcome that addiction, get out of debt, or receive that deserved promotion. You're stuck." Don't believe those lies. The enemy thinks he has you surrounded, but the Most High God has him surrounded. God knows every attack, difficulty, and unfair situation that's going to happen.

When you feel like you're surrounded, come back to the place of peace and say, "I know my God is surrounding what's surrounding me. He's bigger than this opposition. I will not be discouraged or worried. The forces for me are greater than the forces against me."

PRAY & DECLARE

Father, You know everything that the enemy surrounds me with. Thank You that You are bigger, greater, and more powerful than any of these enemies. I believe that the forces for me are greater than any that are against me. In Jesus' Name, Amen.

OCTOBER 28

Agree With God's Words

The angel answered, "The Holy Spirit will come on you, and the power of the Most High will overshadow you. So the holy one to be born will be called the Son of God. . . . For no word from God will ever fail." "I am the Lord's servant," Mary answered. "May your word to me be fulfilled."

LUKE 1:35–38, NIV

Words are powerful. A teenage girl named Mary became pregnant, not by a man but by the power of God. The angel Gabriel appeared to her and said, "Mary, you are highly favored! You will conceive and have a baby without knowing a man. He will be the Messiah, the Son of God." When God wants to create, He doesn't use material things; He uses words. Mary could have said to the angel, "That's impossible. It's never happened before." Instead she said, "Be it unto me even as you have said." She was in agreement with God.

When God puts a promise in your heart, just agree with Him. Declare: "Be it unto me even as You have said."

PRAY & DECLARE

Father, Your promise to Mary was that she had found favor with You and she would give birth to Your Son. Thank You that no word from You has ever failed. I believe that Your words to me will be fulfilled. In Jesus' Name, Amen.

OCTOBER 29

Hope on in Faith

Against all hope, Abraham in hope believed and so became the father of many nations, just as it had been said to him, "So shall your offspring be."

ROMANS 4:18, NIV

God gave Abraham a promise of a baby son when he was seventy-five years old, but he was one hundred before he saw the fulfillment. Abraham had all kinds of opportunities to quit believing, yet he hoped on in faith. In the face of the impossible circumstances, he stayed focused on how big God is rather than how big the problem was.

You may feel like there's no reason to have hope in a promise of God. In the natural, it's not possible, but we serve a supernatural God. Some promises take time. While you're waiting, it's easy to start believing the lies that the problem is too big. Keep God-inspired hope stirred up. You're not moved by what's not happening. You know what God promised is on the way. You don't consider your circumstances; you consider your God.

PRAY & DECLARE

Father, thank You that because You are supernatural, I can hope on in faith even when I can find no other reason for hope. Thank You that what You promised me is going to come to pass. I declare that I will not be moved by what's not happening. In Jesus' Name, Amen.

OCTOBER 30

Beautiful in Its Time

He has made everything beautiful in its time. He has also set eternity in the human heart; yet no one can fathom what God has done from beginning to end.

ECCLESIASTES 3:11, NIV

Solomon wrote that there was *"A time to be born and a time to die. A time to plant and a time to harvest"* (Ecclesiastes 3:2, NLT). He was saying, "Life is going to have its ups and downs." After listing the different seasons of life, he says, *"He has made everything beautiful in its time."*

You're going to go through things that are unfair — people who do you wrong, setbacks in your health and finances. It's easy to live discouraged, but as you are empowered by the gift of faith within you, in time God will make all things beautiful. God is working behind the scenes. He's going to resolve the bad break, the loss, or the mistake you made. Beauty is coming, restoration is coming, healing is coming, favor is coming.

PRAY & DECLARE

Father, thank You for Your promise that You make everything, not just some things, beautiful in its time. Thank You that my story doesn't end with a deficit or a negative. Thank You for Your gift of faith within me. By it I will keep moving forward, knowing You are going to work it all out for good. In Jesus' Name, Amen.

OCTOBER 31

Your Safe Place

You have not handed me over to my enemies
but have set me in a safe place.

PSALM 31:8, NLT

King Saul had been trying to capture David in the wilderness for years and finally was closing in. But just as Saul was about to attack, a messenger delivered an urgent message, saying, "Saul, hurry home. The Philistines are attacking our land." Saul and his men turned around and left, and they never did capture David. God knows how to keep you in a safe place. Even when it looks like it's too late, He knows how to distract your enemies. He knows how to change people's plans, how to turn the trouble, the sickness, or the opposition around.

We all have things trying to stop our destiny, but God has put you in a safe place. You may have difficulties in your health, your finances, or your marriage. You could live worried, but when you know you're in a safe place, where God has you hidden, you can live in peace.

PRAY & DECLARE

Father, thank You that no matter what challenge I face, I can stay in peace, knowing that You have a safe place for me. I declare that You are my hiding place. In Jesus' Name, Amen.

November

NOVEMBER 1

Don't Be Bullied

So then, surrender to God. Stand up to the devil and resist him and he will flee in agony.

JAMES 4:7, TPT

The enemy is a bully. Bullies are loud, intimidating, liars, and try to threaten you to control you and keep you down. Yet praise be to God that through Christ we can stand up to the enemy and say, "Your intimidation and threats don't move me. You have no power over me. I know who I am, and I know whose I am. You may seem big, but God and I are a majority. I will not live worried or let your lies play in my mind."

The way you defeat the enemy is by saying what God says about you. When the enemy says, "You'll never break out and rise higher," by His power you can declare, "The path of the righteous gets brighter and brighter, and that's my path. My greatest victories are still in front of me."

PRAY & DECLARE

Father, thank You that Your Champion, Christ Jesus, lives within me and He is far more powerful than the enemy. Thank You for breaking the enemy's power. I will walk in the liberty by which Christ has set me free. In Jesus' Name, Amen.

NOVEMBER 2

Covered

He will cover you with his feathers, and under his wings you will find refuge; his faithfulness will be your shield and rampart.

PSALM 91:4, NIV

The enemy has schemes and strategies to try to keep you from your destiny. People or a sickness or bad breaks may be set in motion, headed to your address with your name on it to cause you trouble. But because you made the Lord your God, you are under the shelter of the Most High. The Scripture says He covers you with His wings. He'll hide you from things that could have brought you down, and you didn't even know it. You're not at risk. You don't have to worry that at any moment something bad can happen. God has you covered.

And if trouble does come, you're still covered. That difficulty is not how your story ends. God has the final say. He's not only going to take care of what's trying to stop you, but He's going to bring you out better.

PRAY & DECLARE

Father, thank You that You have a secret place, a safe place, where I can dwell, covered with Your feathers, under Your wings, and abiding in peace. Thank You that You control what trouble comes my way. In Jesus' Name, Amen.

NOVEMBER 3

Tune Out the Doubt

And they were deeply offended and refused to believe in him. Then Jesus told them, "A prophet is honored everywhere except in his own hometown and among his own family." And so he did only a few miracles there because of their unbelief.

MATTHEW 13:57–58, NLT

There's always a battle taking place in our mind. Thoughts come whispering that are negative, discouraging, and alarming. *You're not going to get well. You don't have the talent to get that job. You can't pass that college course. You can't break the addiction.* If you dwell on those thoughts, you can get talked out of what you're believing for.

Don't take the bait. You can't always stop the negative thoughts from coming, but you can tune them out. Don't give the doubt the time of day. Keep your mind focused on God's Word, and you will be filled with faith, filled with hope. What you're facing is not too hard for our God. There is no problem He can't turn around, no dream that He can't bring to pass.

PRAY & DECLARE

Father, thank You for being the God of miracles, and You will prevail no matter what negative thoughts whisper in my mind. Help me to tune out those thoughts and keep my mind filled with faith and hope. In Jesus' Name, Amen.

NOVEMBER 4

Shoes of Peace

Stand therefore, having fastened on the belt of truth, and having put on the breastplate of righteousness, and, as shoes for your feet, having put on the readiness given by the gospel of peace.

EPHESIANS 6:14–15, ESV

The Scripture tells us to put on the armor of God, including the shoes of peace. You may walk through difficulties you don't understand. There's going to be plenty of opportunities to live upset and afraid in this life. But don't worry, you can arm yourself with peace and strength for the battle.

Don't fear the unknown or lose sleep over what doesn't make sense. God has equipped you, empowered you, and anointed you. No weapon formed against you will prosper. Keep walking in faith, knowing that you're wearing those shoes of peace. Trust when you don't understand, and you'll walk into blessings, healing, freedom, abundance, and victory like you've never seen. When you trust God when it doesn't make sense, you're going to come into favor that doesn't make sense — new levels of influence, joy, leadership, resources.

PRAY & DECLARE

Father, thank You for being the God of all peace and for giving me shoes of peace to walk in. Thank You that You walk with me through whatever I go through. I refuse to allow what I don't understand to get me upset. In Jesus' Name, Amen.

NOVEMBER 5

No Condemnation

He will again have compassion on us, and will subdue our iniquities. You will cast all our sins into the depths of the sea.

MICAH 7:19, NKJV

A lot of people are down on themselves because of past things they've done wrong. They're so focused on their past that it poisons their future. We have all sinned, but quit thinking about all the things you've done wrong. When you live guilty, you're in agreement with the enemy, the accuser. He'd love for you to go through life feeling wrong about yourself. He knows you were created to soar, which is why he works overtime trying to make you feel guilty, whispering, "You don't measure up. You failed again. You'll never be free." Yet you can declare: "No, thanks. There is no condemnation for those who are in Christ Jesus. I'm forgiven. My past is over, my present is secure, and my future is bright!"

PRAY & DECLARE

Father, thank You that I am forgiven and redeemed by the blood of Your Son. Thank You that the price for my sins has been paid once and for all. I receive Your love and forgiveness and refuse to live under guilt and condemnation. In Jesus' Name, Amen.

A little faith is
like a little match
that can ignite a
huge fire.

NOVEMBER 6

Hidden

They passed the first and second guards and came to the iron gate leading to the city. It opened for them by itself, and they went through it. When they had walked the length of one street, suddenly the angel left him.

ACTS 12:10, NIV

Peter was arrested for sharing his faith and put in prison. King Herod ordered sixteen soldiers to guard him and had him chained between two soldiers in his cell. The night before Peter was to go on trial and likely be executed, an angel appeared, woke Peter up, and suddenly Peter's chains fell off. The angel said, "Come with me." The prison doors opened of their own accord. They walked past one set of guards, then a second set, and yet none of them saw Peter.

God won't let dire circumstances stop His purpose. He has angels watching over you right now, protecting you. He knows how to open doors that you can't open, how to get you out of problems that look impossible, how to blind the eyes of those who are trying to hold you back.

PRAY & DECLARE

Father, thank You that You supernaturally open doors and make things happen that I can't make happen and don't deserve. I will rest in You. In Jesus' Name, Amen.

NOVEMBER 7

Rise Up

"But Lord," Gideon replied, "how can I rescue Israel? My clan is the weakest in the whole tribe of Manasseh, and I am the least in my entire family!"

JUDGES 6:15, NLT

When the Angel of the Lord told Gideon that he was to rescue the Israelites from the Midianite army, he immediately said that wasn't possible because he came from a disadvantaged family, weak and poor, and he was the least among them. Sometimes the reason we don't feel that we can accomplish a dream is because we were raised by people who were negative, insecure, and dysfunctional. Anytime you try to move forward, there are voices telling you what you can't do and how it's not going to work out. You start to believe when they say, "This is just who you are."

No, that is not who you are. As with Gideon, you're "a mighty hero," and God's favor is on your life. He's called you to take yourself and your family to a new level. Through Christ you can rise up and step into who you were created to be.

PRAY & DECLARE

Father, thank You that I am not limited by my past, by dysfunction passed down through my family. Thank You that my weakness is turned to strength by the power of the Lord Jesus within me. In Jesus' Name, Amen.

NOVEMBER 8

Freedom

"So if the Son sets you free, you will be free indeed."

JOHN 8:36, NIV

Many people struggle with an addiction to something. Perhaps you've tried to stop, with no success. Thoughts have told you that's just who you are. No, that's not who you are, that's what you do. Who you are is a child of the Most High God. You weren't created to be addicted. You were created to be free, and this is a day for breakthroughs. You are free in Christ. What's held you back in the past will not hold you back any more. Chains are being loosed right now; strongholds are coming down. You're about to step into freedom that you've never seen. What used to be a struggle is about to get easier. The strength of what's coming against you has been cut off, and its power over you has come to an end.

PRAY & DECLARE

Father, thank You that when Christ conquered death on the cross, He broke the power of every negative thing that's trying to hold me back. Thank You that I am free and the chains have fallen off. I believe and declare that the Son has set me free. In Jesus' Name, Amen.

NOVEMBER 9

A Heart of Compassion

If anyone has this world's good (resources for sustaining life) and sees his brother and fellow believer in need, yet closes his heart of compassion against him, how can the love of God live and remain in him?

1 JOHN 3:17, AMPC

When two blind beggars cried out for Jesus to have mercy on them, it says that *"Jesus stopped and called them"* (Matthew 20:32, NIV), then He healed them. Jesus was always willing to stop and help any person in need. He could have easily said, "Listen, I have a schedule to keep." But no, Jesus freely gave of His life.

Through Christ, know that your heart of compassion is open. It's actually a joy to be willing to be interrupted and inconvenienced if it means we can help meet someone's needs. We can help initiate a healing process in his or her life. As we open Jesus' heart of compassion within us — without judging or condemning — and simply have an ear to listen, we can pour out God's love and make a difference in that person's life.

PRAY & DECLARE

Father, thank You that You have poured Your love into my heart through the Holy Spirit. Thank You that You have opened my spirit to be compassionate and kind and merciful to others like You are. In Jesus' Name, Amen.

NOVEMBER 10

What's Your Name?

"No longer will you be called Abram; your name will be Abraham, for I have made you a father of many nations."

GENESIS 17:5, NIV

Abram was ninety-nine years old when God appeared to him and said that he and Sarah were going to have a baby. Both of them were way too old, but God did something unusual. In addition to giving them the promise, He changed Abram's name to Abraham, which means "father of many nations." Every time someone said, "Hello, Abraham," they were saying, "Hello, father of many nations." When he had no child with Sarah, they were speaking faith into his destiny, and during the following year, baby Isaac was born.

That's why it's so important to start calling yourself what God says about you. What you continually hear gets down inside. You will become what you believe. Every time you say, "I am blessed. I am prosperous. I am healthy." It's getting deeper inside, it's changing your self-image, it's reprogramming your mind.

PRAY & DECLARE

Father, thank You that You alone have the right to name me because I am Yours. Thank You that You call me blessed, redeemed, forgiven, healthy, overcomer, and a masterpiece. I will call myself what You call me and live out who You say I am. In Jesus' Name, Amen.

Something
powerful
happens when
you are good to
somebody else.

NOVEMBER 11

By Invitation Only

"Do not be afraid, for I have ransomed you. I have called you by name; you are mine. When you go through deep waters, I will be with you. When you go through rivers of difficulty, you will not drown. When you walk through the fire of oppression, you will not be burned up; the flames will not consume you."

ISAIAH 43:1–2, NLT

When you face adversity, is your typical prayer, "God, get me out of this"? There's nothing wrong with that prayer, but you can invite God in. Sometimes the miracle is in what God wants to do *in* the situation. There's power in praying: "God, come into this hospital room, come into this troubled relationship, come into this anxiety." More powerful than God bringing you out is when He comes in and gives you favor despite who's trying to push you down. He gives you strength you can't explain and the grace to outlast and overcome the challenge.

God says that although adversities are going to come, He will be with you in them. Are you trying to get out of the fire God is going to take you through? Are you fighting the fire, wondering why it happened? Everything will change as you start inviting God in.

PRAY & DECLARE

Father, You promise to be with me through life's fires. I know that You're with me in every challenge in my life. In Jesus' Name, Amen.

NOVEMBER 12

Be Secure in Who You Are

"Let him not deceive himself by trusting what is worthless, for he will get nothing in return."

JOB 15:31, NIV

Many people can't feel good about themselves unless they prove to other people that they are important. They are always having to outdo, outperform, outdrive, and outdress somebody else. If you live in a proving mode, it's as though you're running on a treadmill that never stops. As soon as you prove to one person that you're okay, you'll see somebody else you need to impress. It's a never-ending cycle. Rest and allow yourself to get off that treadmill. It's very freeing when you realize you don't have to prove anything to anyone.

Are you trying to prove your value by who you know, what you wear, or what you drive? Because you are a child of the Most High God, you can be secure in who you are. You belong to God. You don't have to prove anything to anyone.

PRAY & DECLARE

Father, thank You that I can feel good about myself because I am Your child. Thank You I don't have to prove anything to anyone. I declare that I am secure because I belong to You, the Most High God. In Jesus' Name, Amen.

NOVEMBER 13

Down Is Not Your Destiny

As for me, I look to the Lord for his help; I wait for God to save me; he will hear me. Do not rejoice against me, O my enemy, for though I fall, I will rise again! When I sit in darkness, the Lord himself will be my Light.

MICAH 7:7–8, TLB

When we're in difficult times, it's easy to feel like the prophet Micah. He gave a list of negative things that happened to him — bad breaks, lack, injustice, betrayal. It was very depressing. But he went on to say that he wasn't giving up. He may have been knocked down, but in the middle of the difficulty, he was speaking victory. He was saying, "This problem didn't come to stay; it came to pass. God being for me is more than the world being against me. I will arise."

Things may be coming against you, but know this: God didn't create you to be overcome; He created you to be an overcomer. Down is not your destiny. Get ready to rise!

PRAY & DECLARE

Father, thank You for the call to rise up in the midst of my difficulties. Thank You that You created me to be an overcomer and speak victory. I declare that I am looking to You, and I know that I will rise. In Jesus' Name, Amen.

NOVEMBER 14

Divine Attitude Adjustments

Put on your new nature, and be renewed as you learn to know your Creator and become like him.

COLOSSIANS 3:10, NLT

As followers of Jesus, we put on what has already been given to us. This includes our attitude. If you're always finding fault, critical of your spouse, or focused on what's not working out, you can access His fresh new attitude that already lives within. Don't wait until something big happens, until a relationship ends. Make the change now. Release anything that's weighing you down and causing you to be sarcastic, condescending, or finding fault.

Life is too short for you to live it sour and discouraged, letting your circumstances dictate your attitude. Every morning, you can proclaim: "This is the day the Lord has made! I'm going to put on my new nature in Christ. I'm going to be positive; I'm going to see the good."

PRAY & DECLARE

Father, thank You that You have given me this day as a gift to live for You. Thank You that I can start this day with a fresh new attitude because You dwell in me and have given me a new nature. I'm going to be my best and make the most of this day. In Jesus' Name, Amen.

NOVEMBER 15

End the Debate

Dear friends, we are already God's children, but he has not yet shown us what we will be like when Christ appears. But we do know that we will be like him, for we will see him as he really is.

1 JOHN 3:2, NLT

When the Israelites headed toward the Promised Land, they were excited that their dream of freedom had come true — until Pharaoh came chasing after them with his chariots. Pharaoh was saying, in effect, "You're my slaves. I'm taking you back." God was saying, "You're My children. I'm taking you into freedom." This debate was playing back and forth: "Are you a son? Or are you a slave?"

That same debate can take place about you. One voice is saying, "You're a slave." The truth is saying, "In Christ, I'm no longer a slave, I'm a son. I'm a daughter. I'm not a slave to my past, to the people who hurt me, to lack. I'm a child of the Most High God."

PRAY & DECLARE

Father, thank You that You have made me Your child and that I am no longer a slave to anything. Thank You that You redeemed me, and You're taking me forward into freedom. In Jesus' Name, Amen.

You are always there to recalculate my route when I make mistakes.

NOVEMBER 16

Stay in Faith

"Look, I go forward, but He is not there, and backward, but I cannot perceive Him; when He works on the left hand, I cannot behold Him; when He turns to the right hand, I cannot see Him. But He knows the way that I take; when He has tested me, I shall come forth as gold."

JOB 23:8–10, NKJV

I've learned that our character is more important than our talent. We can have all the talent in the world, but if we don't have strong character, we won't go very far. Too many people let frustrations cause them to get sour, lose their passion, and slack off. Through the power of Christ within you, you can activate faith in overcoming ways, even when you can't see what God is doing.

Keep being good to people, keep giving it your best, and have an excellent spirit. Nothing may be happening on the outside, but something has and is happening inside. God has changed you. You might not be able to see Him, but You will come forth as gold.

PRAY & DECLARE

Father, thank You that when I can't see what You're doing, I still have every reason to trust You. Thank You that difficulties will pass and that I will come forth as gold through it. In Jesus' Name, Amen.

NOVEMBER 17

Ignite the Promises

For indeed the gospel was preached to us as well as to them; but the word which they heard did not profit them, not being mixed with faith in those who heard it.

HEBREWS 4:2, NKJV

God has given us hundreds of powerful promises that say we'll live an abundant life, we'll be healthy and whole, we'll experience favor, increase, restoration, and on and on. But as encouraging and inspiring as the promises are, on their own they won't do you any good. They're just nice, encouraging words. Through Christ, you can add in the one ingredient that activates the power, that makes the promises come alive and become what God says, and that's faith.

Faith is like adding rocket fuel. It ignites the promises, and powerful things happen. When you believe, angels go to work, supernatural doors will open, you'll defeat giants. When you believe, you'll accomplish dreams much bigger than you thought.

PRAY & DECLARE

Father, thank You for the promises You have spoken in Your Word and to my spirit. Thank You that I can speak words of faith that agree with Your promises and ignite them to come to pass in my life. I believe that as I mix in my faith, You will do things I've never seen before. In Jesus' Name, Amen.

NOVEMBER 18

Don't Be a People Pleaser

Owe no one anything except to love one another,
for he who loves another has fulfilled the law.

ROMANS 13:8, NKJV

Some people are experts at putting their demands on you and trying to keep you doing and saying what makes them happy. They play upon a false sense of responsibility and thinking that says, "I've got to keep them fixed and cheered up." The only thing you really owe people is to love them. That doesn't mean you have to keep everyone happy or let people put their demands on you. That's carrying a debt you don't owe. Always be respectful and kind, but if you go through life trying to please everyone, the one person who won't be happy is you. Come out from under that debt.

If people are controlling you, it's not their fault; it's yours. Go the extra mile, but don't be a people-pleaser.

PRAY & DECLARE

Father, thank You for the love that You have put in my heart and for the love You want me to share with others. Help me to recognize when others are trying to make me feel responsible for keeping them happy and meeting their expectations. In Jesus' Name, Amen.

NOVEMBER 19

Don't Be Moved

"None of these things move me; nor do I count my life dear to myself, so that I may finish my race with joy, and the ministry which I received from the Lord Jesus, to testify to the gospel of the grace of God."

ACTS 20:24, NKJV

Life is too short for you to go through it drifting, feeling negative, discouraged, and passionless. Through faith — the assurance of things hoped for — you can stir up hope and keep anchored to it. When you're anchored to hope, you're not moved by worry because you know that God is fighting your battles. You may have a disappointment, but you don't get bitter. You know that weeping may endure for a night, but joy is coming in the morning.

To be anchored to hope doesn't mean you won't have difficulties; it means that when those difficulties come, you won't be moved. Nothing big or small will move you or cause you to pull up your anchor. There will be waves and winds, but you're consistent — your hope is in the Lord.

PRAY & DECLARE

Father, thank You that my faith and trust are anchored to You. Thank You that I don't have to be moved by the tests and troubles I face because I know that You are fighting my battles. I declare that my hope is in You. In Jesus' Name, Amen.

NOVEMBER 20

Make Room for More

"I know your works. Behold, I have set before you an open door, which no one is able to shut. I know that you have but little power, and yet you have kept my word and have not denied my name."

REVELATION 3:8, ESV

The moment you accept that something negative is the norm, that's when a stronghold in your mind is formed that can keep you from your destiny. The first place we lose the battle is in our own thinking. If you think you've reached your limits, you have. If you think you'll never get well, you won't. You have to change your thinking and stir up your faith.

God has given you gifts, talents, and great potential. Pray and believe that doors are going to open that no one can shut. That you are going to connect with the right people and talent and opportunities that will thrust you into a new level of your destiny.

Dream big. Believe big. Pray big. God has explosive blessings coming your way.

PRAY & DECLARE

Father, thank You that I can leave behind any negative mindsets and make room for the increase You want to bring into my life. Thank You that You open doors and new opportunities that will take me to new levels. I believe this is a new day to break free from limitations. In Jesus' Name, Amen.

When God wants to create, He doesn't use material things; He uses words.

NOVEMBER 21

Be Patient

For the gifts and the calling of God are irrevocable.

ROMANS 11:29, NKJV

When Moses was a young man, God put the dream in his heart to deliver the Israelites out of slavery. But he got in a hurry and stepped out of God's timing, killing an Egyptian who was mistreating a Hebrew slave. He spent forty years on the back side of the desert in hiding. It looked as though that one mistake disqualified him from God's calling. I'm sure he often thought, *You're a failure. You missed out.* But at eighty years old, God came to Moses and said, "Now you're ready. Go deliver My people."

God doesn't judge you by one mistake or by five thousand mistakes. His calling on your life is irrevocable. You may be tempted to count yourself out, but God has already counted you in. That mistake doesn't determine the rest of your life.

PRAY & DECLARE

Father, thank You for the calling You put in my heart and that my mistakes and failures cannot nullify it. Thank You that I can rest in Your irrevocable gifts and calling and be patient, knowing that You are at work within Me. In Jesus' Name, Amen.

NOVEMBER 22

Feel Like You're Going Backward?

"I am the true vine, and my Father is the gardener. He cuts off every branch in me that bears no fruit, while every branch that does bear fruit he prunes so that it will be even more fruitful."

JOHN 15:1–2, NIV

We all go through times when we feel like we're going backward. Things were going well, but then we lost a major client, our child got in trouble, or a friend walked away. We wonder, *What did I do wrong?* When we have things in our life that are not productive, God will cut those things away so we can put our energy into things that move us forward. The only way to get from "fruit" to "more fruit" is to be cut back. That means there are times when you're doing the right thing and, seemingly, the wrong thing happens. Instead of getting discouraged, recognize that just as there are seasons of growth, there are seasons of pruning. God is preparing you to bear even more fruit.

PRAY & DECLARE

Father, thank You for times of pruning when You cut back something in my life so I can bear more fruit. I believe You're making me even more fruitful. In Jesus' Name, Amen.

NOVEMBER 23

Freedom

"So ought not this woman, being a daughter of Abraham, whom Satan has bound — think of it — for eighteen years, be loosed from this bond on the Sabbath?"

LUKE 13:16, NKJV

This lady who came into the synagogue where Jesus was had been bent over for eighteen years. She had been bound by the enemy for so long that I'm sure she thought it was permanent. When Jesus called her a "daughter of Abraham," it meant she was a part of the covenant that God made with Abraham. She wasn't just any woman. She had privileges because she was in the family line of Abraham.

As with her, you're not just anyone. You're a child of the Most High God. You have rights because of who you belong to. You weren't created to be bound by sickness, an addiction, or any limitation. Get ready, because the chain breaker is about to step in. If Jesus were here today, He would look at you and say, "You are loosed from what's holding you back. Your day of freedom has come."

PRAY & DECLARE

Father, thank You that You have come into my life as my Savior, as my provider, and as my healer. Thank You that my chains are gone and I've been set free. In Jesus' Name, Amen.

NOVEMBER 24

Words of Life

Who have sharpened their tongues like a sword.
They aim venomous words as arrows.

PSALM 64:3, AMP

David referred to some people's mouths as sharp swords and their words as venomous arrows. Are you encouraging people, making them stronger and more confident, or are you putting others down, leaving them wounded and scarred? Many times we can recover from a physical wound quicker than an emotional wound.

If you're a parent, speak words of life, faith, and encouragement to your children. Yes, you must correct them, but don't do it in an angry, disrespectful way. Don't say derogatory things that are going to damage their self-esteem. Correct them in love, with a kind spirit. Don't cut them up with negative, hurtful words at any age. Let's be parents who speak words of life, who push our children into their destiny, and who help release their dreams.

PRAY & DECLARE

Father, thank You that You created me to speak words of life, faith, and encouragement to everyone, and especially to my family. Help me to be aware of the words I am speaking and to tame my tongue before I speak words that could harm. I believe that You will help me to speak in a way that builds up. In Jesus' Name, Amen.

NOVEMBER 25

When You're Surrounded

I lay down and slept, yet I woke up in safety, for the Lord was watching over me. I am not afraid of ten thousand enemies who surround me on every side.

PSALM 3:6, NLT

You would think that being surrounded by ten thousand enemies would have David feeling worried. But he went on to say, "*Victory comes from You, O Lord. May you bless your people*" (v. 8). He was saying, "I could be overwhelmed by my enemies, but I'm not falling apart because I know that God is surrounding what's surrounding me." David saw his enemies, but through his spiritual eyes he also saw the Most High God fighting his battles.

As with David, you may feel surrounded by enemies — depression, sickness, lack. You don't have the people connections or the finances. You could easily accept it and think, *It's not meant to be.* Here is the key: What you see with your physical eyes is not the only thing that's surrounding you. As you open your eyes of faith, you'll realize the troubles and opposition are surrounded by our God. You're surrounded by favor, healing, and angels.

PRAY & DECLARE

Father, no matter what trouble I face, I can stay in peace knowing that You are surrounding every trouble and opposing situation that's surrounding me. I declare that I am surrounded by You. In Jesus' Name, Amen.

God makes everything beautiful in its time.

NOVEMBER 26

Is It Really Too Hard?

Then the LORD said to Abraham, "Why did Sarah laugh and say, 'Will I really have a child, now that I am old?' Is anything too hard for the LORD? I will return to you at the appointed time next year, and Sarah will have a son."

GENESIS 18:13–14, NIV

Abraham was ninety-nine years old when the Lord told him that within a year he would have a son. He and Sarah were way too old to have a baby. It was so far out that when Sarah heard it, she laughed out loud. Has God ever put something in your heart that seemed so unlikely, so big, that your first reaction was to laugh? He whispers in your spirit that you're going to live in a nice neighborhood, lead your company in sales, see your family restored, or get your health back. If Abraham had only looked at it logically, he would have given up. But Abraham was empowered by one thing: he believed. "Yes, it's impossible, but God can do the impossible. It defies the laws of nature, but God supersedes the laws of nature."

PRAY & DECLARE

Father, thank You for the dreams, the promises, and the potential You put inside me. Thank You that nothing You call me to is really too hard for the Lord Most High. In Jesus' Name, Amen.

NOVEMBER 27

Keep Your Cool

Don't sin by letting anger control you.
Think about it overnight and remain silent.
PSALM 4:4, NLT

God made us as emotional beings. Just because you feel something doesn't mean you have to act on it. You may feel anger, which is okay, but don't lose your temper. Keep your cool. You may feel offended, but don't give in to it. You may feel tempted to compromise when your flesh says, "I have to have it, the feeling is so strong," but you don't have to get on board with that feeling.

You think you can't control it, but God wouldn't tell us to be angry and not give in if He hasn't empowered us to keep our cool. Ask yourself, "If I follow what I'm feeling, is it going to move me toward my destiny? Is it profitable for that moment?" If not, know that God's reservoir of self-restraint is right there for you to access.

PRAY & DECLARE

Father, thank You that one of the fruits of the Spirit working in me is self-control. Thank You that I don't have to be a slave to feelings that have tried to control me for years. I believe that You have given me the power to overcome. In Jesus' Name, Amen.

NOVEMBER 28

Seasons of Isolation

For God alone my soul waits in silence and quietly submits to Him, for my hope is from Him.

PSALM 62:5, AMP

After David was anointed to be the next king of Israel, he spent years of isolation carrying for his father's sheep. Nobody knew who he was or was watching him. He felt lonely, overlooked, and forgotten. This was an incredibly important time in his life. He took care of the sheep as though he were taking care of a nation. He risked his life to kill a lion and a bear. He was faithful in obscurity.

In seasons of isolation, deal with the issues God brings to light. Do the right thing when it's hard; keep a good attitude when people are not treating you right. God's doing a work in you. It's an opportunity to grow, to get stronger. By His sovereign grace and power, He is preparing you for the new, expansive opportunity He has for you.

PRAY & DECLARE

Father, thank You that You are always working in my life to shape my character and prepare me for what You have in store for me next. Thank You for the seasons of isolation and obscurity where You are sovereignly working Your way within me. In Jesus' Name, Amen.

NOVEMBER 29

Setbacks Are Setups

Then the Lord said to Moses, "Tell the Israelites to turn back and encamp near Pi Hahiroth . . . They are to encamp by the sea, directly opposite Baal Zephon. Pharaoh will think, 'The Israelites are wandering around the land in confusion, hemmed in by the desert.' And I will harden Pharaoh's heart, and he will pursue them. But I will gain glory for myself through Pharaoh and all his army, and the Egyptians will know that I am the Lord."

EXODUS 14:1–4, NIV

God told Moses to tell Pharaoh, "Let My people go." But God knew that Pharaoh would refuse, so He hardened his heart so God could bring great glory at Pharaoh. God was setting up the odds to be against the Israelites so He could show His favor. In a similar way, you may not like it that some people and circumstances have come against you; it isn't fair, but it is ordained by God — not to stop or defeat you, but so God can show out in your life. It's a wonderfully freeing paradigm shift to ask, "Why am I facing these odds?" Then watch and see — it's just a matter of time before God turns around those obstacles and releases His glory for you to behold.

PRAY & DECLARE

Father, thank You that You are going to use the obstacles in my life to show me Your favor and bring glory to Your Name. Thank You that You are turning my setbacks into Your divine setups. In Jesus' Name, Amen.

NOVEMBER 30

Yesterday's Baggage

"Oh, what joy for those whose disobedience is forgiven, whose sins are put out of sight."

ROMANS 4:7, NLT

We all make mistakes, and some are very painful. Maybe you need to bury mistakes you made. You've lived feeling guilty and down on yourself long enough. Have a funeral and put it behind you. No more talking about it. No more letting the accuser make you feel unworthy. When the defeat, the mistake, or the hurt comes back up on the movie screen of your mind, change the channel. Have the attitude, "I'm not living in regret and rehearsing failures. I'm moving forward!"

How much time and energy are you giving to the negative things of your past — the guilt, the offenses, the blame, the discouragement? You only have so much emotional energy each day. When you spend that energy on negative things, rehearsing your failures and being down on yourself, that's energy you should be using to move forward. Drop yesterday's negative baggage. Let it go.

PRAY & DECLARE

Father, thank You that You've given me the power to stop the negative things from my past that play and replay in my mind. By Your power, I refuse to continue to live in regret and to be down on myself. In Jesus' Name, Amen.

December

DECEMBER 1

He Comes to Your House

Jesus said to him, "Today salvation has come to this house, because this man, too, is a son of Abraham. For the Son of Man came to seek and to save the lost."

LUKE 19:9–10, NIV

A despised tax collector named Zacchaeus had heard how Jesus healed the sick and opened blind eyes. When Jesus stopped in the crowded street to speak to him, time stopped for Zacchaeus. He expected Jesus to condemn him for his dishonesty and cheating as a tax collector, but Jesus said, "Zacchaeus, I want to go to your house and have dinner." When Zacchaeus heard those words, something inside said "He loves you." Jesus was making this point: You don't have to first clean yourself up for salvation to come to you. You don't have to have it all together for God to love you. If that were the case, none of us has a chance.

PRAY & DECLARE

Father, thank You that even though You know everything about me, You still invite Yourself to come to my house for dinner and bring the gift of salvation. Thank You that it's not about my performance, but it's about Your love. Welcome to my house. In Jesus' Name, Amen.

DECEMBER 2

Overtaken by Blessings

"And all these blessings shall come upon you and overtake you, because you obey the voice of the LORD your God."
DEUTERONOMY 28:2, NKJV

God has things in your future that are much bigger than you've imagined. The odds may be against you, but God is for you. We ask God for things that seem reasonable to us. We ask for our healing, to get out of debt, to meet the right person. That's good, but God has blessings that you've never asked for or even thought of. If He showed you all He has in your future, it would boggle your mind.

Because you have a heart to know and trust God, you won't have to go after promotion; promotion will come after you. You won't have to chase blessings; blessings will chase you. New doors are going to open, the right people will show up, and the problems will turn around.

PRAY & DECLARE

Father, You've promised that blessings are headed my way and overtaking me. Thank You that You have blessings that are beyond my imagination. I love listening and following the voice of the Lord within me. In Jesus' Name, Amen.

DECEMBER 3

It Will Be Undeniable

You prepare a feast for me in the presence of my enemies. You honor me by anointing my head with oil. My cup overflows with blessings.

PSALM 23:5, NLT

You may have some obstacles in your path today that have you feeling stuck. There's no way you'll get well, pay off your house, or go back to school. God is about to display His awesome power, not just so you can see it, but so other people can see it. When David says, "*You prepare a feast for me in the presence of my enemies,*" that's not private.

God is going to show out so the opposition and the critics will all see you promoted, honored, in a position of influence, in a public display. That's why you don't have to prove to people who you are or waste your time trying to convince people who are not for you to like you. Keep running your race, honoring God, and at some point, He's going to show out in such a way that your critics can't deny the favor on you. People are going to know the Lord is on your side.

PRAY & DECLARE

Father, thank You that You have Your ways of preparing feasts for me when I face opposition and critics. Thank you that You will display Your awesome power through me. In Jesus' Name, Amen.

DECEMBER 4

Get the Who Right

"Look at the birds of the air; they do not sow or reap or store away in barns, and yet your heavenly Father feeds them. Are you not much more valuable than they?"

MATTHEW 6:26, NIV

We all face challenges in life that we don't know how they're going to work out. We may wonder, *How am I going to get well, meet the right person, or make my dreams a reality?* Here's the key: The HOW is not as important as the WHO. When you know who you are, a child of the Most High God, crowned with favor, with royal blood flowing through your veins, then the WHO will override the HOW. Your Heavenly Father created the universe and has ways of doing things that you can't see. You belong to Him, which means you can live from a place of peace, knowing that your Father has a solution to that problem that's stressing you out.

PRAY & DECLARE

Father, thank You that just as You feed the birds of the air, You will provide me with exactly what I need for every season I am in. I choose to rest, knowing that WHO You are is in control of HOW my needs will be worked out. In Jesus' Name, Amen.

DECEMBER 5

What You Can't See

For His anger is but for a moment, His favor is for life; weeping may endure for a night, but joy comes in the morning.

PSALM 30:5, NKJV

If you add up the negative things in your past, at times the negative is much heavier than the positive. It's easy to look back at an illness, a loss, or a setback and get discouraged or lose your passion. The problem is, you're only looking at your history of negative things. What you can't see is what God has in your future. He wouldn't allow the difficulty if it was going to leave you in a deficit. There are things in your future that God has ordained for you — promotion, healing, divine connections. The joy that is coming is going to far outweigh the disappointment, the pain, the loss.

God will use opposition to strengthen you. We can actually celebrate our tribulations knowing that God is using them to produce perseverance, character, and hope.

PRAY & DECLARE

Father, thank You that in times when the negatives are much heavier than the positives, I can know that it's only for a night. Thank You for Your promise of joy that is coming. I believe that You will always bring me out of the night and into the light. In Jesus' Name, Amen.

The way you
defeat the
enemy is by
saying what God
says about you.

DECEMBER 6

Winter

For everything there is a season, a time for every activity under heaven. A time to be born and a time to die. A time to plant and a time to harvest.

ECCLESIASTES 3:1–2, NLT

We love harvest season. We love when we're seeing favor, prayers answered, new opportunities. But every season is not harvest. We may not like winter, but it is necessary. Without the leaves coming off, the tree would never develop new buds. In the winter, something is happening that you can't see. The tree is gathering up sap. The roots are going deeper. It's being prepared to handle more fruit in the spring. If there weren't these different seasons, the tree wouldn't reach its full potential.

Don't complain about the winter seasons in life — the times when you don't see any growth, you're stuck at the same level at work, nothing is changing in a relationship. You're wondering, *What's wrong? Where is all the fruit?* Nothing is wrong; you're in winter. Something is happening inside. You can't see it, but God is getting you prepared for bigger opportunities, more favor, greater honor.

PRAY & DECLARE

Father, thank You that You change times and seasons, and You're not limited to the right conditions to be in place in order for You to bless me. Thank You that You're always working behind the scenes on my behalf. In Jesus' Name, Amen.

DECEMBER 7

Call Out

"Call to Me, and I will answer you, and show you great and mighty things, which you do not know."

JEREMIAH 33:3, NKJV

Throughout the Bible, we read that our God is a God who is close to us. One of the names we have for Him is "Immanuel," the God who is with us. We also read how He is the Good Shepherd — the God who knows His sheep, cares for His sheep, and is close to His sheep. We are those who are the sheep of His pasture. By faith we are adopted in and called sons and daughters of God.

The fact that we can call to the Lord and He will answer us is an incredible gift. It is an expression of His kindness to His people and a reminder that He is not distant. He is ever near. He is always there. He is right by your side. Call to the Lord today, beliving that He hears you, and that He is mighty to save and able to answer. He loves you very much.

PRAY & DECLARE

Father, thank You that I can always call out to You. Thank You that You hear me and You answer me and that Your heart is toward me. In Jesus' Name, Amen.

DECEMBER 8

Testing Your Character

Until the time that his word came to pass,
the word of the LORD tested him.
PSALM 105:19, NKJV

Before your dream comes to pass, God will test your character. God gave Joseph a dream that he would be in leadership, but his brothers took away his coat of many colors that represented his father's favor and sold him into slavery in Egypt, where he was falsely accused and put in prison. These weren't just random bad breaks; God was testing him. It wasn't fair, but Joseph didn't get bitter. His brothers took his robe, but they couldn't take his favor. They took his freedom, but they couldn't take his anointing. They took him from his home, but they couldn't take his dream. All these steps prepared him to become the prime minister of Egypt.

Testing is not a pressure to pass or fail. It's like metal being tested by passing through a fire. The impurities are released and discarded, and the pure gold comes forth.

PRAY & DECLARE

Father, thank You for the training and preparation process that You are taking me through even now. I believe that Christ's character within me will come forth, and the dreams You have placed within me will come to pass. In Jesus' Name, Amen.

DECEMBER 9

Flourish

And because I preach this Good News, I am suffering and have been chained like a criminal. But the word of God cannot be chained.

2 TIMOTHY 2:9, NLT

After years of great missionary travels, planting churches, and seeing miracle after miracle, the apostle Paul spent the last years of his life in prison. He could have become sour, thinking, *Is this how it's going to end? Stuck in a prison?* But Paul knew the prison couldn't keep his gifts from coming out. While he was in captivity, he wrote several books of the Bible that would change the world and still encourage us two thousand years later. He gave us scriptures that we all quote today: "I can do all things through Christ." "God will do exceedingly abundantly above what we ask or think." "Be strong in the Lord and the power of His might." Paul flourished in ministry even in prison.

PRAY & DECLARE

Father, thank You that You are the Most High God and that Your work in my life is greater than any of the forces that might try to hold me back. Thank You that I can flourish wherever I am planted and the Word of God within me can never be chained. In Jesus' Name, Amen.

DECEMBER 10

A Surely Mentality

Surely goodness and mercy shall follow me all the days of my life; and I will dwell in the house of the Lord *forever.*

PSALM 23:6, NKJV

In today's scripture, David was saying, "I am confident that good things are coming. I am confident that this situation is turning around." It's very powerful when you add the "surely" to what you're believing for. When thoughts tell you that you'll never get well, say, "Surely, Lord, good health is on the way." When they say, *You'll never get out of debt*, say, "Surely I will lend and not borrow." When they tell you, *You'll always struggle with that bad habit,* say, "Surely I will break this addiction. Surely freedom is coming."

What you're up against may look too big. You could be filled with worry and doubt. Try a new approach. Start adding some "surely"s to what you're believing for. When you have this surely mentality, you're going to see some "surely"s come to pass. Don't let the circumstances fool you. Surely goodness and mercy are following you. Surely God is about to bless you and show you favor that you've never seen.

PRAY & DECLARE

Father, thank You that through Christ I have this surely mentality that leads to victory. Thank You for Your goodness and mercy that will fill my day today and every day. In Jesus' Name, Amen.

He has angels
watching over
you right now,
protecting you.

DECEMBER 11

Don't Drag Your Feet

I want each of you to extend that same intensity toward a full-bodied hope, and keep at it till the finish. Don't drag your feet. Be like those who stay the course with committed faith and then get everything promised to them.

HEBREWS 6:11–12, MSG

When God brought the Israelites out of slavery in Egypt, He said the Promised Land was theirs to go in and possess. He promised they would defeat every enemy and come into abundance. But when the ten spies came back with the report that the people were too big and powerful, the Israelites became afraid and wanted to go back to being slaves. Instead of staying with a committed faith in the promise, they dragged their feet in unbelief. What happened? They never made it into the Promised Land.

God's promises give us hope. That hope will sustain and empower you. Be encouraged in your faith. Don't shrink back. Take His promises and know they will come to pass.

PRAY & DECLARE

Father, thank You for the promises that You always lead me to triumph through Jesus. I'm not dragging my feet. My feet are moving forward in faith, empowered by Your promises. In Jesus' Name, Amen.

DECEMBER 12

Ask Big, Pray Big, Believe Big

"O Lord, please hear my prayer! Listen to the prayers of those of us who delight in honoring you. Please grant me success today by making the king favorable to me. Put it into his heart to be kind to me."

NEHEMIAH 1:11, NLT

God gave Nehemiah a dream to rebuild the broken-down walls of Jerusalem, which seemed impossible. Nehemiah was a cupbearer to the Persian king. He wasn't a builder and didn't have any resources, funds, a building crew, or influence. But Nehemiah prayed a bold prayer and asked God to put it in the king's heart to help him. He chose to believe that the God who asks you to do difficult things is the same God who makes a way when there is no way, and that's exactly what God did.

To accomplish your God-given dreams, ask big, pray big, believe big. You're going to need other people to open doors. Have you ever prayed, "God, put it in people's hearts to help me and show me favor"?

PRAY & DECLARE

Father, thank You that the dreams You have put in my heart are always possible. Thank You that I can dare to pray big, to ask big, and to believe big. In Jesus' Name, Amen.

DECEMBER 13

The Good Fight

Fight the good fight of the faith. Take hold of the eternal life to which you were called when you made your good confession in the presence of many witnesses.

1 TIMOTHY 6:12, NIV

Some of the difficulties we complain about, the challenges we don't like, are meant to prepare us for greater favor, influence, and opportunities. Quit telling yourself, "It's too hard. They did me wrong. I can't put up with this." Instead of trying to pray away all the things that make you uncomfortable — the people who get on your nerves, the delays — try a different approach and say, "God, help me to keep a good attitude in the midst of these challenges. Help me to stay in faith when people aren't treating me right. Help me to fight the good fight of faith and resist the temptation to compromise, to take the easy way out. Thank You for Your power within me to rise above all that swirls around me."

You can handle every difficulty through Christ. You have been armed with strength for every battle.

PRAY & DECLARE

Father, thank You for the abundance of grace You give me to go through every difficulty and challenge I face. Help me to fight the good fight through Christ Jesus and to overcome what has overcome me. In Jesus' Name, Amen.

DECEMBER 14

The Hands That Rule the World

The smoke of the incense, together with the prayers of God's people, went up before God from the angel's hand.

REVELATION 8:4, NIV

When you pray, your prayers rise before God. When you pray, God not only listens, but He answers. Angels are dispatched, chains are broken, favor is released. You can send up prayers for a loved one and stand in the gap while they're off course, not making good decisions. You can go to God on others' behalf and ask Him to send healing, to send comfort to them in a loss, to help them find a job. God has entrusted us with something incredibly powerful. When you ask God for their needs, your faith can move mountains.

PRAY & DECLARE

Father, thank You for the powerful vision of prayers rising before You. Thank You that You have entrusted me with the faith to pray for others' needs and dreams. I believe that Your blessings through my prayers make a difference in the people around me and in the world. In Jesus' Name, Amen.

DECEMBER 15

Helping Others

"But love your enemies, do good, and lend, hoping for nothing in return; and your reward will be great, and you will be sons of the Most High. For He is kind to the unthankful and evil. Therefore be merciful, just as your Father also is merciful."

LUKE 6:35–36, NKJV

Joseph was sold into slavery by his brothers and working for a man named Potiphar. Rather than focus on his problem and be bitter, Joseph was so faithful that he was put in charge of Potiphar's household. Later, after he was falsely accused and put in prison, rather than focus on his problem, he was so excellent that he was put in charge of all the prisoners. When Pharaoh needed his dream interpreted, Joseph stepped in to help, and he was made the prime minister of Egypt as a result.

Notice that while you're working on someone else's problem, God is working on your problem. You can't sow a seed without reaping a harvest.

PRAY & DECLARE

Father, thank You that You destined me to help other people solve their problems. Help me to keep my eyes open for the people and opportunities You bring me to serve. I believe that as I take my hands off my problems, You will put Your hands on them and help them. In Jesus' Name, Amen.

You are free
in Christ.

DECEMBER 16

Yesterday, Today, and Forever

Jesus Christ is the same yesterday and today and forever.

HEBREWS 13:8, NIV

Our God is the same yesterday, today, and forever. He is always with you and for you. What He's done for others, He can do for you. The same God who displayed His favor in Scripture is still at work today. He can open new doors of favor, line up supernatural appointments, and bring new increase and provision just as He did for Abraham, Joseph, and Elijah.

And when God pours out His favor, it won't be just a drizzle. It's going to be a flood — a flood of ideas, a flood of good breaks, a flood of talent, and a flood of opportunities for you to increase your influence in amazing ways. Don't shrink back in doubt. Keep believing, keep hoping, and keep praising. The same favor that was in the Scripture is available to you.

PRAY & DECLARE

Father, thank You that You are the same in Your character yesterday, today, and forever. Thank You for Your favor and blessings that are available to me each and every day. I believe and declare that a flood of ideas, good breaks, and talent is coming my way. In Jesus' Name, Amen.

DECEMBER 17

Put Your Feet Up

For he raised us from the dead along with Christ and seated us with him in the heavenly realms because we are united with Christ Jesus.

EPHESIANS 2:6, NLT

God said that He would make the enemies of Christ His footstool. It's a picture of the rest of faith we can have because we are joined to Christ and seated with him in the Heavenly places. When we face difficulties, the first thing we should do is put our feet up. We come back to that place of peace. Thoughts may tell you why you'll never get well, how your family will never be restored, or why your dream will never come to pass. That's the enemy trying to deceive you into standing up. He knows that when you're seated in peace, what may have been meant for your harm becomes your footstool. Instead of being a stumbling block, it's going to be a stepping-stone to take you to His divine blessings.

PRAY & DECLARE

Father, thank You that I am seated with Jesus today. Thank You that Jesus has defeated every enemy and made them a footstool that I can rest my feet upon. Thank You that you turn footstools of rest into stepping-stones of blessings. In Jesus' Name, Amen.

DECEMBER 18

Hold Tightly, Hold Loosely

"Woe to those who quarrel with their Maker, those who are nothing but potsherds among the potsherds on the ground. Does the clay say to the potter, 'What are you making?' Does your work say, 'The potter has no hands'?"

ISAIAH 45:9, NIV

Many years ago, Victoria and I were certain we'd found our dream house. We prayed over it, thanking God that it was ours, and made an offer. But the seller rejected our offer. We were deeply disappointed, but if we're only going to be happy if God does it our way, that's not trusting Him. A few months later, we purchased another house. A few years after that, we sold half of that property for more than we paid for the whole property and built a new house there. God blessed us in ways greater than we'd ever imagined.

We believe in praying bold prayers for our dreams. Learn to hold tightly to what God puts in your heart, but hold loosely to how it's going to happen. Don't be discouraged because it hasn't happened the way you thought. God is working out His plan for your life.

PRAY & DECLARE

Father, thank You that You are the Potter and that my life is being shaped by Your hands. Thank You that I can come to You with bold prayers for my dreams, but not hold tightly to how You make it happen. In Jesus' Name, Amen.

DECEMBER 19

The Battle Turns

The very day I call for help, the tide of battle turns. My enemies flee! This one thing I know: God is for me!

PSALM 56:9, TLB

We all go through times when we don't think we'll win our battles, seasons of darkness when nothing is changing. You may have been believing for a long time for things to change in your marriage, your finances, or with an addiction, but the obstacle seems permanent. But praise be to God! Today's scripture says that the moment you prayed in the dark, the battle turned.

All the forces of darkness cannot stop what God has promised you from coming to pass. You may not see anything improving, but my challenge is to trust Him in the dark. The sun is going to come up sooner than you think. The battle has already turned. Daybreak is about to happen. Get ready for favor, breakthroughs, freedom, promotion.

PRAY & DECLARE

Father, thank You that You hear every prayer that I whisper in the dark. Thank You that in the unseen realm You turn the tide of the battle because You are for me. I believe and declare that nothing can stop what You have promised me from coming to pass. In Jesus' Name, Amen.

DECEMBER 20

Every Good Thing

And God is able to bless you abundantly, so that in all things at all times, having all that you need, you will abound in every good work.

2 CORINTHIANS 9:8, NIV

Every good thing comes from your Father. The source of blessing is the Lord. When doors opened that you couldn't open, when you were at the right place at the right time, when you met that person and fell in love, that wasn't a coincidence; that was the source. You weren't being lucky when that person put in a good word for you and you got the promotion. God spoke to that person, telling them to be good to you. They may not have even known it was God, thinking they just suddenly had the desire to help you.

Yes, He is the source who is making it happen. There are no lucky breaks or coincidences. The Most High God is the One who put them there.

PRAY & DECLARE

Father, thank You that You are the source of every good thing in my life. Thank You that You are blessing me abundantly so that I always have what I need to abound in every good work. I live today overflowing with an attitude of thankfulness and gratefulness. In Jesus' Name, Amen.

I'm no longer a
slave, I'm a son.
I'm a daughter.

DECEMBER 21

Be a Blessing

Do not withhold good from those to whom it is due,
when it is in your power to act.
PROVERBS 3:27, NIV

When you know you can be a blessing, when you have the resources to help a person in need, or when you can teach them the skills you've learned, don't put it off. You may think, "I can't help them. I have to focus on fixing my own problems." But when you make sacrifices to help other people's dreams come to pass, God will help make your dream come to pass. As you bless others and show them favor, God is going to bless and favor you.

Don't live focused only on yourself—your problems, sickness, trouble at work. Go and be a blessing to someone in need. Sow a seed with your finances or a word of encouragement. When you help solve their problems, you're setting a miracle in motion for yourself, and God is going to solve your problems.

PRAY & DECLARE

Father, thank You for what You've brought me through that I can now use to help others solve their problems. Thank You that I have something to give, some blessing to impart. I believe You will make my dreams come to pass. In Jesus' Name, Amen.

DECEMBER 22

A Little While

And after you have suffered a little while, the God of all grace, who has called you to his eternal glory in Christ, will himself restore, confirm, strengthen, and establish you.

1 PETER 5:10, ESV

The Scripture never says that if you have faith, you'll never have any suffering, never have things that aren't fair or situations that aren't turning around. But it says the suffering is for "a little while." Don't believe those lies that what you're going through is permanent. That suffering didn't come to stay; it came to pass.

You have been chosen and called by the Creator of the universe to overcome every obstacle. The forces that try to stop you are no match for the God of all grace. God Himself is going to restore you. The Most High God is going to suddenly turn things around. When it's your time, you're not going to come out the same . . . you're going to come out better.

PRAY & DECLARE

Father, thank You that the difficulties I go through are but for a little while, and You have purposed to use them for my eternal good. Thank You that You are the God of all grace and that You will restore, strengthen, and finish Your work in me. In Jesus' Name, Amen.

DECEMBER 23

Do Not Be Afraid

Once you were like sheep who wandered away. But now you have turned to your Shepherd, the Guardian of your souls.

1 PETER 2:25, NLT

When we look at all the natural disasters, sicknesses, and accidents going on around us, it's easy to live worried and afraid. We think, *What if we face another pandemic? What if my business doesn't make it? What if my child has an accident?* If you were on your own, you would have valid reasons to be afraid. But you're not in this by yourself.

The Most High God is the Guardian of your soul. When He breathed life into you, He didn't just put you on the earth and say, "Good luck." He guards you from forces of darkness and shields you from trouble. You don't have to be afraid. God knows how to keep harm away. And if it does come, He knows how to restore what was taken.

PRAY & DECLARE

Father, thank You that I have turned to You, my Shepherd, the Guardian of my soul. Thank You that I need not fear. When things come against me, I know that You have me in the palms of Your hands. In Jesus' Name, Amen.

DECEMBER 24

Sing With the Angels

Suddenly, the angel was joined by a vast host of others — the armies of heaven — praising God and saying, "Glory to God in highest heaven, and peace on earth to those with whom God is pleased."

LUKE 2:13–14, NLT

On the night Jesus Christ was born, shepherds were out in a field near Bethlehem when an angel appeared to them and told them the good news about His birth. Then suddenly, a vast host of angels appeared who were praising God. The Scripture tells us that there are angels in Heaven singing God's praises day and night. Think about this: When you praise God, you are joining with the angels in Heaven! What an awesome thought that we can be one with the Heavenly hosts when we worship. As you celebrate the birth of Jesus during the Christmas season, take time to rejoice with the angels that the Son of God came to us to save the world.

PRAY & DECLARE

Father, thank You for the birth of Your Son. Thank You that I can join with the angels and give You all the praise and glory for what You've done. I come before You and bow my knees and heart and offer You my worship. In Jesus' Name, Amen.

DECEMBER 25

The Gift Too Wonderful for Words

But when the fullness of the time had come, God sent forth His Son, born of a woman, born under the law, to redeem those who were under the law, that we might receive the adoption as sons.

GALATIANS 4:4–5, NKJV

Beyond the Christmas lights and presents, beyond the music and great food, God reminds us that in the fullness of time He gave us the most wonderful gift that has ever been given — the gift of Jesus.

The apostle Paul was so overwhelmed at the thought of all that God has given us that he wrote, *"For it is by grace you have been saved, through faith — and this is not from yourselves, it is the gift of God"* (Ephesians 2:8, NIV). Jesus is God's perfect, indescribable gift. Jesus, the Savior of the world, who brought the promise of unconditional love, unending hope, and eternal life to every person who believes in Him.

PRAY & DECLARE

Father, thank You for the perfect, indescribable gift of Your Son Jesus, who is too wonderful for words. Thank You for the gift of eternal life, the unending hope found in Him, and the unconditional love You have given me. The gift You've given so graciously is what I want to share with the world. In Jesus' Name, Amen.

Dream big.
Believe big.
Pray big.

DECEMBER 26

Word Builders

Now the people complained about their hardships in the hearing of the Lord*, and when he heard them his anger was aroused. Then fire from the* Lord *burned among them and consumed some of the outskirts of the camp.*

NUMBERS 11:1, NIV

One reason the Israelites never made it into the Promised Land is that they started complaining about their challenges. Because of their negative words, they wandered in the wilderness and went around the same mountain for forty years. If you're not speaking grateful, beneficial words that edify and build others up, do yourself a favor and zip it up. If you're critical and condescending, you'll keep going around your own mountain for forty years. You can't be disrespectful to your spouse or your coworkers and become all you were created to be. You can't talk behind people's backs and reach your Promised Land.

Proverbs 18:21 says that life and death are in the power of the tongue. My question is, are you speaking life or death to your future?

PRAY & DECLARE

Father, thank You that You created me to speak words of gratitude, faith, and encouragement to everyone, and especially to my family. Help me not to just zip my lips before I speak words that could harm, but to use my words to edify and build others up. In Jesus' Name, Amen.

DECEMBER 27

Say So

Whoever dwells in the shelter of the Most High will rest in the shadow of the Almighty. I will say of the L*ORD*, *"He is my refuge and my fortress, my God, in whom I trust."*

PSALM 91:1–2, NIV

It's significant that the psalmist didn't just say, "I'm going to stay in the shelter of the Most High, and that will keep me protected." He says, *"I will say of the Lord."* What you say is powerful. You can't go around talking defeat because negative talk is like bait. It attracts the enemy. It can open the door to difficulties.

Start declaring you're protected and thanking God that there's a hedge around you. There's a power infusion as you speak out what God has already placed within you. It's Heavenly fuel for your earthly engine. And it's available 24/7, in every circumstance. Yes, say what God says about you.

PRAY & DECLARE

Father, thank You for being my refuge and my fortress, my God, in whom I trust. I speak it out loud because I know it's true, and I believe that You will deliver and protect me. I declare that I will rest in Your shadow and dwell in Your shelter. In Jesus' Name, Amen.

DECEMBER 28

It's Not Too Big

"How will this be," Mary asked the angel,
"since I am a virgin?"
LUKE 1:34, NIV

When the angel told Mary she would give birth to the Messiah, she asked how it would be possible since she was a virgin. She was talking about the physical, but I believe there's a deeper meaning to her question. God's promises are not dependent on man. You don't have to have a certain person to fulfill your destiny. You don't need someone with power to help you catch a break. God's promises are not dependent on who you know or who you don't know. The main thing is to know Him.

God is the all-powerful Creator of the universe. What He has spoken over your life may seem impossible. It may look too big. But do as Mary did and simply believe.

PRAY & DECLARE

Father, thank You for Your promise to Mary that her giving birth to Your Son was possible because nothing is impossible for You. Thank You that Your promises to me are equally possible because You control all things. My eyes are on You alone to do what no person can do. In Jesus' Name, Amen.

DECEMBER 29

The Greatness of His Goodness

Oh, how great is your goodness to those who publicly declare that you will rescue them. For you have stored up great blessings for those who trust and reverence you.

PSALM 31:19, TLB

When you look back over your life, you can see the goodness of God. There were the times when He made a way when you didn't see a way. You were at the right place at the right time. You made mistakes that should have held you back, but God in His mercy covered you. He brought you out, and now you're blessed and fulfilling your purpose. It was the hand of God. He's been working behind the scenes in your life.

Take time every day to acknowledge how great His goodness has been in your life. It will be refreshment to your bones and inspiration to your spirit as you declare His goodness. Acknowledging His blessings is a tremendous blessing!

PRAY & DECLARE

Father, thank You that Your hand has been upon my life in so many ways. Thank You for the countless blessings You have brought me and for all You are going to do as You take me forward. I stand in awe of Your goodness to me. In Jesus' Name, Amen.

DECEMBER 30

More Than You Can Carry

King Jehoshaphat and his men went out to gather the plunder. They found vast amounts of equipment, clothing, and other valuables — more than they could carry. There was so much plunder that it took them three days just to collect it all!

2 CHRONICLES 20:25, NLT

When King Jehoshaphat and the people of Judah were surrounded by three major armies, they humbled themselves and asked God to save them. God miraculously gave them a mighty victory, and they didn't even have to fight. They could have returned home thanking God for their deliverance, but our God exceeds our expectations. He blesses us with vast blessings.

You may have obstacles in your path and challenges coming against you. Stay encouraged. God is not only going to bring you out, He's going to have some spoils there. He's going to bring you out better than you were before. He's going to exceed your expectations.

PRAY & DECLARE

Father, thank You for Your hand of protection on my life and how You answer my prayers. Thank You for how You go beyond my requests and exceed my expectations. I believe and declare that You will not only bring victory but spoils and vast blessings as well. In Jesus' Name, Amen.

DECEMBER 31

Leave It Behind

I press on to take hold of that for which Christ Jesus took hold of me. . . . I do not consider myself yet to have taken hold of it. But one thing I do: Forgetting what is behind and straining toward what is ahead, I press on toward the goal to win the prize for which God has called me heavenward in Christ Jesus.

PHILIPPIANS 3:12–14, NIV

In this new year, God has made a powerful way to leave anything from the past that keeps you from moving ahead. Say goodbye to the things you didn't understand, offenses you're hanging on to, or bitterness that lingers. Say goodbye to being argumentative, sarcastic, and seeing the worst. Say goodbye to guilt and regrets, to a wrong self-image, to feeling inferior. Say goodbye to any relationships that you know are wrong and causing you to compromise.

Embrace who God says you are. You are fearfully and wonderfully made. You are a masterpiece. You're forgiven and redeemed. God has something better ahead. It's going to be a bountiful, abundant, flourishing year.

PRAY & DECLARE

Father, thank You for the new year that is right in front of me. I say goodbye to all the negative baggage that would try to keep me from moving ahead. I look forward to the new things You're doing in my life this coming year. In Jesus' Name, Amen.

ABOUT JOEL OSTEEN MINISTRIES

Joel Osteen Ministries, rooted in Houston, Texas, is an extension of the legacy built by John and Dodie Osteen, who founded Lakewood Church in 1959. Originally meeting in a modest feed store, Lakewood has grown into one of the largest congregations in the U.S., attracting people from all walks of life. John Osteen's leadership touched millions through his television ministry, which reached over 100 countries, and his influence as a pastor's pastor. His wife, Dodie, also played a key role, especially with her testimony of miraculous healing from cancer, which has inspired countless people.

When John passed away in 1999, his son Joel stepped into leadership, despite his background in television production. Joel's transition into senior pastor marked a new era for Lakewood, with the church's global influence expanding significantly. Under Joel's leadership, Lakewood's outreach grew, broadcasting to over 200 million households, and the church became a beacon of hope for millions seeking encouragement and inspiration.

Joel's wife, Victoria, serves alongside him, contributing to the church's leadership and vision. Their daughter, Alexandra, continues the family tradition, leading worship and contributing to Lakewood Music. With a focus on uplifting messages and practical teachings, Joel Osteen Ministries aims to reach new generations, inspiring people worldwide to rise above their challenges and live their best life through faith, hope, and love.